The
Rebel Angels
among Us

"On a visit to Timothy's home in a remote part of New Mexico, I had occasion to witness him in the deep communion with Georgia that was required to generate this series of unforgettable volumes. There he sat in the utterly unique home he himself had designed. Around him was perhaps the most impressive private library I have ever seen, and his own visionary art lined the walls. I knew then what I know now: Timothy Wyllie stands in a class all by himself as a contributor to the emerging literature influenced by the Urantia Revelation. His literary and artistic legacy will remain invaluable for decades to come."

BYRON BELITSOS, AUTHOR OF *YOUR EVOLVING SOUL:*
THE COSMIC SPIRITUALITY OF THE URANTIA REVELATION

PRAISE FOR OTHER WORKS IN THIS SERIES
BY TIMOTHY WYLLIE

"*Confessions of a Rebel Angel* is Timothy Wyllie's magnum opus. This saga is brilliant, arresting, and fulfilling, a true story of the esoteric secrets that fester in the human heart and are now awakening the human spirit. Georgia, a juicy and witty rebel angel, comes to us through Wyllie's engrossing and engaging prose—a totally balanced story of humankind's evolution and struggles with the forces of the dark and the light. If you want the real truth about the fallen angels, read this book!"

BARBARA HAND CLOW,
AUTHOR OF *AWAKENING THE PLANETARY MIND:*
BEYOND THE TRAUMA OF THE PAST TO A
NEW ERA OF CREATIVITY

"*Awakening of the Watchers* is the latest masterpiece to be released by the always inspiring Timothy Wyllie. This book expands you and compels the reader to go deeper into the mystery that is all around and within us. A captivating read that is hard to put down."

PAUL SAMUEL DOLMAN, AUTHOR OF *HITCHHIKING WITH
LARRY DAVID: AN ACCIDENTAL TOURIST'S SUMMER OF
SELF-DISCOVERY IN MARTHA'S VINEYARD*

"*Revolt of the Rebel Angels* and its series is recommended to everyone who is interested in where we have been and where we are going as a planet and as individuals. It will explain a little of what is out there. I can hardly wait for the next volume."

NEW DAWN MAGAZINE

"Timothy Wyllie's *Awakening of the Watchers* is a memoir of the dimensional ecology of the Lucifer rebellion and the Process Church that creates a living dialogue between the New Earth density and we the reader—the individual soul—a bottom line in any Universe."

ALFRED LAMBREMONT WEBRE, AUTHOR OF *THE OMNIVERSE:
TRANSDIMENSIONAL INTELLIGENCE, TIME TRAVEL,
THE AFTERLIFE, AND THE SECRET COLONY ON MARS*

"Timothy Wyllie's *Wisdom of the Watchers* is an enthralling read. Wyllie is an eloquent author with a discerning wisdom of the world. This book has the benefit of being practical and enlightening like a wonderful intertwined subjective journey. Truly awe-inspiring."

E. A. JAMES SWAGGER, AUTHOR OF *THE NEWGRANGE
SIRIUS MYSTERY: LINKING PASSAGE GRAVE
COSMOLOGY WITH DOGON SYMBOLOGY*

"In *Wisdom of the Watchers* Timothy Wyllie and his guide, Georgia, continue the deep revelations of the hidden histories and lost legacy originally detailed in *The Urantia Book*. *Wisdom of the Watchers* is the nexus of a history and destiny that is both personal and universal."

RANDY MAUGANS, OFFPLANET RADIO HOST

The
Rebel Angels
among Us

THE
APPROACHING
PLANETARY
TRANSFORMATION

TIMOTHY WYLLIE

Bear & Company
Rochester, Vermont

Bear & Company
One Park Street
Rochester, Vermont 05767
www.BearandCompanyBooks.com

Text stock is SFI certified

Bear & Company is a division of Inner Traditions International

Cataloging-in-Publication Data for this title is available from the Library of Congress

ISBN 978-1-59143-366-8 (print)
ISBN 978-1-59143-367-5 (ebook)

Printed and bound in the United States by Lake Book Manufacturing, Inc.
The text stock is SFI certified. The Sustainable Forestry Initiative® program
promotes sustainable forest management.

10 9 8 7 6 5 4 3 2 1

Text design and layout by Virginia Scott Bowman
This book was typeset in Garamond Premier Pro with Baskerville and Myriad Pro
used as display typefaces

Some books are crooks
they steal your time
but worse than that
some melt your mind
of all the books I've ever read
I prefer the ones that raise the dead.

JASON BARENHOLTZ, INSPIRED BY
THE WRITING AND FRIENDSHIP
OF TIMOTHY WYLLIE

Contents

∩

Timothy's Spiritual Legacy, Continued

An Update for the Reader

In Timothy's last book, *The Secret History of the Watchers,* I alerted the readers that Timothy had passed on from this life in October of 2017. I also shared the "succession plan" that Timothy and I had discussed in regard to carrying on his legacy—though Timothy and I always cringed when that word was mentioned, as there is both a finality and an arrogance that is often perceived by readers when using it. I would therefore like to take this opportunity to reintroduce myself and update you, the reader, on the status of Timothy's "outreach." I would also like to touch briefly on the meaning of Timothy's works.

Again, my name is Daniel, and Timothy and I shared a "surrogate" father and son relationship. As I mentioned in the previous book, Timothy directed me to "reach as many people as possible. If my writing, my art, and my music inspires them, I want to be in their homes."

Timothy and Georgia had completed three more books in the *Confessions* series by the time Timothy passed. The first—the aforementioned *Secret History of the Watchers*—was already in the editing phase when he passed and was published in 2018. I personally owe a great deal of gratitude to the whole Inner Traditions team, who demonstrated nothing but the highest levels of professionalism, caring, and *patience* when working with me—a novice—in getting the book to the readers. They helped picked up the baton with such a fervor—and in such a loving way—that I felt I was working more with a supportive family than a publisher interested only in putting a book out for a few shekels.

The final two books—both untitled—were complete and on Timothy's computer, right where he left them. Both manuscripts were submitted to Inner Traditions and were—not unexpectedly—picked up for publication. The book you are holding is the first, and the last book—Volume 8—is due out in 2021.

Timothy's new website, timothywyllie.com, is finally up and running. Please feel free to visit it. Though it is not yet 100 percent complete at the time of this writing, I will continue to flesh it out until it is. Timothy had more than four hundred drawings alone, and each of his pieces—books, artwork, interviews, articles, and so on—will have its own page. So please enjoy what *is* on there throughout the process!

Over the past couple of years, I have been inundated with emails asking for information on ordering prints, original artwork, and so forth. I am happy to announce that you can now order a print directly from the site, or contact me for additional information on originals (or anything else). I do not maintain Timothy's originals, which are in the care of Timothy's lovely "artner," June Atkin, but she and I work together closely, and I am glad to serve as an intermediary for her.

Taking on the management of Timothy's body of work has been interesting (to say the least). I knew many of his friends and family members already, but I have met so many more folks throughout this process. I see the impact Timothy's books and artwork have on some individuals, and it reminds me of how Timothy and I came to meet—and of the impact he has had on my life.

It puts a smile on my face when someone sends Timothy an email with the same questions, confusion, desperation, and *awakening* that

I experienced, and it feels good to share what I have learned with them—which brings me to a very important point that Timothy always conveyed: we are all on our own path, and there is no "right" or "wrong" on our personal journey.

There are some people who, in a haughty fashion, criticize Timothy and what lies within the pages of his books. To their surprise, I am sure, Timothy respected their differences of opinion and actually *loved* good, intellectual discourse—as well as respectful arguments. He lived life like a child in a candy store, and all of us were the magnificently interesting pieces of candy within that store to be explored.

Dear reader, you would be tickled to learn that Timothy kept notes on *each and every* person who contacted him. He cared. Back before the days of computers, smartphones, and contact lists, Timothy would keep a Rolodex of names, contact information, and tidbits of interest regarding each individual.

I keep the notecard he created when *I* first contacted him nearly thirty years ago. It simply reads, "Daniel Mator . . . impatient young man." Thus, the adventure began!

I share this with you because all Timothy cared about was sharing *with you* what he and Georgia experienced. What you do with that information is totally up to you; Timothy had no expectations of his readers. As he would say to me, "Daniel, all I can do is point in a direction . . . you have to do the walking." It would—because of his accurate assessment of my impatience (I'm getting better!)—drive me nuts sometimes, but it is in that walk where we learn the most about ourselves. And that walk is a personal, unique one that only *you* can experience.

So I speak on behalf of both Timothy and myself when I say that I sincerely hope this book contains *something* that assists you in finding answers about yourself and the world in which we live. Though I already knew Timothy and many of the personal exploits contained within these pages, it has still done that for me.

Note to the Reader
Regarding a Glossary of Terms
and the Angelic Cosmology

In this work the author has coined or provided specialized definitions of certain words, some of which are derived from *The Urantia Book,* a key source text. A complete list of these terms and their meanings has been provided in the glossary at the back of this book for your ready reference. The reader will find a brief overview of the angelic cosmology, also drawn from *The Urantia Book,* in the appendix.

An Emergent Understanding

The Twin Threads, Collaborating with
a Watcher, a Ventriloquist's Dummy,
Writing for an Audience

Those readers familiar with Georgia—the watcher with whom I collaborate—and her *Confessions* series will know that the two basic threads weaving through her narrative sometimes veer away in different directions, but they also sometimes synchronistically comment upon one another. As I don't plan out these volumes in advance, it's as much a surprise for me—as I would hope it is for the attentive reader—to see how these threads entwine and inform one another.

This volume perhaps more than any other brings the threads together so that each reveals aspects of the other that—up to that point—had remained hidden from me. Of the many factors that keep me interested in this long project, these synchronicities are the ones that fascinate me the most, as they are both unexpected and always deeply meaningful.

I admit to sometimes feeling a little too revealingly exposed by Georgia, but I have had to recognize in a very real sense—something I've long considered in the abstract—that it's best to consider my life as an experiment. But I suppose I have always thought of it as *my* experiment.

When I explored the potential for cetacean telepathy I was mostly in the ocean swimming with dolphins. I felt that I was actively using my body and my neural networks in an experiment from which I would be the beneficiary. I was the one with the record of my interactions with both wild and captive dolphins, while the dolphins may or may not have noted those occasions for themselves.

Writing with Georgia appears to be an extension of that. After all, she is participating in using my body and my neural networks. Yet at the same time, this is also a completely different experience for me. Here, unlike those ephemeral telepathic moments with dolphins, Georgia and I are leaving a snail's trace of printer's ink (or binary digits) that—word by word, sentence by sentence, paragraph by paragraph—exposes the precise state of our relationship, moment by moment.

In retrospect I can now understand that the two books (*Adventures Among Spiritual Intelligences* and *The Return of the Rebel Angels*) I wrote previously in conjunction with angels were a preparation for this collaboration with Georgia. In the previous books I would simply be aware of Zophiel or Zadkiel's presence and would get a pleasant frisson of affirmation whenever I got the words right.

Writing with Georgia is very different. After invoking her, the words always seem to be there. Even if they ooze out more slowly on some days than on others, she has never failed me. My job is simply to be patient and open. Yet it isn't anything like taking dictation, nor is it similar to automatic writing. Georgia insists that we are more fully collaborative than that.

So, what am I in this collaboration? I have the fingers, obviously, but I also act as a grounding for Georgia. I'm part research assistant, part source of anecdotes and examples, part butt of Georgia's dry humor, and part subject of her experiment. In fact, I now feel that I'm as much Georgia's experiment as I am my own. I believe I have been able to come to terms with this—as much due to Georgia's infinite consideration for my defects and limitations as anything I've done consciously to deserve this privilege. One of our running jokes is that Georgia is the ventriloquist and I, naturally, am the dummy.

As I've previously stated, neither Georgia nor I initially had any intention of publishing her "confessions." We were both writing them entirely for our own understanding. It was only when others read the first volume and believed it would have some general value for a wider readership that we both agreed to publish.

I was curious, to begin with, to find out whether writing with an audience in mind would impede the delicate process of working with a discarnate entity. Writing for an audience is quite a different experience. It can be as if I have a noisy crowd looking over my shoulder, each one demanding that a different word be used or another direction be taken. So I've been overjoyed to discover that Georgia's presence has remained consistent, and her voice has proved mercifully stronger than my own self-consciousness and timidity.

> *Let a divine being approach you! It may be nothing or everything. Nothing, if you meet it in the frame of mind in which you confront everyday things. Everything, if you are prepared and attuned to it. What it is in itself is a matter which does not concern you; the point is whether it leaves you as you were or makes a different person of you.*
>
> RUDOLF STEINER, *CHRISTIANITY AS MYSTICAL FACT*

> *Abandon the search for God, and creation, and similar things of that kind. Instead, take yourself as the starting place. Ask who is it within you who makes everything his own saying, "My God, my mind, my thought, my soul, my body." Learn the sources of love, joy, hate, and desire . . . . If you carefully examine all these things, you will find God in yourself.*
>
> HIPPOLYTUS, *THE REFUTATION OF ALL HERESIES*

The essence of the meaning of human existence is to be found not in a system of supposedly supernatural laws presided over by institutionalized authority, but instead in the experience of the individual heart and soul.

STEPHEN E. FLOWERS,
LORDS OF THE LEFT-HAND PATH

1

The Path to Breaking Free

Returning from Death, the Dalai Lama's
State Oracle, Life on Atlantis, Rebirth of the
Copper Trade, Twin Souls, Childhood Trauma

Mein Host Timothy's second life began when he returned from the
dead that rainy November afternoon in 1973—although he wouldn't
really understand this until he was more fully disentangled from the
imbroglio that he had created for himself.

His disappointment at hearing nothing back from Mary Ann—the
apex leader of the Process Church—about his near-death experience
(NDE) had created the first tiny crack in his conviction that she was
the incarnate Goddess. But he quickly repressed the thought. He clearly
didn't want to believe that she might have been playing him for a fool
all along. I could see it in his emotional body how firmly he pushed
down his moments of doubt. Besides, he had his work to distract him.

The New York Chapter of the Process Church on Manhattan's First
Avenue—now the Foundation Faith of the Millennium—was becoming
progressively busier as public interest in the New Consciousness movement brought in a wider set of people. It had been under my ward's
leadership that the Chapter had moved toward solvency, and I could see
that my ward thought he needed to play the game out. I don't believe

it ever came to him to leave the community at that point. Whenever I have heard him subsequently speak about it, he has always said that life in the Chapter was "terrifically stimulating and challenging," and he was "enjoying it far too much to leave." As a side note, I have also heard him claim that he was getting a certain vengeful pleasure from showing up the Four, each of whom, in turn, had run the New York Chapter into the ground before my ward had taken over.

I've come to think in retrospect that Mein Host was in a position of leadership in which he simply couldn't live with himself were he to let everyone down. If he gave any thought to the idea of leaving the community—and escaping the clutches of his dark Goddess—he must have known that such a situation would have to be very carefully crafted. Yet I saw no sign that this thought had ever crossed his mind as he settled back into his regular everyday life. Besides, his mind was filled with other matters—Tibetan Buddhism being only one of them.

Mein Host was no expert on Tibetan Buddhism, but—unlike many Westerners—he had at least read the Tibetan Book of the Dead as a result of his entheogenic explorations in the early 1960s. Having joined the community in 1965 and choosing to set aside entheogens, I doubt if he'd given any further thought to Buddhism until the afternoon two small, elderly Tibetan monks and their translator sat in front of him in his office.

What occurred then has continued to puzzle him, so I hope my view of that encounter will illuminate what has long concerned him.

There had been no warning, no phone call, no appointment; just Sister Marion—Timothy's assistant—knocking at his office door and asking him if he had the time to meet with "a couple of very odd-looking little brown men in skirts." Marion was an instinctive xenophobe.

After being introduced by the translator as monks Nechung Rinpoche and the slightly older Drepung Rinpoche, the pair in their saffron and brown robes sat down, both on the edge of their chairs with their backs rigidly straight and their nut-brown, oval faces sweetly impassive.

It was Nechung Rinpoche who did the talking. He spoke through their translator, who was standing slightly behind and between them. The Rinpoche explained that he was the senior monk of the Nechung monastery, and among his responsibilities was the care of the Dalai Lama's State Oracle.

My ward leaned forward with interest when he heard about the State Oracle. I don't believe he knew about this mediumistic practice descending from the pre-Buddhist Bön shamanism. And he certainly wouldn't have known—if indeed the monks even knew—that Bön shamanism itself was descended from a tradition brought to Tibet in one of the Lemurian diasporas between forty thousand and fifty thousand years ago.

Nechung Rinpoche went on to explain that the State Oracle was always consulted by the Dalai Lama before any important decisions were made, and it was the result of one of these psychic consultations that had brought them to his office. I saw a mixture of interest and confusion on my ward's face, and I could feel that he liked these men. He was at ease with them, and when I looked at his emotional body I could see how it was harmonizing with those of the two monks.

The Rinpoche went on to explain that the oracular consultation in question had concerned ways of introducing Tibetan Buddhism to the West. I noticed Drepung Rinpoche tilt forward slightly at this point, his left hand gripping the edge of the desk, his skin like tanned leather stretched thin over skeletal knuckles. Nechung Rinpoche had paused, and I could feel something unspoken pass between the two monks before he continued.

Here it comes, I thought.

It was in the course of this consultation with the State Oracle, the Rinpoche continued, that Mein Host's name had been pronounced by the Oracle as a person who would be helpful to their cause. Would he therefore help them?

This wasn't the kind of request that came in every day, and my ward has since said that he would have probably helped them without any prompting from the State Oracle. Of course, he was flattered! Who wouldn't be? The Dalai Lama's State Oracle, no less.

And, as we know, my ward has shown a weakness for being flattered. Yet, being half aware of this vulnerability in himself also must have brought up some reasonable doubts. *His* name! His *name*? It was such an improbable claim, as he said to Juliette (Mein Host's Process confidante) afterward—and whatever did they mean by *his* name, anyway? What name? Father Micah? Father Jesse (as he was now called)?

The name Micah had been originally given to him by Mary Ann, and now he'd used the opportunity of the community's renaming to rename himself. Jesse was the name he had chosen, although I don't believe he ever knew why he picked that particular name. He would always say that he "just liked the sound of it—all that snaky hissing."

"But you didn't ask, did you?" Juliette was smiling.

"Ask what?"

"I bet you didn't ask them whose name the Oracle used," she was laughing now, already aware of his answer.

So the situation stood. The name really didn't matter; he was going to do what he could for the monks because he liked them and respected them as fellow exiles. Although they didn't share a common language, they seemed to have a natural and unspoken resonance with my ward. More than once I caught the three of them giggling away at some shared unspoken joke. He said afterward that one of the characteristics he loved was the old monks' humor.

It was a perfect match. The Foundation Faith had the facilities, the Tibetan Buddhists had the message and the intention, and New York was ready for what they had to say. This combination led to two extremely successful conferences—as well as a series of seminars—delivered by these two eminent Buddhist monks. My ward wasn't to discover just how eminent they both were until many years later.

The Nechung monastery was indeed the seat of the State Oracle and a monastery devoted to a tradition so ancient that the place was still known as the Demon Fortress of the Oracle King. The Drepung monastery was close by in Tibet. These were two of the most senior

Rinpoches who'd managed to get out of Tibet. They really *were* following the direction of their Dalai Lama, as demonstrated by the gift of a white, raw-silk, mantilla-like scarf, delivered with the Dalai Lama's gratitude by Nechung Rinpoche to Mein Host after the last of the seminars.

So I can now put my ward's mind to rest. The State Oracle had indeed spoken of a person who would be of help and who could be found in Manhattan. The State Oracle also described the neighborhood and even the building—or so I heard—in which this person could be located. But there was never any name. No Father Micah, no Father Jesse. Sorry about that, old friend!

This distortion had arisen by way of the translator who'd known previously of Father Jesse and the Foundation Faith and who took advantage of his position as a go-between to pump up what was already a remarkable synchronicity into an offer impossible to turn down. If the Dalai Lama's State Oracle had spoken of him by name—*by name!*—how could he possibly refuse? How could *anyone* refuse?

However, from what I observed at the time, the two elderly monks knew nothing of their translator's manipulative ploy. I chose not to look any deeper into this, charmed as I was by the monks' quiet nobility and their resolute sense of purpose.

Yet, I'm bound to observe that both monks were highly intelligent and sensitive men and well trained in the subtle arts. In retrospect, since they are now long dead—and probably reincarnated somewhere in the West—I suspect they knew perfectly well what was going on. And they would have justified their small deception, no doubt, in much the same way as those in the community had rationalized so many of their own self-serving deceptions—as the end justifying the means.

I was aware that it never felt right to my ward that the State Oracle might have actually spoken his name, but he liked the monks and didn't want to believe they would lie to him so baldly. As the subject never came up again, it slipped into irrelevance until he had to revisit the interaction with the Tibetan monks for the book he wrote in 2009 about his time with the Process. It was then, so many years later, that the unlikelihood of his name being issued from the mouth of a trance medium on the other side of the world was undeniable.

Yet, there were still those two beautiful, pure, ancient beings, sitting in his office in front of him, their placid faces unreadable by a Western eye. Surely they couldn't have been lying straight to his face.

Still, in all that time, I don't believe it ever occurred to my ward that it was the translator's lie, distortion, or the man's embroidery—however he thought of it—that was responsible. As for the monks, yes, they knew about it, but they considered the deception irrelevant, assuming that it was simply how business was conducted in the West.

Please forgive my digression. Or, make of it what you will if you find value in it as metaphor. I wished merely to relieve my ward's mind on the matter that had continued to puzzle him.

The Foundation Faith of the Millennium was always purely a creation of Mary Ann. Now, with Robert (one of the founders of the Process and former husband of Mary Ann) and Verona (a Processean with whom Robert was romantically involved) well out of the picture, never to return—and their having given up on the idea of re-creating the Process in their image—Mary Ann was able to exploit the schism, as it came to be called, very much to her advantage. Although numerically it could barely be called a schism.

Life for most in the community—and for many of the junior members who knew nothing of its inner workings apart from the existence of an abstract Omega—remained much the same. This was despite the rewritten rituals, different colored uniforms, renamed magazines and newsletters, and the abrupt refocusing solely on Jehovah. A few people who would have left anyway at some point dropped away from the periphery; a few others joined up as there was no longer mention of Lucifer or Satan.

All of which suggested to me that it was never really the belief system that attracted people to the community; it was the personalities of those already involved. The belief system was the reason they would have given themselves to engage their rational (or irrational) minds, yet it would be in their emotional bodies that decisions such as whether to join the community would be made—and most would be unaware of this. Most wouldn't consciously know they were taking challenging aspects of themselves and seeing those qualities in others who appeared to have resolved them. In light of this, there should be no surprise that there was a lot of psychological projection involved.

As Mein Host was projecting his Goddess onto Mary Ann—who had willingly accepted the projection because, no doubt, she agreed with him—others, in turn, would project their dreams and desires onto my ward, as they would fixate on other of the senior Processeans who were more visible to the public. Most of this projection—because it was occurring on an emotional level and was largely unconscious or otherwise repressed—seemed to hang in the air like a steamy fog.

I observed that my ward chose to remain detached from much of these emotional shenanigans, which only succeeded in making him appear even more of a tempting morsel to women of a certain nature (*because* of his unavailability). However, he was far too busy to take much note of any of this. He had now accumulated a small battery of secretaries and assistants, all anxious to keep any outsiders from penetrating the shell within which he was able to keep working, to keep creating and coming up with moneymaking ideas. Of course, other senior Processeans were doing much the same in their own domains, but my narrative concerns my ward and only speaks of other people when they cross his path or affect him in some significant way.

I have no doubt that Mein Host appreciated this partial isolation, even if it meant overlooking or tolerating Sister Marion's bullying, officious ways. There were a few occasions when—through some skillful angelic coordination—certain people were able to make it through the shell surrounding him. In this way—although neither person knew it at the time—he would come to meet other rebel angel incarnates such as himself, and have a chance to work closely with some of them.

One of these was a remarkable woman who appeared in the New York Chapter one afternoon early in the spring of 1974. Her name was Hilda, and their recognition of one another was as immediate as it was unexplainable. It would emerge that Hilda's organizational efficiency, her wide network of contacts, and her well-established and much tested (as it turned out) psychic abilities, would position her ideally to collaborate with Mein Host for the next phase of his journey.

* * *

I have to be careful that I don't overstate my reactions to what I observed as I moved around Atlantis. I've always found it hard not to compare the quality of mortal life on Earth to what I found on my journeys to Zandana. And I had just returned from one of those visits.

The two planets were at roughly the same level of advancement at the time of Lucifer's revolution, but, based on my recent time there, it was quite obvious that Zandana had now drawn far ahead. Of course Zandana was not entirely without its problems, but they faded into relative insignificance when held up against what had been happening on Earth since the revolution—and under Prince Caligastia's stewardship.

Yet of all those many millennia of turbulence, it was what I was observing on the island of Atlantis that I found the most disturbing. The sight of all those incarnated rebel angels really shook me up, I can tell you. It was the last thing I expected to find. No one had ever warned us that this might occur, and I confess I was shocked. I hadn't yet known the possibility of a mortal incarnation was going to be open to rebel angels. This was still about seventy-five years before the second of the three disastrous natural catastrophes that befell Atlantis, the third of which entirely destroyed the island four millennia later.

At first appearances, admittedly, life on Atlantis seemed to be working like a well-oiled machine. It was evident that Prince Caligastia's midwayers had taken over and must have been in control for at least five hundred or six hundred years. Moving around the narrow streets, it looked to me as though the midwayers were consolidating their power on the island. A sure sign of this was the psychological condition of so many of the normal human beings—the "first-timers"—who were walking around in seemingly fugue states of consciousness.

I recognized the hand of Caligastia in this. I had seen it before, long ago, when the Prince was pushing his midwayers to develop those tragically—and criminally—premature, technological societies that ended in rendering much of North Africa and the Middle East uninhabitable for tens of thousands of years.

Men and women were moving around and fulfilling their everyday tasks as though hypnotized. No, they weren't quite automatons. They had feelings. They loved their children. They submitted to their superiors. They suffered with little complaint; as they also betrayed little of their joy. If anything, the various slaves I observed were actually more relaxed and expressive than their masters—or any of the free men I watched working at their stalls in the open marketplaces.

After seeing the quality of the goods for sale or for show, it didn't take me long to realize how wealthy the Atlantean society had become. The people must have built themselves up again on what had remained after the catastrophes of the thirteenth and twelfth millennia.

Impressive, I thought. But then I saw the copper. It seemed to be everywhere. It was shaped into pots and pans and every manner of cooking utensil, as well as gongs and finger pipes and an assortment of other small instruments. There were copper ornaments and intricate copper jewelry studded with precious stones, but most obviously, copper had been beaten into large, thin sheets and used as an external covering on the facades of the largest and most important buildings.

Evidently the copper mining in North America had started up again after a long hiatus. I knew most of the miners had been recalled after the disasters to help with the rebuilding work on the island, so here was another sign that the economy was prospering. The harbors were busy with boats. The larger, oceangoing vessels—some of which were unloading at the docks—were laden with copper ingots. Other, smaller vessels were making for the mainland and the various trading ports around the Mediterranean.

Moving closer to one of the harbors I could see boats bringing in tin from deposits in northern Spain, Portugal, and Cornwall, in southwest England. I have written previously at greater length about some of the discoveries made in metallurgy during the earlier eras of planetary life. The search for a stronger metal has always been another sure indicator that a particular species is showing signs of entering a technological period, and thus a time when genuine progress can occur. We were told in the lectures on Jerusem that this would have been prompted by a nexus of a number of different threads—from opposable thumbs to innate mortal curiosity, a familiarity with fire, and the demand for better weapons. There is a small minority of advanced aquatic cultures that places little or no reliance on an externalized technology born of their planets' metals but who need to use other methods to develop their cultures.

Different metals tend to be widely distributed over the continental landmasses on a planet such as Earth. Most of it is far underground with only a rare seam of gold, silver, copper, or tin reaching the surface, sometimes to be weathered away and washed down in streambeds as tiny pieces.

Until temperatures of the various metals—all with different melting points—are raised to precipitate liquidity, nothing of particular substance can emerge. Iron, in its turn, was generally found only in meteorites, and that was rare enough. However, copper and tin both have lower melting points than iron and are far more common.

Thus, in each of these technological surges—and I'm not including Lemurian technology here—bronze most often became the first combination of two metals to produce a serviceably hardened metal for the blades and points in the drive for evermore effective weapons. But finding the appropriate metals in quite different locations in the world—and then combining them in correct proportions to create the alloy known as bronze—required a sophisticated and wide-ranging organization.

As with the later development of the temperatures necessary to smelt iron ore and the techniques to anneal it into an even tougher metal, the technique of alloying copper and tin to produce bronze was one of the most closely held secrets of the age. During the eighth and seventh millennia it was the Atlanteans who held those secrets, and it was only they who possessed the oceangoing boats to transport the raw materials. To be able to move tin in bulk from the mines in Cornwall and Devon, and to ship the copper from the Great Lakes region of North America, required a large and efficient fleet, bold sailors, and excellent logistics.

No other culture on the face of the planet during the seventh millennium possessed the wealth or the skills to have accomplished these feats of invention and transport on such a massive scale. This had long made the Atlanteans the dominant power in Western Europe, the Middle East, and the Mediterranean region, as well as most of North and West Africa.

Yet, as wealthy and well organized as Atlantis had clearly become, there was always the issue of all those incarnate rebel angels and what they were planning. It wasn't until I penetrated the labyrinth of caves and lava tubes—some natural and some hollowed out in the foothills to form an interconnected series of laboratories—that I realized what those plans might entail.

* * *

The arrival of Hilda into my ward's life produced a remarkable increase in efficiency and doubled the amount of work coming out of his office. It also created the kind of waves expected when an interloper appears to be favored above those who feel they have served long and loyally.

It was inevitable in the hothouse atmosphere of a (largely) celibate community that the emotional bandwidth would be a fog of conflicting desires. Sister Marion had been doing a savagely effective job of keeping people away from my ward—members of the general public as well as the various assistants and secretaries then working for him. But how

Hilda came to be working alongside Father Jesse in his office (in his office, no less!) requires a little explanation, as Hilda, unknown to my ward, was part of a small team of incarnate angels commissioned to rescue him from Mary Ann's web of control.

Hilda, like the others in the rescue team, was only marginally aware of this motive and had other reasons for wanting to involve herself with the community. What I found amusing as I watched this parade of half a dozen young women—in all cases they were young women—who presented themselves over the next few years was that each one differed from the others in very specific ways. It was as if a benign Goddess was showing my ward a number of distinct aspects of herself. Some of these women may have believed this involved seducing him away from the community, while others tried to dazzle him with their psychism or the depth of their occult knowledge.

Among these women Hilda was exceptional; not only, as my ward put it, "for *what* she brought to the party, but for *how* she brought it."

It had started for Mein Host one afternoon while sitting alone in his office, gobbling down the lunch brought from the Cavern (now known as "J's Place") by Sister Marion. He was feeling somewhat overwhelmed by the pressure of work and wondering, so he tells me, what he could do about it. He'd recently had the chance to examine a form of systems analysis found to be helpful for complex engineering projects—in this case he says it was for a British submarine—in which significant events were plotted along a series of parallel timelines indicating what needed to be done and when.

Spending the afternoon creating a similar systems analysis of the many various projects now falling under his aegis, it became "startlingly obvious" (his words) that he was lacking one key individual who would enable the flowchart to work. He was very clear about the qualities this person needed to possess. He smiled when he wrote down that he hoped it would be a woman. She would need to be mature and intelligent, and it would be good if she was widely read and familiar with psychology, parapsychology, and spiritual and magnetic healing. It would be helpful if she had an artistic temperament and yet was personally well organized. And, of course, she would need to be available to work with him without expecting a salary.

My ward must have known it was a tall order to find all these qualities in one person, so he did what he intuitively felt was the correct action: he "asked the Universe"—as he so often did throughout his life—for the right person to appear to fill the post.

I take notice, although in retrospect, that this was the first time he'd actually consciously created (or rather co-created, as he would later come to understand) a future reality that would be fulfilled with a remarkable fidelity. He would use this approach at a number of key watershed moments in his future life when he would have no personal preference as to which course of action to take. By then, however, he would have a better idea with whom he would be co-creating his future realities.

In this case, the result manifested within twenty-four hours when Hilda stood at the bottom of the long staircase up to J's Place, a slightly puzzled expression on her freckled face and asking for a Father Micah. Completing the symmetry to this elegant synchronicity, it just happened to be Father Micah (now Jesse)—rarely out his office—who was standing at the top of the staircase to answer Hilda's question. He had no idea of what was going on behind the scenes. He also did not yet know that he was a rather different person after returning from his NDE only a few weeks earlier.

* * *

Hilda fulfilled the qualities Mein Host hoped for in a working colleague to a truly remarkable degree. She was slightly older than him—in her late thirties—which at his age of thirty-three my ward would have thought of as a grand amount of additional life experience.

Hilda naturally had her own reason for turning up at the New York Chapter and asking for a certain Father Micah, though my ward didn't learn what it was for some weeks. After climbing the stairs to where my ward stood waiting, and then meeting each other for the first time, the energy flowing between them was so pronounced that the reason she'd given herself for being there must have seemed irrelevant.

I must confess that observing this encounter made me somewhat nervous, too. It was clear to me that the meeting had been "arranged" by their companion angels, although at that time I didn't know the true purpose of Hilda's function in my ward's life.

Strange though it may sound, companion angels can never be absolutely certain as to how their arrangements are going to turn out, and this holds particularly true when incarnate angels are being guided to meet one another. There is good reason for this, although it may seem surprising. Of the 7 billion souls currently living out their mortal lives on the face of this planet in the early part of the twenty-first century, a mere 120 million of them—but more coming in every day—are incarnate angels. Though this may seem like a large number of incarnate angels, in reality it is still a very small percentage of the overall population.

Under normal circumstances incarnate angels are generally unaware of their angelic heritage, but they tend to be all too aware that there is something very different about them from most of the people in their lives. If they can negotiate their childhood relatively intact—which can frequently be extremely challenging—they tend to emerge with strong and charismatic personalities. Many normal mortals can be readily affected by such personalities. They often want to emulate or follow the incarnate or their words. Sadly, they can also slip into idolizing them.

Incarnate angels also possess what might be thought of as metafunctions. Depending on which stage an individual rebel angel is experiencing in their own arc of development—which may have involved multiple previous incarnations—a metafunction uses an individual's particular talents to reach a wider field of influence. In some cases this is made very obvious. Take Keith Richards of the Rolling Stones or the late John Lennon, both being rebel angel incarnates at different stages of their own development, and both having a profound and lasting influence on the world around them.

However, most angelic incarnates live less visible lives, and much of the effect they have on others occurs on a more modest—or even on a subconscious—level. And here's the most important point: because of their spiritual natures, incarnate angels are uniquely open to angelic guidance in a way normal mortals are not. Angelic incarnates, therefore, can become invaluable assets to the planetary Overgovernment should serious catastrophes need higher levels of angelic management.

It's for all these reasons that incarnate angels are generally not encouraged to become involved—unless there are specific reasons for doing so. And this is where the risks lie and when the sparks can fly.

This was not the case when my ward was greeting Hilda. There was quite evidently a deep level of mutual rapport, but neither of them would have been able to say what it was. Here is Hilda, describing those first moments in her own words: "We knew we were connected that first, fateful day when we laid eyes on each other. It wasn't exactly 'love at first sight' but rather a recognition that embraces a consciousness beyond human love. Stratospheric one might say—certainly not common and at times bizarre."

This might be rather overstating the immediacy of the connection from my ward's point of view. Remember, he had already accumulated a crew of young women who felt similarly about him, thus the experience wasn't quite so exceptional for him. As time passed, however—and as they came to know each other better—it became quickly obvious to him that Hilda was made of different stuff than the others; although, once again, he could never have articulated what that difference was.

Hilda, with her greater sensitivity, appears to have had a clearer view of what was happening between them. Once again, here she is describing her feelings when she looked back on those times: "In human lineage, Micah and I couldn't be more different. During World War II, I was brought up on Central Park West in New York City, while Micah was being reared in London. We didn't meet, in this world, until both of us were in our thirties. Micah and I never fell in love. We fell into each other's lives without expectation, without any future promise, without anything but the rather uncommon knowledge that we were somehow the same, perhaps even twin souls—Micah occupying a male body and I, in female form. But energetically we were each male/female, complete unto ourselves."

I believe from what I have observed of human love that the sensation of being twin souls is not an unusual one. True or not, many quite normal human beings can feel this about one another, and the concept of twin souls, or a single soul that has split into two, has always been the stuff of romantic dreams. Had Hilda left her thoughts at that they could be dismissed as mere romantic idealization, but to do so would thoroughly underestimate Hilda's prescience.

Here is how she continues in her brief summary of her feelings about Mein Host: "Since gender wasn't a factor in our coming together, we surmised that we were both androgynous—which in all probability makes us angels. Angels wouldn't need each other though they may want to be together from time to time to compare perspectives.

"Micah and I share the knowledge that we have been created from the same seed, perhaps not terrestrial, but certainly originating from the same Source. Stepping outside of the human context, which we often do, we both recognize our celestial origins."

These observations were made by Hilda many years after the events she describes. She and Mein Host have known each other for more than thirty years, intermittently being drawn together, as Hilda addresses: "Ours is certainly not your typical 'boy meets girl' story. In all our threescore years of encountering each other, there has never been a moment when we actually considered dating, courtship, marriage, or children. We often discussed the unusualness of our attraction. I still find Micah's very tall (well over six feet), very slender, well-delineated, very well-endowed body very enticing. But most of all I am drawn in by his icy blue eyes, long snow white hair (white from the day I met him), and extraordinarily handsome face. His startling appearance, British by birth, has always felt familiar . . . perhaps because he reminds me of an almost-transparent Nordic extraterrestrial being I recall encountering before meeting Micah. Many close encounters later, Micah's resemblance to my alien acquaintance triggered immediate recognition. Regarding Micah as not of this world has made it easy for me to view him as a metaphysical rather than a physical partner."

My collaborator is going to have to deal with any temporary embarrassment at my inclusion of Hilda's admiring comments. Sorry, my friend, but I insist. I want to use Hilda's actual words to suggest the complex intertwining of feelings of one incarnate angel as she tries to come to terms emotionally and spiritually with another incarnate angel, when neither of them are consciously aware of being angels.

Here she opens up on a more delicate subject and yet, once again, it illustrates something of these angel-to-angel relationships when they are lived in truth: "For thirty years, in this lifetime, Micah and I have circled around each other, often in different time zones and different geographical spaces, but always in touch, though rarely touching. Over our many years of interacting, we enjoyed only one brief sexual adventure that never repeated itself. Even in our one-time tantric twining, our bodies never consummated our relationship. But when you are racing at psychedelic cyclone speeds along the edge of the world, the last thing you can imagine is stopping to spread your legs. However, you can suck in the tail of the snake in your mouth as it winds its way round. This breathtaking trip opened many inner doorways as we ripped through the veils of our lives.

"Observing and interacting with Micah has always and still assists me to move beyond earthly inhibitions and boundaries, holdovers from an abusive childhood."

That should serve to draw a brief psychological sketch of Hilda and suggest something of the relationship she has with Mein Host. Physically, she was an attractive slim woman of medium height, well formed, and with an electric vitality. She had her auburn hair shortish, just curling over her collar, and wore minimal makeup on her lively, expressive face. There was something slightly masculine about her ways, which gave her the androgynous quality she herself pointed out earlier.

It emerged at some point that Hilda's father was known to most Americans who listened to the radio in the 1950s and '60s. Her father turned out to be a subject about which Hilda wasn't prepared to discuss. She clearly had an extremely complex and ambivalent relationship with her father, and I thought my ward was wise to avoid trying to probe. As it turned out, the sexual and physical abuse she underwent was so serious that it would take many more years of inner work before she would fully come to terms with what occurred at the hands of her parents. Besides, it really is Hilda's story.

She writes well, and my ward considers her a fine poet, so hopefully one day she'll publish the truth of what she endured as a child and how she managed to survive. It's an appalling story that needs to be told in full and be made more publicly available than anything I will include here. It will be far better written by her in her own words, and it should be told in her own time.

There are some important insights to be derived from my brief portrait of Hilda Brown, and I include them because her chosen lifetime will be somewhat similar to many other incarnate angels, in both male and female bodies.

While not every abused child is an incarnate angel, almost all incarnate rebel angels undergo some form of abuse, deprivation, or abandonment in childhood. I believe this is the consequence of a choice made prior to incarnation and is regarded as a bold and effective way of burning off karma. The nature of the abuse will relate to what an individual angel needs to learn or accomplish in their lifetime, and it will depend on what stage they've reached in their own Multiverse career. While choosing to experience a traumatic childhood doesn't hold true in every incarnate angel's case, there will inevitably be times in the life of certain ones when they'll likely wish they'd gotten the unpleasantness over with when they were young.

It is a common psychological observation that serious childhood trauma can produce states of dissociation, which can then later lead to a particular psychic sensitivity. I suggest there is a deeper truth: the psychic sensitivity is the angelic sensibility; the childhood trauma is the method chosen to activate that sensitivity, and dissociation is the means by which this is achieved.

2

The Rise of Discourse

Generating Resonance, Atlantean Slaves,
the Collapse of the A-Team, the Virgin Messiah,
the Schism, Sirian Overlords, the Countess

There was a shiver in the aether, and there was Astar—one of my sister watchers—phasing into the astral domain beside me, from where I was observing life on Atlantis.

Astar had made a particularly detailed study of the Lemurian civilization, and when the islands of Mu had finally disappeared under the waves of the Pacific, she had followed one of the smaller groups of Lemurian survivors to Atlantis. As far as I knew, she'd been on the island ever since.

Whereas I am more of a wanderer, Astar seems to prefer to stay in a specific location for as long as that one civilization endures. Only then will she move on to the next up-and-coming civilization, and she'll remain there studying that until it, too, collapses or disappears.

"I am of the opinion," I heard her voice in my mind—there was always that slightly haughty edge to her tone when I hadn't seen her for a while—"that in observing the rise and fall of a single civilization I will better be able to determine the dynamics and flaws of mortal cultures that can develop under such isolated conditions."

"And you plan to submit your report to Prince Caligastia—or perhaps to Jerusem?" I queried. It was a provocative question, and I thought it only half-jokingly. I didn't expect her to flip it back at me.

"What do you think, Georgia? What would you do?"

Truth is, I really didn't know what to think, let alone what to do—but then I'm not expected to submit a report.

It was obvious that Prince Caligastia had a tighter hold on Atlantis than ever, and—through his midwayers—he loosely controlled most of the other developing cultures in India, throughout the Middle East, and in parts of Europe.

Vanu and Amadon, now long gone—and their grand Lemurian experiment, which had once spread around the world, becoming the root culture from which so many others have descended—now only remained an influence in small settlements in South America and Tibet, in some regions of Eastern China, and on some of the Pacific islands.

I relaxed when I saw that Astar was now smiling.

She asked, "You didn't truly believe I would hedge my bets, did you?" But it wasn't a question, or at least not a question I was prepared to answer. As would frequently happen when I was with Astar, I learned more about myself and my own ambivalence from what would pop into my mind. It used to irritate me. I'd perceive it as Astar's pulling rank on me. But then I had to admit that she was actually doing me a favor by reflecting back to me my deeper state of mind.

And it was true. I had arrived back from Zandana with unusually mixed feelings. After hearing what Prince Janda-chi had to say about Prince Caligastia dragging all the other revolutionary worlds down with him—and then finding the Prince had put his ascension gridlock in place—had been a nasty shock. It seemed only to confirm Prince Janda-chi's worst predictions.

Astar and I were in one of the larger subterranean chambers the Atlanteans had enlarged from the maze of lava tubes and converted into a laboratory. A quick look around established that among the mortals working in the chamber there were a few incarnate angels. They appeared to be working alongside the normals. Mind you, neither the incarnate angels nor their regular mortal colleagues would have been able to readily discern any noticeable difference between them, apart from what I could see was a certain social awkwardness on the part of the incarnate angels. Had I known the diagnostic term at the time, I might have considered the latter as having some form of Asperger syndrome.

Astar was pointing out the various devices being developed as we moved between the long bench tables. As you'll be aware, I don't have much of a head for science, so I couldn't make any sense of what I was seeing.

"Resonance," Astar broke into my thoughts again. "They're working on ways of generating resonance—high-frequency vibrations—in matter."

"Like Lemuria? Like what they used to do?" I knew that Vanu had passed along some of the secrets of manipulating matter using sound.

Astar's tone had grown wistful. "That's what's so sad. They know the legends of the ancients. They know it's possible to levitate massive blocks of stone, but they don't know how the ancients did it. They think it must be something to do with sound, but—as you can see—they're trying to make it happen using those mechanical devices."

Looking closer, I could see inside some of the devices a huddle of interlocking gears—cogwheels of varying sizes—that seemed to terminate in a large quartz crystal.

Astar said, "They are attempting to excite the crystal. Do you see? But they'll never do it mechanically. They've lost the secrets of sound. Other people might have retained more of the ancient knowledge, but you can see here they haven't . . . not for all their advancement."

I couldn't tell from Astar's tone if she was disappointed or relieved at what she'd called a scientific dead-end. What surprised me was that she had made no reference to the incarnate angels I was watching working here in the laboratory—or those I'd seen in the marketplace earlier.

"They're not helping . . . not at all, the arrogant fools!" I don't think Astar knew I could hear her thinking—she'd not closed down the channel. She was as angry as I'd ever heard her, maybe angrier. "They think they know best—but they know nothing! Absolutely nothing!"

I was taken aback at Astar's sudden vehemence, and my startled reaction must have reminded her of my listening presence. Her tone was more measured when she reached out to me again. "Like my Prince Caligastia, I had great hopes for the successful reimprinting of the grid. I thought we could make up for all the setbacks if humans could be recycled back onto this planet for their next life. It would be good for us, good for them, good for everyone. That's what I thought . . . but look at what we got!"

She paused, and I wondered whether she was going to get angry again. She was clearly far more emotionally invested in the fate of the Atlantean civilization than I was, which was one of the hazards of specializing in a single culture. It was also evident that, like Caligastia, Astar had underestimated the ingenious response of the Multiverse Administration (MA). By reincarnating rebel angels in place of the normal mortal ascension program, MA had outwitted the Prince's plans, while at the same time giving the rebel angels an opportunity to experience a third-density life.

Astar broke into my thoughts, angry again. "And look what happens when they take a mortal lifetime! They forget everything they ever knew. They become dulled. Fools. And we had such high hopes."

I wondered if this wasn't Prince Caligastia's line of thought that Astar was parroting. But as I watched the so-called scientists in the laboratory more carefully, I couldn't help noticing a certain hesitancy in their movements that was then covered up by a bullying, know-it-all attitude. More than once I saw them shouting angrily at the incarnate angels and, in one case, one of them received some very harsh blows. It looked like they were getting blamed for all the scientists' failures and their ugly moods.

I was starting to see what Astar meant.

I think, in retrospect, that most of us underestimated the effect of a third-density reality on the more sensitive angelic system. Of course none of us knew such a risky hybridization experiment hadn't been tried before. What was it that the angel Joy once told my ward? "Placing an angel into a human vehicle is like squeezing a rainbow into a Coca-Cola bottle."

A glamorous enough comparison, I'm sure, but it didn't start to describe the actual difficulties an angel faced in one of their early mortal incarnations. Astar had gone on to explain that when the rebel angels first started appearing some four centuries earlier, they really had been imbeciles. "Like silly children," she'd said, "who had never grown up."

According to Astar, it had become slightly better over the years, but it was when she told me to observe more closely that I got my next shock. All four angel incarnates in the lab were actually working at the most mundane of tasks: clearing the debris off the benches, sweeping the floor, and serving the needs of the scientists! They were the slaves!

I'd managed to get the whole incarnated angel business upside down. I thought the angels would bring their genius with them into their mortal incarnation, but it was quite the opposite. The density, especially in the emotional bandwidth, was too much for them.

This business of "density" is difficult to explain to those who live their everyday existence within it. Perhaps an example from my ward's experience will make the concept of density more tangible.

In the late 1980s, Mein Host was living in New York City and was contacted by a group from Sedona, Arizona, calling themselves the "A-Team" and requesting contacts for a proposed tour they planned for Manhattan in a few months. The A-Team claimed to be extraterrestrial walk-ins and that much of their teaching involved the subtle manipulation of sound. They came with impressive credentials for what they were able to accomplish with their precisely modulated vocalizations.

My ward, who'd already come to know several walk-ins—one with whom he had traveled extensively and knew as a brother—was open to helping out the A-Team. He took them at their word and put them in touch with the appropriate people. Hotels and venues were fixed up for them, and the city's alien cognoscenti waited with some interest to hear what these folk from Andromeda had to show them.

A couple of days before the first seminar, the A-Team flew in from Sedona. My ward, his function fulfilled, had heard nothing more from them until he received a phone call on the day of the seminar to tell him that the A-Team had all returned to Sedona the previous night. They had spent barely twenty-four hours in Manhattan before their crippling headaches and state of mental confusion had driven them back to Arizona.

They had been prepared to pay off the venues and lay out the exorbitant fees to change their tickets, just to get out of the density of Manhattan as fast as possible. It seemed their more refined sensitivities were simply unable to tolerate what they themselves called the "emotional density of the city."

I have heard people questioning why extraterrestrials don't make themselves more obvious; why they're not seen walking around the planet alongside humans. There are, of course, some extraterrestrials who are doing just that—and bless them for taking on the assignments. However, for most advanced off-planet races, spending any time on a third-density world is an extremely uncomfortable experience. Most prefer to avoid it.

The density is not as discombobulating an experience for incarnate angels because their mortal human bodies are already attuned to third-density frequency domains. But it is why—although you might feel us or sense our presence—you will never actually see a watcher, or any angel, within any of humanity's third-density domains.

What I witnessed on Atlantis with Astar was a group of incarnate angels at early stages in their reincarnational cycles, whose material bodies at that time reflected their difficulty with adapting to the density. When I contemplated the implications of this, I found that rebel angels could expect to undergo who knew how many lifetimes in these limited—and limiting—mortal vehicles before they could achieve any degree of reasonable parity that would allow them to live unrecognized alongside normal mortals.

I realized to my horror that—if I was ever to achieve mortal incarnation—I, too, might have to face a few such humiliating incarnations. The idea of spending lifetimes being dismissed as simpleminded or discarded as mentally unbalanced or being enslaved—as I observed occurring on Atlantis—appalled me.

I became considerably less enthusiastic about the prospect of entering mortal incarnation, I admit to you, when I observed those poor, simple creatures being bullied by a lot of arrogant, all-too-human, self-proclaimed Atlantean scientists.

* * *

It was one of the rare occasions the Omega—one of Mary Ann's many titles—had ever come down to Manhattan after she and Robert had settled into Mount Chi, their house in Westchester County. Now that Robert was gone, and Mary Ann was the sole center of the community, it was even more unusual to find her one afternoon, sitting together with most of her inner circle in the fancy living room of the priests' residence on East 49th Street.

They'd been drinking their coffees and smoking their cigarettes while discussing the goings-on in the various chapters as they normally did at such meetings—though such meetings were normally conducted at Mount Chi. This had created an atmosphere of nervous anticipation among the small group as they cleaned and dusted the 49th Street house in preparation for the unexpected visit—a tentativeness that lingered on well into the meeting.

Mary Ann clearly enjoyed playing the anticipation for all it was worth and put off until late in the evening what she'd obviously come down to Manhattan to disclose. And when she did, it was to introduce the most preposterous idea—in my opinion—that she had ever proposed. It was also one of the most revealing, because by the time the idea had played itself out, Mary Ann never raised the subject again. I suspect even she, who was shameless, may have been embarrassed in retrospect.

However, as they sat around the living room, she was quite serious about her instruction to her inner circle: she told them to go and find the Messiah! Yes, indeed! They had to go out there on the streets of the city and bring back the Messiah!

You might imagine that this order would startle most groups of young people living at the tail end of the twentieth century, but, by now, Mary Ann's inner circle had been tempered into tougher material. They may have thought it absurd, as did my ward, but they weren't about to say anything about it. By that time they knew better than to question Mary Ann. As my ward said later, "However silly the idea was, because it came from Mary Ann, it had to be about *something*!"

They quite reasonably asked how they would know the Messiah. Mary Ann then defined the Messiah as a young man between twenty-five and forty years old, who was pure and unblemished—and who was also a virgin. Yes, a *virgin*! In the 1970s! In the midst of the sexual revolution! That was going to limit the contestants.

They were to go out and search for the Messiah and meet back a couple of weeks later to report on their progress, or to produce the Messiah if they'd found him, of course. I don't think there is any need for me to dwell at any length on the various situations in which my ward and the others found themselves as they went about their sacred search. You can, I'm sure, imagine their state of mind as Mein Host and his pair for the day were standing outside a theological seminary trying to spot a likely candidate and wondering how they were going to pop the question: Are you a virgin? And then, of course, the most important question—and what the search was all about: "Are *you* the Messiah?"

Of course the mission strained credulity. Even in the unlikely chance they might find a virgin, wouldn't a man who answered "yes" to the Messiah question automatically disqualify himself from truly being the Messiah? For if a shaman who claims to be a shaman is no shaman, then a messiah who claims to be the Messiah is no messiah.

Surely the real Messiah would be self-evidently and obviously messianic. You wouldn't have to *ask* the man who he was; the knowledge would beam out of his eyes, wouldn't it?

Manhattan might not be considered the most likely place to find the Messiah, and the eight people scouring the city for a couple of weeks ended up with no reason to disagree. There'd been a number of embarrassing incidents as it turned out that very few people ever got beyond the virgin question. It seemed that certain privacy issues came up.

Mein Host didn't appear to throw his heart and soul into the search for the Messiah. Although I never saw him express his opinion openly about it, he clearly thought it was a pointless mission; and I don't believe he ever even approached a prospective virgin. Besides, he was far too busy to spend much time on such a fruitless endeavor. Hilda's daily presence at a desk in his office had the beneficial effect of bringing out the best in him. I've observed that my ward often does his best work when closely collaborating with another person—as he is now collaborating with me.

I observed this behavior with interest as I could see this dismissive reaction to an instruction from his Goddess—although he'd kept it well hidden—was something of a first for him. It could have been her complete lack of acknowledgment of his NDE—or it could have been an aftereffect of his NDE—but the crack in his conviction was widening.

When the second meeting came around, Mary Ann took the trouble of coming down to Manhattan again—something I don't believe she ever repeated. She was obviously wanting to make a point. She would have already known that no Messiah had yet been found, so it had to be something she believed of paramount importance.

It turned out to be an equally harebrained idea.

"If the Messiah can't be found out there in Manhattan, then perhaps the Messiah is among us," was the gist of Mary Ann's spiel, which she delivered while looking around the small group, from person to person, with a curious intensity in her green eyes. Mein Host commented on it afterward to Juliette when they were comparing notes on the meeting. He told her it gave him "a cold shiver down his backbone" when Mary Ann looked at him like that and that he "hoped to hell she wasn't going to pick on him!" He was no virgin, and he certainly had no pretensions of messiahhood, but as he agreed with Juliette: "You never knew with Mary Ann."

A perceptive insight. And considering what happened next, not without reason. Having quickly established that the Messiah was not sitting in the living room alongside her, Mary Ann's attention turned to Father Jonathan, the young Priest who was currently leading the Boston Chapter.

Jonathan—the younger brother of my ward's friend and fellow architect Richard—first entered my narrative when he'd defied his parents and joined the Process as a seventeen-year-old. It had taken a wrongly addressed envelope revealing the opposition's courtroom strategy—and a brilliant defense by the eminent psychologist Ronald Laing—to have the parents' case dismissed and for Jonathan to stay in the community.

Jonathan was a beautiful young man. He was tall and slim with the same blond, almost white, hair as his brother Richard. He was immensely earnest and dedicated to both Mary Ann and to building up the Process. He would push himself hard, harder than most, because he'd never want it thought that he was riding on his brother's—his older and far more senior brother's—coattails.

In manner, Jonathan was somewhat slow-witted—"not the brightest bulb in the billboard"—to quote my ward, who liked the man without ever having been particularly close to him. They were seldom, if ever, in the same chapter together.

When Jonathan first joined the community I know my ward wasn't the only one who thought the seventeen-year-old might be slightly mentally retarded. Yet he'd lasted the course with the rest of the hard-core members. He'd pulled his weight and taken his knocks with the best of them, and he'd risen through the ranks to take charge of a chapter. No small accomplishment.

He was also acknowledged to be one of the best donators in the community—his looks being much to his advantage—and he was clearly an inspiring leader. His chapter was by now bringing in an inordinate amount of money each week.

The money raised by different chapters was invariably the standard by which they were judged. A chapter might be doing great work in social outreach—it might have a fine band or be running successful and well-attended courses and classes—but if they weren't bringing in good money, then something was thought to be seriously amiss.

As the weeks passed, Mary Ann began speaking more and more enthusiastically about Father Jonathan's leadership and the Boston Chapter's ever-burgeoning income. Mary Ann's style was to boost someone's success, while simultaneously using that success to berate and humiliate those who were not as successful.

It did seem that magic was afoot. The Boston Chapter under Father Jonathan was not just consistently pulling in more money than the other chapters, it was making substantially—no, vastly—more. Week after week. More and more. Nobody could deny it. Father Jonathan was making miracles happen.

So I doubt if anyone in the inner circle was altogether surprised when Mary Ann announced that it was Father Jonathan who must surely be the Messiah!

It must have been hard for my ward to suppress his laughter when he heard this. Like all of them—except, it seemed, Mary Ann—Father Jonathan, for all his financial acumen, would never have even made the top 100 of possible messiahs. If anything was more absurd than walking the streets of Manhattan stalking the Messiah, it had to be in considering that Father Jonathan might be "the One."

No doubt the Oracle would have reasoned that as Jonathan had joined the Process at such a young age he would have to be a virgin. He was never present at any of the group-sex shenanigans, and he possessed the kind of simple innocence that might be expected of a virgin.

Within a week Father Jonathan found himself being moved to

Mount Chi to join the Four in their wing of the Oracle's house. And, of course, to become subject to the relentless questioning Mary Ann no doubt would have demanded to assure her of his authentic messianic status.

I wasn't present when the truth came out, but it must have been an unpleasant shock for Mary Ann because nothing was ever said again about Father Jonathan being the Messiah. And Jonathan soon found himself demoted—sent to another chapter—and would spend the next few years in disgrace, out on the streets every day, donating.

The truth was bound to leak out sooner or later, however much Mary Ann would have liked to keep it under wraps, and then it was only to the select few of the inner circle. It was not only that Father Jonathan was no virgin, but the reason the Boston Chapter was doing so spectacularly well was that Father Jonathan had been cavorting with the pretty young donators. Or, as Mary Ann might have been heard to mutter through her teeth, "The bloody man was running a bloody harem."

Mary Ann, like many autocrats, lacked any appreciation of irony—especially when the joke was on her. That she could ever have thought such a "profligate womanizer" (her words) was a virgin, let alone the Messiah, might well have exposed her as shortsighted at best, and very possibly a bit crazy, too.

There was, of course, a double irony here. Not only was there Mary Ann's comical error of judgment but also the very way he was getting the best of his donators was sexual . . . in a celibate community! The masters of the other chapters who had been straining hopelessly to compete with the sexually excited girls of the Boston Chapter—while faithfully following the group's celibate standards—found themselves suddenly vindicated.

Jonathan was generally popular among the inner circle and being Richard's brother had brought him in closer contact than others with the senior leadership. Yet because he joined some three years after the Process originally started, he had never been considered part of the Omega's inner circle. In such a rigidly hierarchical community—regardless of his connections—Jonathan was still regarded as relatively junior. In short, the man was definitely not top management material.

I'm sure it was the extraordinary financial success of one so junior, and presumably inexperienced, as Father Jonathan that was so shocking as well as irritating for those who had been harshly treated by Mary Ann for their financial failures. Those of the inner circle may have liked Jonathan as a person, but there wasn't one among them who didn't take a certain pleasure from seeing him fall so thoroughly from grace.

His punishment was long-lasting and severe. He was evidently one who, like my ward, had deified Mary Ann, so spending years in exile—denied from ever seeing his Goddess—was the harshest of all penalties. My ward may have had his ups and downs with Mary Ann, but apart from those three days he spent sitting in disgrace outside Xtul, he had made himself far too useful to be exiled to the boondocks.

My ward is hoping I'll throw some light on this curious—even for them—and revealing episode. Could Mary Ann really have believed the Messiah was to be found living and working in Manhattan? Failing that, did she really believe for one moment that Jonathan might be the Messiah for whom she was looking? What was behind her insistence on finding such a Messiah?

Mary Ann, I tell him—as if he didn't know—was an extremely complex person. An aspect of the woman that my ward never witnessed—nor indeed had anyone else except perhaps Robert in his time—was the emotionally deprived little girl who was not allowed to grow up naturally. Being forced to learn the art of emotional manipulation at such a young age, she'd successfully locked away her tenderness and innocence, but she had never removed it.

It is difficult for my ward to acknowledge what he never witnessed in the woman; and besides, his conviction that Mary Ann was the Goddess would have blinded him to her other qualities. However, placing her behavior in context, she had only just managed to get rid of

Robert, the man she'd been desperately trying to mold into the Messiah for at least a decade with no success. The man had run off with his paramour. You'd have thought she'd have given up on the Messiah business after that hopeless and humiliating failure. But that does not take into account this immature, emotionally needy aspect of Mary Ann. It was a part of her she kept so well hidden that she couldn't even see for herself the absurdity of her search—or the lunacy of the instructions she had given to find this virgin Messiah. Then to double up on her foolishness, to cast poor Father Jonathan in that impossible role—a role he strives to this day to fulfill—and to so cruelly abuse him for her famous prescience, was asking for a very firm rap on the knuckles.

Mary Ann wasn't used to being this wrong, and she evidently wasn't about to start now. She was, of course, absolutely furious with Jonathan when she learned the truth of his sexual improprieties, yet with never a word about her own part in all the foolishness.

And that was that. There was no more talk about the Messiah. Perhaps Mary Ann was affirming for herself that she didn't need a messianic partner—or that there wasn't a man out there with the right credentials (credentials she defined). Not that she would ever have played second fiddle to the Messiah even if she did find him— although I rather think that any messiah worth his salt wouldn't want to couple his destiny to one such as Mary Ann and her little cult of true believers.

Yet Mary Ann may have drawn a single lesson from the Messiah affair that she would apply with her usual complicated mixture of motives. And it would be no surprise that it would be Mein Host who would fall into her trap.

* * *

Autocratically organized societies have a way of being aggressive and warlike. Atlantis was no exception. Whereas they had once been known throughout the Mediterranean region for their piracy, now their aggression was more ordered and almost entirely marshaled behind their vast merchant empire based on copper, tin, and other metals—like silver and gold—that the Atlanteans considered of less importance.

Their trading relations with the people of Crete had remained relatively stable, and there was a certain amount of artistic and intellectual cross-pollination as well as migration between the two islands. However, there was a constant rumble of hostility between the civilization that was emerging in the lower Nile Valley from the ashes of the previous culture, which had been ravaged by drought when the climatic conditions had changed so radically four millennia earlier.

Astar explained that the Atlanteans, the Sea People, had then taken pity on the people of the Nile estuary and that so many Atlanteans had emigrated to Egypt between the eleventh and seventh millennia that the region had become an extension of the island kingdom. They brought their beliefs and their gods with them, along with their ways of life, their customs, their symbols, and their architectural and construction techniques. What had once been a small colony of Atlanteans in Egypt had become, over the millennia, a force to rival their parent culture.

Here, in broad strokes, is how Astar explained the way this change in the balance of powers came about. She pointed out something that would never have occurred to me: the Atlanteans, she stressed, were the epitome of an island culture. No one had ever invaded their island kingdom, and the only catastrophes they'd ever faced were natural disasters—the responsibility for which they lay at the feet of their gods. You might say that the innate sense of insularity bred deep into all island populations became, for the expanding Atlantean settlements in Egypt, both a curse and a blessing.

Astar explained that the Atlantean settlers were psychologically, and therefore culturally, unprepared for the combination of the strength of the local traditions, inherited mainly from the Land of the Two Rivers, and the influence of traditional entheogenic shamanism. They attempted at first to impose their more advanced ways—a symbol of which became the massive carved figure of the Sphinx and a number of stepped pyramids that have long since been reduced to rubble, their stones used to re-create or emulate the original structures some seven millennia later. These original stepped pyramids in Egypt were direct, though distant, descendants of the monolithic stepped pyramids of Lemuria.

The conceptual brilliance of the Sphinx at Giza, Astar said admiringly, lay in its monumental projection of implacable authority and its statement of permanence. In carving the figure out of the living rock of the plateau—even when additional blocks were needed, they were cut from the rock on the site—the makers ensured its most fundamental property would be permanency and indestructibility. In spite of being lashed by floodwaters and the monsoon rains—which resulted from the radically altering climatic conditions and the constantly changing course of the Nile River—and despite the earthquakes that rippled regularly through the region destroying lesser structures, the Sphinx remained, age after age, and is far more ancient than the Giza Plateau pyramids, having survived now for almost twelve thousand years.

Egypt, because of its pivotal geographical position, was always a confluence of different cultural influences. Within eight hundred years of the arrival of the first Atlantean colonizers, the subsequent rapid expansion of power was seen to have benefited from a variety of cultural influences from the South and East. By the mid-eighth millennium, Egypt had grown to rival the island nation that had originally spawned it. So by the time Astar and I were surveying the vessels coming and going from one of the harbors within the inner ring, we could see that a number of these boats were carrying armed troops.

One of the ways the two cultures had grown apart, Astar told me, lay in how the kingdoms were ruled. The Atlanteans had always carried an ancestral memory from their Lemurian forebears of Vanu and Amadon, who were remembered as the Divine Twins. On Atlantis this was used to establish the divine right of kings, as well as setting a pattern of pairs—four pairs—or the eight primary deities of the Atlantean religious system.

When the Atlanteans first colonized Egypt it was a belief in these eight gods and goddesses that accompanied them. However, in the melting pot of all the different belief systems centering in the Nile Valley, the Atlantean deities had yielded to other cultural and religious influences enough to have formed what was essentially a new and separate religion from their mother culture. In Egypt the priest caste rose to power with their assimilation of many of the shamanic practices from India and the East. It was only later—when it became clear that the people needed their figureheads—that they started empowering ruling families to become the pharaonic dynasties that dominated the later eras.

What we were watching, said Astar, was a piece of classic social and religious engineering; a mother culture—as in cell mitosis—extruding its offspring, which then matures and redefines itself according to the indigenous cultural and psychosocial expectations as well as its need to separate itself from its parent.

It was this clash of ideologies that Prince Caligastia and his rebel midwayers were able to use to their advantage. Sad to say, the rebel cause—as promoted by the Prince—remained his basic strategy of divide and conquer.

It was later that same day, and Astar and I were relaxing high on the slopes of Atlas, the great central volcano from which the island received its name—as well as its very substance. A rising full moon was turning the distant ocean into a silvered living being stretching far into the clouded horizon. We hadn't spoken for a long time, bewitched as we always were by the beauty of an unspoiled third-density spectacle. (Note: I use the word spoken *toward a vocal culture to describe initiating a telepathic contact*).

I was already aware of the part played by different extraterrestrial races with a variety of different investments in this planet. It had been the Pleiadian interplanetary arks that evacuated those willing to travel with them from the sinking islands of Mu. There was the Sirian mission that reached out to the people of Atlantis at the time of the first series of natural disasters in the mid-thirteenth millennium.

I had heard the reasons given for defying the planetary quarantine: the Pleiadians had their DAL Universe, and the Sirians had their own traditions to honor with the sun being the fourth star within their domain. And, of course, there were the gourmands from Itibi-Ra, who didn't believe harvesting a few fruit from deep in the Amazon rain forest was really breaking the quarantine . . .

Astar broke into my thoughts as I hoped she would.

"After the disasters of the twelfth and thirteenth millennia—and the Sirian rescue mission had completed its humanitarian task—there was a small group of eight Sirians who stayed behind to aid in the rebuilding of what was still the most potentially progressive civilization on the planet at the time.

"Well, no surprises here: the Sirians stayed on long after the Atlanteans had built up their civilization again. Coming as they did from a more advanced culture, it was inevitable they would have a hand in molding the Atlantean civilization and its belief system along Sirian lines."

Let me interrupt Astar for a moment and clear up an obvious confusion regarding the Sirians, as well as the involvement of a number of other extraterrestrial races with an interest in this world.

There are four ways in which beings of another planetary race can establish a presence on this planet. They can come here in their craft if they have the technology to do so. They can incarnate one of their race into a human body. They can travel here in an altered state of consciousness. And—under emergency conditions—they can walk into a vacated adult body as a walk-in.

Each method has its advantages and disadvantages. For example, though beings might travel here in their light-bodies, they will be unable to interact with the third-density reality. As an aquatic race, the Sirians had limited access to human societies, so apart from a rare appearance in the physical—as when they'd originally come to the rescue of the Atlanteans in the time of the first disasters—they used the serial reincarnational method. Thus, the original Sirian being would return after the death of the physical vehicle to occupy the body of his next in line, and so on. You will see this dynamic reflected in the preoccupation the Egyptian dynastic pharaohs of more recent times held for their death rituals.

Here again is Astar, speaking about another aspect of this increasingly complicated situation: "This will act as a demonstration for other interplanetary races of what might happen if they dabble in the affairs of another world, however noble their initial motives may have been. And the Sirians *were* initially acting from altruism. They might have even gotten away with it if they hadn't been tempted to stay on—again with the best of intentions. That's what got them hooked. They just couldn't resist it. To them the native population of Atlantis were like children who were subject to the whims of the midwayers."

Now that answered a question I had.

We were told in our Jerusem seminars that under normal circumstances one of the essential functions performed by the midwayers was to act as a filter to keep off-planet races from unauthorized meddling. If an entire System of planets has been officially quarantined—not a possibility ever addressed in the lectures, I might add—it stands to reason the planets within that System, like Earth for example, would be doubly protected from outside interference.

What I was being asked to understand from Astar's inference was that some form of reciprocal deal must have been made between the resident Atlantean midwayers and the Sirian overlords. I noticed Astar's reluctance in pursuing this subject as she closed the discussion by saying presciently, as it turned out, "They will not be able to continue in this practice for very long."

Just how long? Astar was unwilling to say.

* * *

I have touched on the subject of celibacy in describing a number of occasions in my narrative of Mein Host's life when his sexual abstinence revealed some significant aspect of human behavior. I've also suggested that by claiming to be celibate, the community was making a public statement very much in opposition to the sexual manners of the day. They certainly wished to *appear* celibate, but as we know that wasn't entirely true.

However, whatever sexual activity existed tended to be tightly organized and prescribed by Mary Ann. There were the weeklong Absorptions (Sacred Marriages) back in London and, more recently, each chapter might have one or two married couples living within its walls. There were occasional group-sex sessions—though there hadn't been one of those for a couple of years (and they would never again be repeated). Other than these rare situations, though—all of which would have been initiated or directed by Mary Ann—the rule of celibacy was followed, dare I say it, with religious devotion.

Celibacy had emerged naturally in the early days of the community and after they'd left England for Nassau. My ward insists that it wasn't because they were antisex—a number of them had already slept with one another before joining the group, as had Juliette and my ward—but because it made life a great deal more simple when they were focusing on the psychic and spiritual dimensions of life.

And there was some truth in this. The collapse of many of the experimental communes and communities that flourished briefly in the 1960s and '70s was a direct consequence of the disharmony resulting from sexual games, petty rivalries, jealousies, and resentments—any of which can easily lead to the inevitable dissolution of the community spirit.

As I've come to observe the Process over the years, I believe there was another dynamic at work. Claiming to be celibate—while knowing there was sexual activity happening behind the scenes—allowed them all the excitement and self-importance of belonging to a secret society.

They were proud of their celibacy. It was a mark of their self-discipline in a self-indulgent age. They didn't get high, they didn't get drunk, and they didn't have sex. They liked to give the impression of being above all that sort of thing. It didn't make them popular, but it did make them interesting.

Mein Host appeared just fine with this. I never heard him complaining about the lack of sex—he'd certainly had no lack of it before joining the group. He'd never enjoyed alcohol, and I believe he was grateful to have done his entheogenic exploration when he was young. His NDE had confirmed for him much of what he'd been shown while in an entheogenically activated altered state. I've heard him say if he'd had the NDE while on entheogens, he wouldn't have entirely trusted its authenticity. Because he was straight when he had the NDE and hadn't used entheogens for at least ten years—with the exception of that spiked acid brownie in Rome—he had no doubt about the utter reality of the NDE.

I can't say that the NDE appeared to have any immediate and obvious effect on him as he went about his life. But, as I suggested previously—on a level of which he was unaware—he was gradually creating a structure that would eventually allow him to ease himself out of the community. However, had you asked him at the time if that was what he was planning, he would have most vehemently denied it and fully believed his denial.

Mary Ann, on the other hand, with her acute sensitivity and having had the advantage, no doubt, of reading my ward's unacknowledged four-page NDE letter, she would have picked up on my ward's ambivalence and decided to tighten the noose.

Mein Host would have said there was no more committed and devoted a member of the community than him—and yet from the very start he was one of the few Processeans to keep up with his contacts and friends in the "world of men." Fifty years later, for example, he is still in contact with Jean, the girlfriend with whom he parted when he joined the group, and he remains in contact with Hilda Brown.

My ward's Gemini nature and his natural charm had made him useful to the community, both as a fundraiser and in his function as public relations officer, and this I could see he took as license—as he put it—to "develop his contacts." This meant that on top of his administrative work—much of which he was then able to delegate to Hilda—he was also regularly spending evenings out "developing his contacts."

Just as he'd been able to meet Allen Ginsberg, Abbie Hoffman, and Timothy Leary in the 1960s—and was free to follow up with Dr. Leary in his tepee at Millbrook—so he was now being taken up by the set of smart and beautiful people orbiting around Mike Todd Jr., the son of the well-known film producer and the stepson of Elizabeth Taylor.

Mike Todd Jr., though affable enough, had not lived up to the promise of his famous name. After an initially brilliant success filming the memorable roller-coaster ride for *This Is Cinerama*—his father's company's introduction of the new wide-screen process—he had a series of failures, some comical and others merely embarrassing. After that he'd largely faded from the industry.

If Michael Todd Jr. will be remembered at all, it's likely to be for introducing the unfortunately named movie format Smell-O-Vision and for producing *Scent of Mystery* in 1960—the only movie to ever use the innovative Smell-O-Vision technology. The title *Smell of Mystery* would never have made the cut!

My ward must have seemed a peculiarity to these sophisticated and jaded New Yorkers. He had no interest in the cocaine offered, and his insistence on his celibacy amazed and amused them. He was an entertaining and worldly conversationalist, and—from the long training all Processeans underwent in excellence of communication—he was also a good listener. They liked having him around. A hip priest was a rarity in their world, and my ward's monkish vows of poverty, obedience, and celibacy—especially celibacy—were often the center of conversation when they would meet for afternoon tea at the Plaza Hotel. To add to my ward's anomalous appearance, this man who lived without sex, drugs, alcohol, or money was wearing a superbly tailored—and obviously very expensive—dark suit. His hair was now short and well cut, he was beardless, and given his suit—a gift from Hilda, who couldn't abide looking daily at his normal tatty uniform—and his long slim form, he had something of the dandy about him.

Mein Host later described to Juliette his times with Mike Todd Jr. as being like "the first Native American to have been brought back to England to meet sophisticated Londoners, to be paraded in front of them, and to be poked and prodded to see who and what he was" and said, "I must seem as outlandish to them—they're always trying to test me to see if I really mean it."

Everyone in Mike Todd Jr.'s circle called Miriam "the Countess." No one knew the Countess's surname, or whether she was indeed a real countess (although my ward hadn't heard her deny it). He would never find out what she did in life, how or if she made a living, or even whether she was staying in New York or just visiting. Mike Todd Jr.'s circle were not the kind of people inclined to reveal a great deal about themselves.

Nevertheless, authentic or poseur, the Countess was one classy dame. She was invariably beautifully dressed in the way of elegant French women and spoke with an accent that even I found adorable. She was clearly conscious of her good looks—she might have been a fashion model at some point—and always made sure to appear at her best. The Countess was also unusually intelligent and genuinely interested in what Mein Host had to stay.

My ward may have justified his evenings spent with Mike Todd Jr.'s circle by believing there would be a sizable donation for the community, but if he was honest he would have had to admit that he was fascinated by the Countess—and that is why he really continued to meet with them. The truth was, he really did not much like Mike Todd Jr. or most of the people who hung out with him. They were a cynical, hard-hearted group who, he was perfectly aware, were using him for this amusement—with the exception, of course, of the Countess.

Mein Host had never spent any time with the Countess apart from when they met with the group. The tearoom in the Plaza Hotel seemed to be the preferred haunt where Mike Todd Jr. could hold forth in the afternoon over cucumber—or Gentleman's Relish—sandwiches and dainty cups of China tea.

My ward has always enjoyed an animated discussion with nonbelievers and pitting his wits against the materialist's arguments. Mike Todd Jr.'s set may have been somewhat jaded and cynical, but they were not unintelligent. They would argue as vociferously as my ward, pointing out, for example, how priestly celibacy in the Roman Catholic Church had led directly to an epidemic of sexual abuse by Roman Catholic priests of the children in their charge.

Of course, my ward could never tell them the truth. He defended his celibacy every bit as vigorously as they attacked, citing how much more psychic it made him, how he could sublimate his sexual energy into creativity, how absurdly oversexualized society had become, and how commercial interests were manipulating people through their sexual fantasies. All of which was essentially true, incidentally.

It is my observation that when subjects as delicate as sexual abstinence arise in conversation, people are apt to express their opinions with increasing volatility as such a discussion proceeds. It was in these discussions that the Countess had emerged as my ward's defender—not that he really needed one—yet he clearly enjoyed the smiles of agreement and support from a beautiful and mysterious French woman to spur him on.

One afternoon within this same time frame, my ward was sitting with Mary Ann and three other Luminaries—which was what the most senior Processeans were now called—in the Oracle's study in Mount Chi. A few weeks earlier Father Jonathan had been exposed for his sexual peccadilloes with the young donators in the Boston Chapter, and he'd be transferred to a junior post in the Chicago Chapter. The income coming from the Boston donators without Jonathan's stimulating encouragement had fallen precipitously, and so talk of sex was very much in the air.

At some point Mary Ann asked the four of them if they missed having sex. There was some shilly-shallying around as each of them tried to work out what Mary Ann was up to. There were some mumbling replies, nobody quite ready to commit themselves one way or another, so Mary Ann kept pressing them for an answer.

Now, few normal, red-blooded young guys when given no choice but to answer honestly whether they missed having sex are going to say "no."

"And what if," Mary Ann asked, "you could just go out there and have sex. Don't make a big deal of it, don't tell anyone, keep it to yourselves . . . what then?"

More mumbling, with no one sure in which direction this was going. I imagine Mein Host was thinking about the Countess and how resolutely and tactfully he had turned away her obvious advances.

"If you need to do it," she chided them, "just go out and do it. That's what I'd do! There's nothing stopping you if that's what you really want. But just keep quiet about it." And then, with a wink, "Remember, we're a celibate order!"

The meeting broke up after that, and on the drive back to New York the four of them compared notes on what they thought Mary Ann was really saying. She certainly sounded like she was encouraging them—they all agreed upon that. And it didn't pass muster to ignore an instruction from the Oracle, even if it came in the form of a suggestion or an encouragement.

But, then again, should they? It was one matter to be paired off for a week of sexual indulgence with another Processean, but quite another—as my ward said—"to pick up some chick for an evening and fuck her."

Was that what the Oracle meant? Nobody was really into one-night stands, they all agreed. On the other hand, there was the Oracle's instruction to go out and do it, and wouldn't it be silly to ignore it and then find themselves berated for being feeble and gutless?

I noticed that my ward made no mention of the Countess during the drive back to the chapter, but I could see from his emotional body that she was never far from his mind.

3

Emergence of the Form

Sirian Serial Reincarnation, Orion Walk-Ins,
Celibate Shtick, In Disgrace Again, Five
Angels, the Sky Dragon, the Serpent Gods

Astar's "not very long" turned out to be a full four millennia before
the practice of serial reincarnation on the part of the Sirians came to
an end. But by then they had set their stamp on the Atlantean empire
and—by extension—the rapidly expanding Egyptian civilization.

Astar said that these millennia of Sirian involvement with Atlantis
created two direct consequences that could have been foreseen. First, it
ensured that the Sirians would have a continuing karmic responsibility with life on this world—which they fulfilled by repeatedly returning here as the Nommo to the Dogon in the fourth millennium, the
Anunnaki to the Sumerians, and the Oannes to the Babylonians.
All were amphibian, and all were spoken about in much the same
manner—and all were recorded as bringing the arts of civilization.
Go to the creation myths of some Pacific cultures, like the Maori of
New Zealand, or the myths of the peoples of Mesoamerica—or even
China—and you'll find some essential, central similarities to Sirian
cosmology. These were either planted by Sirian agents or derived—as
in the case of the Maya—from their Atlantean forebears.

49

Sirian agents have continued to show up throughout history and into the modern era, although since Greek times I've observed that they have primarily used the single incarnation method.

The second of the consequences would also have a profound influence on Western civilization. What happened was that the Sirians opened a window of legitimacy for other extraterrestrial races—some with more predatory motives—to break the quarantine (you'll have noticed that the early Pleiadian involvement didn't create this effect as it was a one-time humanitarian mission). Using the fact that the Earth—as a "decimal planet"—is classified as "experimental," and pointing out that the presence of the Sirians had already broken the planetary quarantine, other interested races argued that they had an equally legitimate cause for being here.

Once again, I wasn't present for the judgment, so I can only infer the court's opinion from what I observed. At least two extraterrestrial races that I know of took advantage of what I assumed was a legal loophole: entities from a planet in the Orion system and beings from two different timestreams of a planet in the binary star system known as Zeta Reticuli.

Discretion was required of all visiting races, and—as this was generally observed—I imagine there were other off-planet interests occurring of which I wasn't aware, perhaps some underwater bases in the Pacific from which their craft might come and go without my noticing. I hadn't spent much time in the Pacific region since the disappearance of the last of the islands of Mu, and that was more than ten thousand years ago!

As an aside, you've no idea how fast time can fly for an eternal being!

I should also point out that since the seventh millennium—when there were only a handful of off-planet races interested in this world—there has been a steady increase in numbers over the millennia. This has been building up through the modern era, culminating in an explosion of interest following World War II that has continued to the present day. I have no access to the current number of extraterrestrial races with a presence on the planet as I write this, but I would expect it to be between seventy-five and a hundred—quite possibly more—with a lot of coming and going.

In the mid-1980s, Mein Host was told by an extraterrestrial contact that some extraterrestrials were encountering for the first time other extraterrestrial races they'd never met before on this planet.

Orion was different.

There had been an intense rivalry between the Sirians and a faction of beings from a world in the Orion system long before they ever encountered each other here. They followed very different religious and philosophical traditions, each dating far back into their own mythic histories. While the Sirians were proud to be dedicated to the service of others, to helping other races stumble into civilization, beings from Orion were devoted to serving the self.

Orion used both the incarnational and walk-in methods when they started appearing in the fourth millennium—although Astar told me that she thought she'd observed a few Orion walk-ins among the priests in the Egyptian renaissance of the eighth and seventh millennia.

Astar again: "We should be grateful that Orion's power was ultimately limited by their insistence on individual self-service. They'll no doubt produce a handful of immensely powerful and aggressive historical figures, but their influence will be unlikely to long outlive them."

This must have made us both thoughtful, because we sat in silence on that gentle slope, the scent of the night-flowering jasmine so powerful we could smell it from our perch in the astral, and the moon now high in the sky overhead, lighting the roofs of the monumental buildings of the city of Atlantis far below us. Most of the city was asleep, but one of the harbors was still an anthill of activity well after midnight.

Astar, still beside me, laughed at the metaphor. The dock workers did look exactly like ants all scuttling about their business. I realize this has become something of a cliché, so while I can't claim originality, I can claim to have made the observation a long time before it ever became a cliché.

It wasn't simply the tiny size of the dock workers and the sailors in the harbor that made them appear so antlike, but it was also the lines of dockhands slowly tracing trails to and fro. They walked from boats to warehouses—barrels balanced on their shoulders, much as ants transport their cut slivers of leaf—along with the return stream that was ducking and weaving to avoid their laden colleagues who were wobbling along in the other direction.

We amused ourselves for a while watching our anthill and pointing out different equivalencies. There were the soldier ants protecting the ships and the warehouses, and there were the scouts ranging around the harbor, but I could feel that Astar wanted me to know more about what was happening beneath the surface of life on the island.

After a while she spoke again, and I heard that divinatory tone that could fall over Astar from time to time. It had been a long time since she last favored me with what I thought of as one of her transmissions.

"What we are observing is a watershed moment in the history of human beings on this world. Much in the future will be found to have been incubated in these very moments of time. There will be disasters to come—and there'll be death and destruction on an unprecedented scale—yet much of what has been so deeply implanted here on Atlantis will spread far across the planet.

"It will become the hidden knowledge passed down through generations in codes, in architectural dimensions, and in double meanings: the nature of Creation and the ways of the Creators, of the lesser gods and the quantum secrets of matter, of the mystery of water, of procreation, and of the heart and the movement of blood through the body. The skills of their advanced metalworking will reach as far as India.

"Yet, I see the island becoming lost to history. They will become the ancient ones spoken of only in whispers, the root culture behind what diffused into the surrounding region throughout the sixth millennium."

She paused again, and it seemed to me that Astar—or whoever might be speaking through her—was considering whether to trust me with her next vision. A decision must have been made, because when she started talking again she was in full singsong mode.

"I see yet more destruction. I see a white fiery serpent in the dark of the sky and waves the size of mountains. I see great Atlantis ravaged with raging floods, of boats reduced to flotsam, of rotting corpses clogging the canals, of all the debris and detritus of a wrecked civilization laid out before me."

Oh, no, not more destruction! When will it all stop? When will human life be able to continue smoothly for once? Is this, too, the product of Caligastia's misjudgments? Why is it that every civilization showing signs of any real advancement seems to collapse before it ever comes to true maturity? Even poor Lemuria, the finest and most harmonious of the ancient civilizations, was swept away—and swept from history, as well.

Astar again, her tone softer and more pliant this time: "Yet Atlantis will rise again to struggle on, a shade of its former glory. It will be a resentful, angry, aggressive culture—defiant of the gods whom they will blame for the disasters that have befallen them—before the island will bring its final disaster upon itself. And like noble Lemuria, Atlantis will disappear into legend, as it will finally disappear beneath the waves of the Atlantic ocean."

And with that Astar was silent, her eyes closed as though she was still in a trance. The crepuscular light of a false dawn announced another day as the planet fell into the warming light of a new sun. The gray mist layering the far horizon slowly fluoresced before burning off in the tropical heat.

I thought of the African mainland far to the East over the ocean, where the sun would already be scorching the parched earth of the ever-expanding Sahara Desert. I remembered one of the times when I was observing a small hunting expedition—in Central Africa, I believe it was—and my terrible frustration when I could do nothing but watch them being torn to pieces by lions. I was trembling again at the thought. Imagine being compassionate and caring by nature and yet being structurally unable to prevent wrongdoing from happening.

I was saved from further self-recrimination when Astar opened her eyes, smiling gently at me. Together we watched the sunlight sweeping down the mountain beneath us in a wide, horizontal swathe, relentlessly eating the darkness before it, and exposing in sudden flashes the roofs and walls of the magnificent houses that crept up the lower flanks and foothills of the volcano.

And yes, it was beautiful. You can tell from my rhapsodic description how taken I was with the new dawn. Natural events in a third-density reality are experienced so much more vividly—because of the extremes of polarization—than in the more diffused monotonal light of the Earth's astral.

I wondered whether Astar was able to hear or absorb what she announced with such prophetic certainty when she fell into trance. I wasn't sure I wanted to repeat back what sounded to me like more bad news. Everything going down in flames yet again. Once more I was troubled by the thought that this wasn't what we risked everything for when we followed Lucifer into the revolution.

"Have patience, dear sister," Astar stated as she reached out and touched my face, stroking my hair with an unusual show of affection. "There are visions I see that I'm unable to express; sometimes I can't understand them myself. These I am not given to share with you."

I must have appeared hurt by Astar so clearly defining the limits of our sisterhood, because when she spoke again, I felt she was reassuring me.

"You will have to exercise great patience," she said again. "You'll witness the deepest truths, extraordinary courage, and terrible tragedies before this game is played out.

"But, hear my words, my sister: when the Greater Truth is revealed, as one day it will be, you shall know there is nothing that has ever occurred, or will ever occur, that will not be transformed into the gold of spiritual wisdom."

Quiet again, Astar sat for a while beside me before rising to her full height, giving me a final smile, which could have been one of encouragement—or the knowing smirk of a Cassandra—before the ether swallowed her up again, leaving me sitting alone with the streets of the city coming alive far beneath me.

I so much wanted to believe the best of Astar. I wanted to believe that my sister watcher wasn't just pandering to my frailties. "There, there! It'll all work out for the best of all."

It was always difficult to tell with Astar. She was that tricky! It has taken me a long time to realize that she was really doing me a favor. To seek such certainty from her was to avoid finding it in myself.

And yet, for all of that, something deep inside me was touched by her faith and wisdom; and—somewhere even deeper—I knew she was right. All would indeed ultimately work out for the best of all.

I just needed to be extremely patient and play my cards right. I believe it was then that I first formed the determination to be present for that very day Astar spoke about, when the glorious Greater Truth would be revealed. It was a resolution I would need to reaffirm with more frequency and with more passion as time passed than I could have ever imagined when I first had these thoughts.

I had no idea it was going to be so challenging.

* * *

Mein Host had a jaunty lilt in his step as he made his way to meet the Countess and the Mike Todd, Jr. crew at the Plaza. It had rained earlier in the day, and the avenues were still slick and shiny, the air clear and washed clean by the downpour. The sun had broken through. It was New York City at its best.

He'd given himself some time so he could stop and look in the windows of the art galleries on 59th Street on his way to the hotel. I don't think he had any doubt in his mind that tonight was going to be *the* night with the Countess. However, because much of what followed was an inner experience, this is my ward telling what happened in his own words: "I felt confident that Mary Ann meant what she said, and it so happened there was this beautiful French Countess whom I'd spent the last month turning down. I realized it must have been driving her crazy—she was the sort of woman who was used to getting what she wanted.

"She was always asking me back to her place after our get-togethers with Mike Todd, and I was always finding excuses to avoid it. She was gorgeous, but I didn't have sex on my mind. I always took the celibacy thing seriously. I never cheated on it. Actually, I don't think anybody did. We valued the state—at least I did. But, hell, I was a kid. I enjoyed sex as much as the next person, and it must have been a couple of years since I'd had any. What would you do?!"

As angels are not sexual beings, I didn't have a ready answer for that. But writing now, thirty-seven years later, I'd like to think I would have plunged ahead—which is exactly what my ward did.

"I didn't want to appear like a flake—after I'd argued so effectively for celibacy—by telling them that now I was not celibate. It would have made my so-called vow sound like a whim. Nor did I particularly want to have this crowd of cynics think they'd won the argument or—perhaps worse—that I needed to have permission to have sex. A man in his midthirties!

"So I sat through the meeting at the Plaza, and when the Countess asked me back to her place—much to her amazement—this time I agreed. We chattered, happily walking back to her place on East 58th Street, both avoiding the subject on both of our minds. I hadn't told her I'd been given permission, of course—that would have been too demeaning—so I decided to continue to say nothing and just see what happened. Besides, agreeing to accompany her back to her apartment would have been clue enough to a woman of the Countess's sophistication.

"So blasé had I become in an effort to appear my normal, casual, celibate self that I suppose I was asking for what happened next. But, at the time, it was totally unexpected.

"Now, of course, the Countess had no reason to think I wasn't still the celibate priest I'd made myself out to be. I thought I made a good case for celibacy. I reckoned I'd find some way of telling her what changed when we got inside. Some hope!

"She ushered me into this very feminine and elegantly appointed room, and—as it was a one-room apartment in midtown Manhattan—there was the bed right there. A shiny brass bed with a mass of oriental cushions at the head and covered in an ornamental bedspread.

"I think I must have been startled by getting hit with the reality of the bed right there, in front of me, so I didn't at once look back to where the Countess was fiddling with the locks on the door. When we both turned to face one another she had a key—the front door key as it turned out—in one hand and a seductive, if slightly predatory, smile on those full, red lips.

"We stood looking at each other for a long time before I made a slight move for the key. The smile broadened and the key went down her cleavage. The Countess had played her hand.

"Now this was interesting, I thought. What's she going to do now? I wasn't going to make a move. I was celibate. Yes, I was still doing my celibate shtick. I needn't have had any concern. The Countess clearly had her plans. She threw herself at me and started ripping off my clothes, my beautiful new suit, shedding some of its buttons in her enthusiasm.

"Now I'd been in this position before with that woman in Toronto, and that time I'd firmly fought her off. Of course it was different this time. I put up enough of a facsimile of defending my virtue and saw that it only increased her passion (and my own excitement). Then it hit me . . . the Countess was really getting off on having her way with a celibate priest. And what's more, the celibate priest was really getting off on being ravished. In fact—without using my full strength—I found that trying to fight her off would induce yet more passion in my soft and increasingly deliciously scented seductress, as her purpose became more and more obvious.

"Now, I dare say there hasn't been a human male at any time in the history of the world who, finding the soft lips of a loving woman sliding up his penis, has tried to push her away. I certainly didn't, and I received one of the finest blow jobs in a long life of fine blow jobs. This then led to an evening of ecstatic lovemaking, the Countess kvelling with pride at her illicit seduction of a priest. I should have known she came from a Catholic culture, and it was probably some long-held rebellious desire of hers to fuck a priest.

"I didn't care about that. She was a beautiful, enigmatic creature, and she was great in bed—that was good enough for me. Besides, I feel she really did fancy me; it wasn't just the priest-fucking thing (although I'm sure that kink sharpened her appetite)."

After a long evening reveling with the Countess in the passion he'd denied himself for the previous few years, my ward returned to the chapter for the evening meeting a happy and rejuvenated man. When his turn came he gave his report on his time with Mike Todd Jr., and he announced that he felt he was getting closer to a substantial donation, but, of course, there was no mention of the Countess.

It was the next day—when the four Luminaries who'd been let off the sexual leash were comparing notes—that Mein Host surprisingly discovered that the other three had not had his good fortune and had returned to the chapter as celibate as when they'd set out.

So the situation stood until that evening, when Mother Cassandra drove down from Mount Chi and asked to see my ward.

Mother Cassandra has previously made her appearance in my narrative as Wendy (her "gray-force" name) in Xtul and then later as she came to play more of a part in Mein Host's life. He had known her for some years before the Process existed—they'd even shared an apartment on Stanhope Gardens in London with five other students. She had always been attracted to my ward, but he'd never shown any interest in her. Although she'd joined the community some months after him, she'd quickly become one of Mary Ann's favorites. So when my ward returned to the fold after his two-year hiatus, Mother Cassandra had by then become the senior matriarch in an increasingly hierarchical organization.

Mother Cassandra had finally got her way with my ward, though in a somewhat unglamorous manner. This had started in Toronto three years previously when there'd been a particular focus on sex, and when my ward had participated in the group-sex gatherings organized and directed by Mary Ann.

Nothing sexual had occurred between Cassandra and my ward during the gatherings, so he was surprised when he was taken aside one day by Mary Ann. She confided that she had a mission for him: Mother Cassandra, she told him, was sexually frigid, and she asked what he could do to warm her up.

I don't know what Mary Ann told Cassandra—neither did my ward—but a few days later the two were in bed together. It had to be very quiet and surreptitious as no one in the chapter could know that two of the most senior members were consorting together when they were expected to remain celibate.

As it's my manner to turn away from my ward's intimate moments, here is his brief description of what followed: "It was true; the woman was terribly closed down. I'd always liked her—she'd been a friend—but she never turned me on. So there was no point in pretending to be romantic or trying to work up some degree of eroticism. I took it as a mechanical problem; one that called for the more precise application made possible by oral sex. It was all pretty dispassionate (from my point of view, anyway).

"It didn't feel like anyone had ever gone down on the poor girl before. She was as dry as a parched throat. Now, I wasn't altogether unskilled in this gentle art. I was fortunate enough to have learned at a young age what pleasure can been given. Surely, I thought, that will warm her up. But no such luck! I'd go at it until I had a rick in my neck. Nothing. Some hopeful moans and some sensual wriggling, but down where I was working away . . . nothing.

"This must have gone on for months, getting together maybe once or twice a week. Still nothing from her, but for me, an endlessly sore neck. I'd decided to say nothing to her about the neck, believing her concern for me would then just be one more obstacle to her potential orgasm. So it went.

"Two people can't meet weekly for what was so intimate and yet so apparently fruitless an activity without developing a certain wry humor about it. I wasn't looking to get any sex out of it. Perhaps that's what made it take such a long time. But, finally, we did it. She had her orgasm—and a few more just to be sure of it—and I reckoned my job was done.

"Nothing more happened between us after that, and I saw no signs that she had any more continuing interest in me than I had for her. It was all very detached. Then I was transferred to New York, and I'd only see Cassandra at meetings up at Mount Chi, where she was living alongside the Four as Mary Ann's factotum.

After one such meeting, she came up to my ward to chat. "I'd no idea what she wanted to speak to me about. She seemed friendly and interested in how I was doing, if I was happy, blah blah blah . . . then, ever so casually, she asked me how it went with the Countess. I'd no reason not to tell her—Mary Ann had only said that the junior Internal Processeans (IPs) weren't to know—so I described my time with the Countess in glowing detail, proud as anything that I'd gone out as instructed and gotten myself laid.

"Then, suddenly, the mood changed. The formerly placid and amused Mother Cassandra turned in front of my eyes into a screaming harridan. She was absolutely furious, and I didn't know why. Had I been too literal in my description of the Countess's sexual arts? Too effusive, perhaps? Certainly it was tactless as I think back on it, but would that elicit such a response?

"Yet, as she spluttered her angry accusations I started making out from the words that it was Mary Ann who was furious with me. I'd let *her* down. I'd betrayed her with some French trollop. I'd disappointed everybody, let everyone down again. Of course Mary Ann had never intended for me, or anyone else, to go out there to whore around, to disgrace the whole community. Was I insane? Did I hate them all so much? Was I so filled with anger? After all Mary Ann had done for me! And on and on."

So, once again, Mein Host was in disgrace—which can be translated as being in Mary Ann's bad graces. It was extremely emotionally painful for my ward because he experienced this isolation as being cut off from his Goddess.

I suspect that for a nonbeliever this might sound trivial or overblown, but for anyone with a firm belief in a supreme being to be forsaken by the God, or the Goddess, was the very worst of punishments.

In my ward's case, the pain of being cut off from his Goddess was increased and deepened (unbeknown to him at the time) by the emotions he repressed as a young child, when his father left the family, never to return. Although he knew by that time that it was his mother, Diana, who had turned his father out of their lives for his infidelity, the boy's deeper and unacknowledged feeling was one of abandonment. His father had abandoned *him*. A three-year-old thinks like that.

He was conscious of none of this at the time. So totally had Diana banished any idea of his father from my ward's mind that he'd given almost no thought to his father in his thirty-five years. When he was in his forties, the truth all spilled out from Diana—but that is for later in my narrative.

Being consciously unaware of the emotional impact of his father's abandonment only deepened the distress of his being abandoned by his Goddess. Yet it didn't last long. My ward had become too valuable an asset to keep in the doghouse for very long.

Mother Cassandra's anger was clearly not an act; she was not merely reproducing Mary Ann's fury and disappointment. I know my ward took note of this because he later asked Juliette if she thought Cassandra might still have a thing for him. Juliette was noncommittal in her answer, but by merely asking the question my ward had answered it for himself.

And Mary Ann; what was she up to?

Was it a simple dominatrix trick? "First you love 'em up, then you reject 'em?" She had definitely sent them out to have sex if that is what they wanted. There was no ambivalence about that, regardless of what Cassandra might have said. I was there. I heard what was said. Besides, all four of them had taken Mary Ann seriously enough to go out and try to obey her instruction.

The other three Luminaries who didn't get lucky—were they being more clever than my ward? Or did they merely display their ineptitude as they attempted in vain to pick up women in a singles bar on First Avenue? A singles bar! My ward had joked to Juliette that those three were probably the only men to ever walk out of a singles bar at the end of the evening without getting laid!

All very funny, but there was far worse to come. Mary Ann made part of his penance the requirement to go back to the Countess to explain what had happened—that it had all been a terrible mistake, and now he was celibate again.

I could see from his emotional body how distraught he was; how he felt he'd led the Countess on. He wasn't permitted to say he'd been set up by Mary Ann, of course, because no one was meant to know about her. So he had to take the whole weight of the humiliation on his own back.

The Countess wasn't having any of this emotionalism. She said she had a wonderful time and hadn't expected anything more. Then, to my ward's astonishment, she broke out laughing and then paused, evidently to consider whether to share the final piece of the puzzle.

"Mon cher, Father Jesse," she smiled, stroking his face as her French accent curved around him like velvet. "It eez better than you think. I won my bet wiz Mike. He didn't believe I could seduce you. Now I haff my rent for zee next three months . . . merci, merci, mon cher!" And she threw her arms around his neck and kissed him three times on the cheek before the truth of what she had said sank in.

Mein Host never saw the Countess again after that last revelation. I don't think it particularly upset him to hear that he'd been the subject of a wager. If anything I think he was amused and rather admiring of the Countess's arts of love.

He was gentleman enough not to tell her that he had his own secret—that he'd not been celibate for that one occasion—and in spite of the struggle he'd appeared to put up, he'd allowed her to seduce him.

What he didn't know was that Miriam, the Countess, was the second of the five angel incarnates who were appointed to soften up my ward and prepare him—without him knowing it was happening—for leaving the community. The Countess, like my ward, was unaware of being an incarnated rebel angel. Yet she fulfilled her function to perfection.

And she got her three month's rent out of it.

* * *

It is a curious sensation having to write concepts like "years past," or "centuries or millennia ago," when to a watcher it isn't really time that is passing. The way we experience time is as a spatiotemporal matrix within which events can occur. As there are many of these spatio-temporal matrices—every one different—we as watchers are trained to observe, we don't think naturally in terms of divisions of time.

This is almost impossible to explain, because all mortals are necessarily locked into the rhythms of their own biology and to the environment in which they exist. You say that everything begins and ends, that everything lives and then dies, and that a rock is thrown before it lands. You live within the biorhythms and the physics of your third-density experience. It is—you might say—for your convenience that the laws of physics and those that govern the planet's biological processes operate within a predictable spatiotemporal matrix. But you must know that yours is only one matrix of many.

While I'm talking time, let me clear up a perennial enigma that will upend the old science-fiction theme of time travel—sorry about this! There are *no* third-density mortals in your future time line. This is not because your time line ends in disaster, but because the Earth is not going to be a third-density world for very much longer.

Besides, there is no need for "beings from your future to return to the past" as everything is proceeding according to plan. Nothing needs to be fixed—as goes the sci-fi trope—and anyway, because of the radical density shift, the prospective time traveler would be unable to manifest in a third-density reality.

While it is still possible—if they have the inclination and the spiritual chops to manage it—for those in the future to touch into the past, it can only be done through the inner worlds of mediums and overlighting. However, this is exceptionally rare as it is generally frowned upon; it serves no purpose for time travelers but to satisfy their curiosity and does very little for those in the present (except to further confuse them).

So, let's say—within this third-density spatiotemporal matrix—event followed event; each event building to the next, and to the next, and to the next, with the same inexorability as the planet circles its sun.

Life on Atlantis for its mortal inhabitants—and I include among them the incarnate angels—through those many orbits, remained much as might be imagined for an aggressive, rapacious, theocratic tyranny. Trade in precious and semiprecious metals had grown rapidly as more and more ships were built and made available for trading. This led to a rise in the power of the Atlantean merchant class and because payment for the metals was frequently made in slaves, their numbers grew, too. As the riches continued to pour into the island's economy, the merchant class became the new aristocracy, and the slaves took over more and more of the everyday work. Probably for the first time in any previous civilization, leisure became a tangible factor of life for this new aristocracy.

Sympathetic resonance experiments continued in the laboratories, but—without ready access to the flow of electricity—their scientists made little progress.

The seven royal lineages of Atlantis—the eighth king had been murdered early on in the Sirian coup—had grown in size over the generations, as the families were both exceptionally fertile and just as long-lived. So much so, that for a while it seemed to me the Sirians were trying to incarnate so many of their agents on the island that it would become a truly effective Sirian outpost in disseminating what they considered their superior civilizing ways.

Even as a watcher, I knew that was downright illegal! No one planetary race can arbitrarily intervene in any substantial way with the progress of intelligent life on another world. Under certain circumstances an off-planet race can drop its pearls of wisdom—generally to selected individuals—but the outright usurpation of the most powerful civilization on the planet was absolutely forbidden.

It had been more than a century since the sky dragon had disappeared, and the warning it had carried with it was long forgotten. That the dragon presaged no disaster when it passed had severely discredited the seers who had foretold catastrophe. In fact, it was very much the reverse. After the comet's passing, the treasure chests of the Atlanteans had been increasingly filled to overflowing.

Thus, when the dragon had reappeared in the night sky, starting out like a tiny white scratch on a basalt boulder but then growing steadily larger so it could be seen during the day, no one on the island seemed particularly concerned. They were all sure that the fiery dragon would be bringing prosperity and good fortune with it, as it had on its previous pass.

Also, by this time, I had observed that the overall Sirian colonization project had been quietly withdrawn. I didn't know whether the Sirians had been warned off by agents of the Uversa court system or if—as a more advanced culture—the Sirians may have had clearer astronomical information on the orbital paths of comets.

This withdrawal of Sirian energy and support left only the royal lineages and their extended families, who—over the generations—had dissipated much of their personal power in overindulgence and frivolous pursuits.

The dragon grew larger, and sometimes at sunset people of the island would gather on the slopes of Atlas and watch while the dragon's long tail turned blood red before disappearing and reappearing again, icy-white, against the night sky. Had they known better they might have understood that the comet was now penetrating deep into the inner solar system. It was traveling on a hyperbolic trajectory at some tens of kilometers every second, and had they been able to make the necessary calculations they might have known that it was going to pass perilously close by the planet.

However, they didn't know better. And there was a sense of worshipful celebration to the small crowd who had stayed silent throughout the dragon's display, only bursting into a cheerful chatter when the clouds blotted out any view of the dragon. It was then that I heard some whispered talk among the men about the return of the ancestral serpent gods: that the fiery dragon was an omen of the coming transformation, and that the ancient promise was being fulfilled.

When the crowd had finally retreated back down the slope I found myself once again alone and in a meditative state. The clouds had cleared. The moon was a finely etched crescent with the planet Venus sparkling close by. Leaning back I could see the comet again, its long tail streaming behind it so that now I could see the braiding of the ionized gases in the comet's tail being blown free by the solar wind.

The peoples' talk of the serpent gods and the ancient promise being fulfilled reminded me of my recurring, waking dream of that serpentine form flicking through the water, and then—much later—when I caught a glimpse of the magnificent creature consorting with the two off-world visitors whose mission appeared to end so poorly for them. (*Note: This refers to the "Adam and Eve" mentioned in previous books, whose function was that of "biological uplifters" on the planet.*) At least, that's what it looked like—another victory for Prince Caligastia.

Yet as I lay there with the sky filling with stars, I recalled Astar telling me how what I was observing—in what I'd called my waking dreams—was in actuality an alternate reality. She'd gone into this long and complicated explanation about alternate time lines and probability theory, most of which went over my head but for one important factor: whatever "real" meant in the grand scheme of life, I knew after what Astar had told me that what I'd seen was real enough.

Had I been a mortal I might have thoughtlessly dismissed the waking dreams as hallucinations or whimsical delusions, but watchers—like many angels—aren't equipped with particularly active imaginations. We can't—as you might say—"make stuff up" in the way that will-creatures like human beings are so remarkably capable. A watcher might well observe an event from a singular and unique viewpoint—and, therefore, others might be tempted to question its veracity—yet to my knowledge no watcher has ever been found culpable of actual data falsification.

I mulled this over, relaxing comfortably on the warm volcanic rock and enjoying the scent of the jasmine and thinking—not for the first time—how curious it was that while I could actually *smell* the scent, I knew my mind was *manufacturing* the gentle pressure of the rock I felt beneath me. How odd that was! That those little scent molecules move so easily through contiguous frequency domains always deeply touches me. It links me with the third-density in an unaccountably moving way.

Once again, I found myself drifting into what I now accept is an alternate reality—and it must be very much like a mortal's waking dream. Although it is using elements of my current experience of where I am and what I'm feeling, the dream is superimposing an entirely different landscape so that I seem to be somewhere else entirely.

I am overlooking a wide plain with a range of mountains stretching away into the distance. People are moving around on the plain, alone and in small groups. A river snakes through the long grasses, while the weeping willows on its banks bow and tremble over the slowly moving water. I can observe people gathering beneath some of the shade trees. It looks like they are receiving teachings. Now I can see the tents; they're like white cones and clustered together in one of the bends of the river.

I find I can move freely in my mind amid this peaceful tableau. I lose my sense of whether this is real. I am there, I think, so it must be real on some level.

It's when I draw near a small group gathered around one of the teachers that I get my first clue as to what I'm watching. The teacher is very tall, perhaps double the height of those listening to his song, and he is swaying sinuously while he is singing. His long blond hair sways along with him, and when he opens his eyes they are gentle and unusually blue. His small audience, perhaps thirty or thirty-five men and women—in itself remarkable to have such an even mix of sexes—sit with their eyes shut, swaying, too, in emulation of their teacher.

I see that other small groups are gathering around these tall, swaying teachers. After a short while the teachers' individual lilting voices seem to join into one melodious whole. There are male and female teachers, all are tall and fair-haired, and they seem to glow with a very light violet sheen. When their glorious voices coalesce there is a sudden shift of vibration, and all their listeners appear to straighten their backs as if they are one person.

It is then that the last tumbler falls into place. I know what I am seeing and hearing.

Of course, these must be the so-called Serpent People; the promise of a teaching race I was shown so long ago, the hopeful result of the infusion of the Helianx genome in that wild dance I'd observed with the two off-world visitors. Yes, that must be it.

Astar had told me at the time she reckoned for a positive symbiosis that the genomic gift would most likely be stored in the mitochondrial matrix of certain eukaryotic cells. I recall her explaining how the genetic infusion would probably need to function on a time-release basis and that to be truly effective it would have to be triggered by certain pre-determined events occurring between the organism and its environment.

So was this one of those consequences? Could these teachers really be the descendants?

And, as I had that thought, I had my answer. At first I thought it was a trick of the light. A sudden burst of luminescence seemed to surround the teacher I was watching while she twisted and turned her long, slim frame. In that one moment I saw the serpentine form of her genetic ancestry overlighting her bronzed, naked body, and I knew her songs were the songs of the Serpent People.

I imagine that is what I needed to know as the vision slowly faded and—once again—I was alone on the slopes of Atlas, the night sky much the same as it was before I slipped into the vision.

I was left with a strange feeling of optimism. I knew the wisdom of the Serpent People ran in direct opposition to the Caligastia tyranny and that there'd been a continual attempt over the millennia by the Prince's forces to eliminate the Serpent People.

There was no nostalgia in the vision. It acted more as a reminder of the continuing existence of the alternate reality. I understood in those moments how these two realities can interweave as needed; how the Serpent People are those who are capable of existing in both these realities.

I knew that however history treats the Serpent People—whether they are revered in one era and maligned in another—that the Helianx genome continues to sleep deep within the cells of humanity, to express itself when necessity calls for its emergence.

I knew the Serpent People would always be part of the planet's great sweep of history. As individuals, they would appear and disappear through the generations of humankind: sometimes as a chieftain, sometimes as a shaman, sometimes an artist, sometimes a seer, and sometimes an inventor, a musician, a statesman, a courtesan, or a dandy.

A wave of gratitude swept through me—a feeling I'd almost completely forgotten. It was as though I had stepped behind the Great Game for a moment; I'd peeked behind the scrim and had seen the goodness of the grand scheme. I saw that however terrible the conditions became on Earth under Prince Caligastia's brutal dominance, the People of the Snake will always be there to be called forth to speak the truth to power.

I now believe it was knowing this that renewed my optimism. I fear it was not going to be an optimism that would last very long. The dragon was drawing closer in the skies over Atlantis.

4

Separated Reality

A Personality Change, Spiritual Healing, Returning to Göbekli Tepe, the Global Grid, Guns in America, Berbers from Atlantis

I have observed that a full human life can have the quality of a woven tapestry. I'm aware this is by no means an original observation. It's been used to describe the most mundane of social interconnections, as it was also one of the metaphors used by the Sirians to describe the interplay of cosmic forces. The metaphor will appear later in a more elaborate form in Mahayana Buddhism as Indra's net.

It was when Hilda finally opened up on what had drawn her to Father Micah in the first place that the tapestry metaphor came to mind. Although it was never mentioned, I have no doubt that Hilda was taking her good time in checking out this Father Micah for herself. So when the truth did come out it was both comical and another stitch in my ward's tapestry.

Bryce Bond was a one-time lover of Hilda's, and they had remained in contact over the years. They had a shared interest in all aspects of parapsychology, but while Hilda was, and is, a natural psychic, Bryce Bond—now some years deceased—was a natural acolyte. He was one of those human first-timers who was compulsively drawn to the inner glow of an incarnate angel yet could never live up to what he expected of himself. Although he was a good-looking man, his dark eyes betrayed his sadness and his disappointment with himself.

Bryce Bond was a minor celebrity in New York at the time, with a TV show on the paranormal featured on one of the local channels, which brought him in contact with many of the leading people in the emerging New Consciousness movement. That is how he would have originally come to know Hilda.

Bryce was a great one for investigating a mystery. And, as such, he was an uneasy mixture of skepticism and gullibility. Let me say what I mean by this, because Bryce was not alone in manifesting this unsettling pathology.

Bryce desperately wanted to be one of those people he regularly interviewed for his show. He might have been thought a mere poseur if he wasn't also a kind and somewhat innocent man—and it would be unnecessarily cruel to paint Bryce solely with that brush. However, the psychological pattern is not a very complicated one and is acted out every day in all parts of the world under the label of envy.

Bryce Bond's very human and misplaced envy—let's call it what it is—of incarnate angels, coupled with his own lack of self-knowledge, contributed to his desire to be one of those people he so admired. Set against this was the caution of someone not too bright, who had never gone through the experiences of an incarnate angel, and who was therefore naturally skeptical. Thus it was that Bryce seemed continually strung out between these two extremes: gullibility and skepticism.

It turned out that Bryce had read of Arthur Shuttlewood's encounter with a certain Father Micah and Brother Joab in Warminster (described in some detail in an earlier volume) and had decided, as Shuttlewood had, that Father Micah (at least) had to have been an extraterrestrial. He must have been both excited and a little scared when he learned that Father Micah was in New York City and could be found at the Process Chapter, because he'd asked Hilda to go in and look him over.

Hilda in turn had reported back to Bryce that her opinion of Father

Micah was that he was one of the Serpent People. This must have further disconcerted Bryce as it was some months before that he plucked up the courage to come in and meet my ward.

It was not an easy meeting for Bryce Bond.

A quick update on this Father Micah, now Father Jesse—the name I'll use from now on as the change of name had more of an impact on my ward's personality than it might have for others who had changed their names when the Process Church became the Foundation Faith. Whereas "Micah" was chosen for him by Mary Ann, "Jesse" was his own choice.

I have noted earlier in my narrative some details of my ward's growing familiarity with the nature of his alternate personalities. He still wouldn't have been able to articulate what happened to him except to say that he felt very different when manifesting a different aspect of his personality. This had never risen to the level of a pathology; he never lost track of who he was or which personality was manifesting. In fact, the Micah personality was the first one he could consciously control and bring forth when he wanted. The Jesse personality turned out to be rather more intractable.

In fact, Father Jesse was the last of these well-defined personalities to emerge, as well as the final one to manifest before my ward finally integrated and assimilated the seven he knew about into a composite whole in 1980.

My ward has since claimed that Jesse was probably the most difficult and troubled of his subpersonalities. This alternate was about being a leader, about experiencing the qualities necessary for firm leadership, and all the impossible decisions and unfortunate compromises. He says it was when he felt at his most detached that he started thinking that the whole human game was a sad and cynical distraction.

Father Jesse was diamond hard in affect: smooth, glib, and polished. He didn't suffer fools gladly, and he was largely unconcerned with the frailties of others. Apparently, poor Bryce Bond was just too tempting a target to resist.

When they finally came to talk, Bryce seemed unprepared to frame the question he most wanted to ask, lest the answer be in the negative. He didn't want to hear that Micah and Joab were not extraterrestrials and that the whole Shuttlewood story was merely a delusionary fabrication. When Father Jesse, enigmatic in his turn, never said anything to either confirm or deny the Shuttlewood interpretation, it left Bryce forever in a state of confused agape.

One of the unintended consequences of keeping Bryce on the edge for so long was that my ward came to know and feel sorry for the man; he never could convince him that Arthur Shuttlewood's story was an absurd exaggeration. To the end, Bryce remained sure that my ward was an extraterrestrial and insisted on interviewing him on tape for his television show. Holding this belief about Father Jesse seemed to be the way Bryce was able to explain my ward to himself. It was how Bryce was able to fit my ward into his realm of understanding.

There was no doubt that Bryce Bond felt special being on conversational terms with an extraterrestrial. He was sensitive enough to feel that Mein Host was different from most other people, yet he had no context within which to place or understand incarnate angels any more than Mein Host did. Believing my ward was an extraterrestrial was the pigeonhole with which Bryce was most comfortable.

Curiously enough, although my ward wasn't consciously aware of it at the time, Bryce wasn't altogether wrong. Mein Host, as an incarnate angel, had lived a number of lifetimes on other worlds as he would discover later in his life, and it may well have accounted for his elusive answers.

It was here that I saw a cruel streak in this Father Jesse in the way he was playing with Bryce—batting him this way and that, enigmatic and never committing himself, and invariably giving the man more to puzzle over. It was clear my ward had decided that if Bryce was going to insist on him being an extraterrestrial—in spite of his attempts to deny it—then he may as well have some fun with it.

"My dear Bryce," my ward liked to say, "if you asked a spy whether he was really a spy, would you trust him if he said no, any more than you'd trust him if he said yes?"

Hilda Brown was a very different matter. She was not only intelligent and organized but also extremely empathic and certainly one of the most sensitive psychics my ward had yet encountered.

As a tribute to Hilda's natural psychism, some years later in the 1980s she was able to psychically lead the police to the evidence required to catch and convict the murderer of a friend of hers. In fact, throughout the 1980s and '90s Hilda became one of those highly valued psychics who counseled the rich and famous, and she quickly established a reputation as being one of the most reliable psychics in the country.

Hilda would become a lot more playful later in her life, but as winter turned to the spring of 1975—and she was daily working alongside Mein Host—she was a picture of serious-mindedness. The pain of the chronic colitis that plagued her previous life had disappeared, and this had stimulated her interest in spiritual healing. When she first encountered Mein Host, Hilda was already studying privately with a well-respected spiritual healer in the city. This became another of the synchronicities that made her arrival that day when she stood at the bottom of the stairs asking for Father Micah so intriguing.

The ability to heal people by the simple laying on of hands had emerged quite naturally and spontaneously among a number of IPs over the previous few months. In many ways healing was an understandable extension of the community's longtime focus on psychic development; it was an ideal marriage of psychism and religion. And, of course, it brought in more and more people as the healers of the Foundation Faith became better known throughout the city! Hilda's knowledge of the field and her wide range of contacts brought in other well-known spiritual healers for seminars and sessions, which added much to the community's credibility.

The healers at the Foundation Faith were wise enough not to directly charge money for healing, and yet the donations continued to roll in regardless. Together with all the other activities—the courses and classes, the conferences and lecture series, the film shows, the magazine sales, and the donations—the New York Chapter was starting to pay its way.

It seemed that the Foundation Faith was finally set to succeed. And the more successful it became, the more challenging and difficult life became for the community.

Trouble was brewing in the wings.

* * *

I could tell from the position of the approaching comet in the night sky that there was still sufficient time before its effects would be felt. So I decided to leave Atlantis for a short while. I determined to return to southeastern Turkey. Göbekli Tepe had been on my mind. I knew it was a key structure in the implementation of Prince Caligastia's subversion of the planetary grid, and I wanted to see what had happened with the site since I was last there.

When a watcher travels with a specific goal in mind, we are able to use the fourth dimension for almost instantaneous arrival. When the aether trembles as my sister Astar appears beside me, she has phased into the astral from the fourth dimension. This form of travel is restricted only to the planet; to travel between the worlds we need to use the Seraphic Transport System.

I'd barely had the thought of going to Göbekli Tepe when I felt a slight shift and promptly popped into the higher astral hovering high above the hilltop where the circular structures should have been clearly visible. Yet I could no longer see the temples; the great circular spaces had been completely filled in with debris.

I dismissed this at first. I'd watched over the millennia as layer had been built upon layer, so I imagined they were simply preparing to create another stratum of structures. But as I dropped lower I could see that wasn't true. Some of the structures were buried under two or three yards of material so as to be completely undetectable from ground level.

I was moving around over the site—marveling at how such a vast complex of structures could have been visible at one moment and then gone the next—when I felt I slight temperature change, and there was Prince Caligastia phasing in beside me with a sly grin on his face.

"Appreciating my handiwork, eh, watcher?" His tone was as self-admiring as ever I'd heard it.

"But, why, my Prince?"

I'd thought it before I could stop myself. The Prince was notoriously averse to being questioned so directly. Yet to my surprise, he seemed to want to demonstrate to somebody just how clever he'd been.

"Now they will never know," he stated. His tone had a shiny, supercilious sheen to it as he gestured toward the restored hillside, his Temple of Death buried deep beneath it. He must have thrown me a gestalt image at that point, because I suddenly perceived/understood what had occurred since I had been here last and while I'd been away on Zandana.

This was the gestalt image as I interpreted it: I see the midwayers who are opposed to Caligastia actively working to negate the Prince's baleful influence on the grid. I see other structures, massive stone erections, placed at key points on the main grid meridians. And, yes, this is having its effect, as I can see the lines of the world bending in accordance with the new influences. They aren't perfect; they simply mitigate some of Caligastia's more audacious revisions of the grid. I don't know what this will mean for normal mortal ascension, and I see that the Prince is also unsure of how the damping down of his revisions will affect the grid long-term. The grid, for all its many purposes, is a delicate affair. It's flexible, yes, but its very flexibility can result in serious imbalances within the biosphere.

This, of course, was the crux of the issue. This was why it was forbidden to interfere with the global grid. It could easily throw the whole biosphere out of whack.

Caligastia had described his adaptation of the grid to redirect souls into a reincarnational cycle as "a minor tweak in the system." This had appeared to hold true in regard to the biosphere, anyway. There'd been none of the terrible storms and earthquakes that might have been expected, but now—with all those additional adaptive structures—I feared for the worst. Did the midwayers really know what they were doing in attempting to thwart the Prince's plans? Was their solution of countering the Prince with structures of their own going to finally push the grid out of equilibrium?

I think it was then that I caught a glimpse of the Prince's strategy. It was classic Caligastia. He had set a trap for the loyalist midwayers, and they'd fallen right into it. Of course the Prince would have known that his opposition—if they hoped to nullify his effect on the grid—would have to resort to structural changes. For that, it would be the loyalists that the MA should hold responsible. He believed his initial refinement—which is how he thought of his "minor tweak"—would become irrelevant in the light of what was sure to be judged by MA's courts to be a far more serious wrongdoing. In his mind, I felt sure Caligastia believed that because he'd done nothing to actively harm the biosphere, his initial refinement of the grid would be overlooked and his problem would simply fade away.

Now I understood the reason for that sly grin on Prince Caligastia's face.

It was when I returned to the island of Atlantis—as I'd promised myself after my brief visit to Göbekli Tepe—that the deeper implications struck me about what the loyalist midwayers may have inadvertently wrought upon the planet. At least, I have to believe what they did was inadvertent; that they really didn't know what they were doing, or—if they did—at least they had some idea the risks. (Note: When I say the midwayers did this or that, I'm placing the responsibility where it lies, because although it was the human beings who built the great stone structures, they did so under the supervision of the midwayers.)

Perhaps it was the growing proximity of the comet that brought these apocalyptic thoughts to mind.

I was aware that the global grid was intimately interwoven with Earth's magnetosphere and that this magnetic sheath around the planet protected the ozone layer from solar wind. No one could be sure how the magnetosphere had been affected by all that tinkering with the grid, and I didn't want to dwell on what might happen if the comet came too close. A weakened magnetic field on Earth would do little to prevent the drag of the comet's gravitational momentum from stripping away the ozone layer and rendering the entire planet susceptible to the solar wind plasma and ultraviolet radiation. If that happened, it would cause the end of the web of organic life on a third-density planet. And unless Prince Caligastia was determined to bring the planet down with him—and I felt he was too narcissistic to try that—surely it was in nobody's interest to see life on the planet completely wiped out.

It would have been comical if it wasn't so tragic to watch the deluded enthusiasm with which the citizens of Atlantis were greeting the approach of the great sky dragon. This held true almost without exception up and down the rigidly hierarchical social structure. I saw only two ships leaving for the mainland carrying a small number of what I assumed were the highborn families whose patriarchs didn't subscribe to the general celebration.

At first, I didn't think much of this small exodus, but then—as I came to contemplate the wider implications of their impulse to escape—I understood something collectively about humanity that I'd never taken in before. Now, suddenly, with those two boats leaving the harbor, it came into focus.

Here we have a small group of human beings who have a fundamentally different point of view from the vast majority. They will have braved the scorn and hostility of their fellows; some might have been roughed up or even killed. And yet here they were—determined and organized enough to sail together solely on the conviction that they were correct—when everyone else was wrong. This was no mere difference of belief; this was life or death as far as the escapees were concerned.

This insight may not seem so unusual to the modern sensibility, but to a watcher it was a singular lesson. It was an appreciation of just how tenacious a mortal being's grip on life must be. Those few Atlanteans were prepared to risk everything, not only in defying the collective but also in making their risky escape, to follow their own inner convictions. It took the threat of death they believed was foretold by the comet's appearance to force them into asserting their personal wills. It is this ever-present threat of death that is entirely foreign to celestials as it will be for all humans, too, after they pass on from mortal life.

A simple issue, you might think. After all, everything dies; just don't think about it.

Simple, perhaps, but it's a state of mind that is almost impossible for a watcher to identify with. I can understand your idea of death in the abstract, of course. It's living under a constant threat of extinction, which must be utterly exhausting and depressing. That's what makes our identification with it so difficult.

My ward suggests that contemporary humans in most of the Western world coexist with the reality of imminent death by denying it, by compartmentalizing it, by attempting to delay it by staying young and healthy, or by focusing on the endless, mindless distractions that fill everyday life. The thought of death is pushed aside; or it is relegated to the subconscious and to the stuff of nightmares. Yet in each case it will tend to leave the individual unusually susceptible to being controlled and manipulated.

The omnipresence of guns in America, for example, or the graphic violence of Hollywood movies or the murders viewed nightly on television do little to lessen the dread of death by rendering it more conscious. If anything, they heighten the fear because so few people know how to effectively release fear-driven thoughtforms. Thus, the dread will build up in the individual's psyche, and it might find release only in an unexpected explosion of violence—"He seemed like such a mild, nice, young man!"—or it might manifest in one of the autoimmune diseases, or it might be suppressed under a quilt of Prozac. As I've heard my ward say more than once: "We're all swimming in a sea of fear down here."

Death in the modern world has become the last taboo as it's also the most pernicious of control mechanisms. And it is made all the more pernicious by how cynically the threat of death is used by the manipulators.

Setting aside the delusion that the modern world has reached the pinnacle of human civilization, the inhabitants of Atlantis were far more similar to contemporary human beings than most would care to admit. They may not have had cars and washing machines and telephones, but their feelings and their reactions to primal emotions were very much the same as yours would be under similar circumstances.

I became so intrigued by those two boats taking the refugees to the mainland that I found myself carried on board by my interest. Have I mentioned how much pleasure it gives me when I get so gracefully transported by my enthusiasms? It's when I know with the clearest mind that I am in the right place at the right time.

I was immediately surprised at how large the boat was. Its three banks of oarsmen all swayed silently in unison, and their oarlocks were muffled with rags as the boat slipped out of one of the less-traveled harbors on high tide and in the dark of the moon. There'd been no one on the quayside to see them off. They had chosen an auspicious time: the birthday of the High King's first wife, when all the citizens would be celebrating and carousing the night away.

The boats had left from different harbors to lessen the chance of drawing attention to themselves and with the hopeful intention of finding each other at dawn the next day.

As I moved unperceived down the central platform I was struck once again by something I'd never seen before. These weren't the poor ragged slaves I'd observed on the Atlantean trading ships. To my astonishment, there were women—and even some older children—among the men at the oars. Then—even more surprisingly—it was evident that the highborn were mixed with those of the lower castes, and all were intent on rowing together to get away from the catastrophe they were sure the omen of the dragon portended.

They rowed silently without talking or making any unnecessary noises until they could no longer see the flaring lights of the city. Then they relaxed their strokes, shipped their oars, and leaned back, some talking quietly to one another, while the men made ready the sails.

I moved to the stern, where three large, red-haired men were gripping the massive cut-timber tiller, while a fourth was staring up at the stars and whispering his commands to the tillermen as the boat slipped through the ocean, carried by the current toward the West African coastline. Although all four kept at their tasks—while those at the oars relaxed and others ran the sails up the masts—I could feel their growing optimism at having escaped the island.

As the glow of dawn spread over the eastern horizon a cheer went up from those on the main deck. Following their gaze I could see the dark form of the other boat in the distance off our starboard bow, limned by the rosy glow of the sky. On seeing the other boat the tillermen needed no command from the steersman to manhandle the tiller, turning the boat toward the sun now peeking over the horizon.

Looking from the stern and back over the ocean north-northwest, I could see the very tips of the highest peaks on Atlantis glowing red and serrating the horizon until they disappeared from view.

The sun was directly overhead by the time the two boats—with much jubilation—linked up and let the prevailing wind and the current carry them south. By sundown of the third day they spotted land on the eastern horizon, but by the next morning the distant cliffs had disappeared. This caused some consternation among those who hadn't traveled this far south. However, the wind changed direction overnight, and by midday on the fourth day they saw land again. People took their places at the oars, and with much singing and joyful cheering they rowed hard for the distant shore. Yet as hard as they pulled—and they rowed almost continually for two days and nights, switching places every couple of hours—the land seemed to recede and then disappear, to reappear again hours later, just as far away. Enthusiasm on the boats would ebb, then pick up at the sight of land, then ebb and rouse itself again. By the fifth time this happened, enthusiasm changed to grim determination to get the voyage over with as fast as possible.

When they were close to shore, the refugees on the two boats were fortunate to find themselves in a wide river estuary that allowed them to row some miles up the river before anchoring in a sheltered bay on the southern side of the river.

Today, the river is barely a trickle that hugs the southern edge of the city of Agadir on the Moroccan coastline before snaking its way up into the Atlas Mountains. The modern city itself now sprawls across the dry riverbed that was once the estuary.

Once they were ashore, set up camp, and rested from the efforts and privations of the voyage, they held meetings to discuss their next action. Again I was surprised at how easily the castes mixed together once they had shared the perils of their escape. They were united by something far stronger than any caste differences: the mutual conviction that disaster was imminent and the desire to avoid it.

Being an island people they were aware of the dangers of remaining at sea level, so within a few days the refugees struck camp and set out to follow the river as it wound through the marshes and wetlands and up into the mountains.

I chose not to follow them as they trudged along, but I must say that it turned out to be a far longer and more dangerous trek than they'd envisioned. Wild animals had picked off a number of the weaker members and, sadly, five of the children fell to their maws before the group even got to the foothills.

I know they must have finally made it to higher ground and established a settlement in the Atlas Mountains, because they eventually flourished and expanded over the following millennia to become the Berbers of North Africa.

On the island of Atlantis, life was reaching a fever pitch of anticipation for the citizens as the dragon drew ever closer.

* * *

It was when the Foundation Faith was starting to be seen as the main healing center in Manhattan that the third of the incarnate angels commissioned with helping to ease my ward out of the community appeared in his life.

Jeanne was a psychic healer of quite a different order than those in the Foundation Faith. Her focus wasn't so much on the laying on of hands—the faith healing practiced by most of the Foundation Faith healers—nor was she a magnetic healer in the way of those who use their own energy to heal others. Her special gift was psychic diagnostics. Due to her unusual perceptual ability, Jeanne was able to "see into" a patient's body. She could see the muscles and ligaments, the veins and the glands, the soft tissues and the nerves, the bones and internal organs—there was nothing in the physical body that was hidden from her inner eye. Doctors in hospitals had used her to diagnose a patient's physical problems when they needed immediate attention and the appropriate tests would have taken too long.

Jeanne told my ward that her psychic awakening had started when she'd fallen on her head as a young girl. By her account, this had made her subsequent childhood a living hell: people accused her of being crazy, or seeking attention, or thinking she was so, so, special. She had become a nun in the silent Carmelite Order to turn her back on the scorn to which she was subjected at home, but after twelve years, that hadn't really worked. She wanted to make better use of her gift in the outside world rather than being hidden away in a convent.

After leaving the church she worked as a psychic in a number of American cities, always leaving and moving on when word of her extraordinary gifts got around and the crowds started piling in and making life impossible for her. She was now in her early thirties and had recently seen her unusual ability affirmed and fine-tuned at the Berkeley Psychic Institute.

Jeanne was a tall, big-boned, blonde-haired woman—as befitted her

Dutch ancestry—with bright blue eyes and an open, honest Midwestern face. No great beauty, Jeanne was a natural devotee, openhearted, good-natured, and with a delightfully simple mental intelligence.

However—like all incarnate angels—Jeanne's emotional intelligence was undeveloped. The intimate relationships she'd had previously—which turned out to be very few—she described as soul-numbing and lacking any real purpose. And, as is true with many incarnate angels, she was childless and demonstrated little desire to have any. It only came out later that she was biologically unable to conceive—as is frequently true for incarnate angels in female bodies.

Jeanne had lived in her inner world for so long—first as an adolescent and then as a nun in the Carmelite Order for the following decade—that there had been little time to experience the real world. She'd had a short affair with a man at the Berkeley Institute, but she said they hadn't been able to really connect. When she met Mein Host it was obvious she had never come across anyone quite like him before. Although she knew he was unavailable, that she was just one of the many women around him, and that he paid no more attention to her than anyone else, she fell helplessly and devotedly in love with him.

It was equally obvious that Jeanne had no way of easily admitting this to herself. She'd had so little experience with romantic love that she had no appropriate way of handling what she was feeling—or of expressing her love. She came in almost every day and volunteered to work for my ward, only to be kept at bay by the ferocious Sister Miriam and given a task that would keep Jeanne away from his office.

As the months passed I could see my ward doing his best to deter Jeanne from her calflike adoration of him, yet there was nothing he could say that would put her off. He was also in the difficult balancing position of having to make sure she maintained her enthusiasm and involvement with the Foundation Faith, while simultaneously attempting to avoid her love-sick eyes whenever he left his office.

She was an extremely determined woman—as shown by the fact that she would still be present and ever-hopeful in two years' time when my ward parted ways with the community. At that point—finally convinced of Mein Host's lack of romantic interest in her—Jeanne would no longer play any part in Mein Host's life. She would have known on some level that the task for which she was angelically commissioned had been completed.

The presence of Jeanne in my ward's life allows me to open up a thread I've not yet had the opportunity to explore. Jeanne was an incarnate angel, yes, but she was not a *rebel* angel. She was one of those angels who'd remained loyal to Gabriel at the time of Lucifer's rebellion. Jeanne was a "good" angel, if you like.

So what was a good angel doing down here in a mortal body?

I didn't know then what I now understand, that there have been a number of Gabriel's angels who have volunteered for mortal incarnation. I cannot claim to understand—even now—the real reasons behind these acts of supreme altruism as I'm not privy to decisions made by Gabriel on behalf of the Multiverse Administration. It is never pleasant for an angel to spend time close to, or on, a third-density planet even at the best of times, but after what occurred on Earth on Prince Caligastia's watch, it's extremely disagreeable, as well as being dangerously disorientating for those not accustomed to the emotional density.

I've heard some watchers suggest that it may have been when Gabriel's loyalist angels realized that the rebels were being given the opportunity to redeem themselves by entering mortal incarnation that they, too, desired the opportunity for a human lifetime. Other watchers have joked that Gabriel's angels were envious and competitive and had no idea what they were getting themselves into. But, regardless of their motives, it's an act of great courage for a loyalist angel to volunteer for mortal incarnation.

I wonder if I have made this point clearly enough: *angels and mortals are two very different species.* Like cats and dogs. Mortals don't become angels when they die, and angels have traditionally never desired or needed to enter mortal incarnation.

The concept of an angel joining the mortal ascension plan would have been quite inconceivable until recently. I can't be sure this symbiosis has never happened before in the vastness of the Multiverse, but I am fairly certain it hasn't occurred so far in this Local Universe of Nebadon. While it is possible this same approach may have been followed in the earlier two rebellions in Nebadon, so little is known about those affairs that no one can be sure.

There are, no doubt, good reasons for this blanket of silence. I can understand it would not have been appropriate for angels such as myself who followed Lucifer to anticipate that a mortal incarnation might lie ahead for us when the troubles blew over. Knowing that such an outcome awaited us would have inevitably colored our decisions at the time. I think we all would have regarded a prospective mortal incarnation with utter horror; to be stuffed willy-nilly into a mortal body was the most horrific punishment we could conceive of suffering.

It is only now—after the chief protagonists in Lucifer's revolution have reconciled their differences—that the opportunity of a mortal incarnation has been seen in a rather different light. I believe that the MA is now placing more emphasis on the positive aspects of joining the mortal ascension line and is presenting it as an opportunity for personal redemption, as well as a gift for services rendered.

However, it was still late in 1975, and Jeanne, the third angel, was continuing to press her romantic case. She liked to be seen as exuding an innocent, virginal goodness. Her attention was always on the positive. She wore flowing, white cotton dresses, giving her a perpetually summery appearance even in the depth of a New York winter.

Before she arrived at the Foundation Faith, she had studied to become a teacher of Rudolf Steiner's sacred dance movement called eurythmy. She would explain in detail how eurythmy was about matching her gestures and body movements to what she was actually saying. She spoke about how all the sounds in speech, all the phonemes, corresponded to particular movements—music, too—and she would be flitting around my ward's office and waving her arms demonstrating what she called the "soul quality" of the feelings she was expressing.

"It was all rather silly," Mein Host told his friend Juliette afterward. "She wouldn't stop flapping around and telling me what it all meant, while every tiny gesture—you know she's not a small woman—causing her to knock into things. Seriously, it went on and on endlessly, and I'd just asked her to tell me something about the damn thing."

"She good, though," Juliette said. "Knows her stuff. She explained it to me, too."

"Think she'd be any good teaching a class in eurythmy?"

"Could be what she's pushing for," Juliette said after a pause. "Yeah! She'll do okay. People'll love her."

Mein Host did give Jeanne her slot in the evening to teach eurythmy, and Juliette was quite right; people did love her. How could they not? Jeanne exuded unrequited love.

More importantly—from my ward's point of view anyway—since Jeanne was throwing herself into her teaching role, she didn't have as much time to focus on her romantic longing for him.

I introduced Sonia earlier in my narrative as the mother of Daniel, the little boy that my ward took care of during the child's fourth year back in London. Sonia had now taken the name Mother Seraphine, and a few months after being transferred to the New York Chapter she'd begun to conduct what she called "angel readings" at the psychic fairs.

These readings, purported to be transmitted from the individual's guardian angels, proved to be so much in demand that Mother Seraphine was able to set up what amounted to a separate agency—the "Angel Ministry"—within the overall organization. I don't believe it's my place to comment on the authenticity of these angel readings, as I'm sure they were helpful to some who received them, and they certainly did no obvious harm.

I raise the issue of Mother Seraphine's Angel Ministry as there are several ironies here. Although my ward did nothing to stand in the way of Seraphine's work with the angels, he was clearly unusually skeptical about it. He said it made him feel acutely uncomfortable, and he wasn't sure why. And because his discomfort—in light of his later work with the angels—has puzzled him to this day, let me address it now.

Mother Seraphine stayed with the community long after my ward left in 1977 and continued living and working with the group until she died in the late 1990s.

My ward had liked Seraphine well enough, but they had never been close. She hadn't been involved in any of the group sessions he'd attended, and although she was a beautiful young woman, he'd never shown any signs of being attracted to her. This was not altogether surprising as Seraphine was also one of the dozen or so incarnate rebel angels in the community. As I've already noted, there is a certain natural avoidance that occurs between rebel angel incarnates, which can rise to an active aversion in some cases. In Mein Host's case it wasn't so much an aversion to Seraphine as it was a feeling of indifference. He once told Juliette that he didn't want to look too closely into the Angel Ministry lest he discover that it was a delusion, or worse, a con.

So the situation stood until sometime after Mein Host and two others published a book on angels in 1992, which became a modest bestseller. He then heard from someone still within the community that Seraphine had been infuriated with the success of his book and particularly angry and envious of my ward for writing it. She was quite convinced that it should have been her.

An intriguing reaction—you might think—especially for someone who claimed such intimate involvement with angels.

However, Seraphine was an example of a particular expression that some incarnate rebel angels choose to follow. These angels actually do have a vague sense of their angelic heritage, yet because of the frightening implications of what it means to be a rebel angel, they choose to turn to the other side and set out to try to manifest the good, kind, angel of their imagination. Nothing really wrong with that—if they are doing some good in their lives—but sooner or later the truth does tend to reveal itself.

In Seraphine's case this revelation came in the form of a sad lie. She claimed my ward's NDE—which he'd written about in a 1984 book—as her own! She went around accusing my ward of having "stolen" her NDE, though how he could have done this was never explained.

The woman had usurped the most transcendent and utterly real event in my ward's life simply to fluff up her own feathers. It was such a sad delusion and the motive for the claim so obvious on Seraphine's part that I'm glad to say my ward didn't have any need to make an issue of correcting her. Besides, he'd seen nothing of the woman for at least fifteen years, and—as I noted previously—the two had never been close. As my ward said later, he knew perfectly well what he knew. Let the poor woman be.

Yet what he has never allowed himself to accept until now was that Mother Seraphine's Angel Ministry was based on little more than Seraphine's guilty conscience and a desire to be the center of attention.

I trust this brief digression has some value above and beyond a simple exposure of one woman's self-delusion, as Seraphine is by no means the only rebel angel masquerading as a pinnacle of goodness. The mass awakening to the reality of angels throughout the 1980s and '90s brought a number of these unfortunate poseurs to the surface. Caveat emptor.

The final irony, of course, is that it was my ward who, since 1982, had been actively working with the angels from the third-density; although I'm sure he hoped that Seraphine was welcomed by the angels when she passed.

5

Striking Similarities and Further Steps

Atlantean Megatsunami, Seeding Rebel Incarnates, a Covert Mission, Aligned with Gabriel, Reality of Angels, a Floating Island

I cannot delay any longer describing the destruction I witnessed on the island of Atlantis and throughout the Mediterranean region when the comet finally swept past Earth.

I suspect the ironist would have noted that the devastation wasn't nearly as bad as it might have been—as those who greeted the dragon with such enthusiasm would have masked their self-delusion by making much the same claim. It wasn't really *that* bad, was it?

But, of course, it *was* that bad—especially for those who lost their lives or whose houses were swept away by the terrible storms. Boats were reduced to driftwood, and the harbors and warehouses were ruined. Marble columns, chipped and broken, lay every which way in the debris-strewn streets. The corpses of humans and animals were everywhere; some of the great squares of the city were so stacked with dead bodies that it was impossible to see the paving beneath them. The elaborate fountains with their sculptures of leaping dolphins in the center of the squares were so heaped with bodies that it seemed the stone dolphins were launching themselves from a sea of death.

Yet many of those who lived on the higher slopes of the mountains did manage to survive the first terrible phase when the waters rose and crushed their city, as had also happened to other devastated coastal cities and settlements throughout the Mediterranean.

It occurred that as the comet reached its closest point to Earth, the rotation of the planet caused the eastern Atlantic to be facing the passing comet. The gravitational and kinetic influences of the comet temporarily distorted the Earth's own gravitational field sufficiently to create a bulge in the ocean. It was this bulge—almost a thousand feet in depth—that swept like a megatsunami across the Atlantic. Impelled by the comet, the water was then sloshed back and forth until the ocean level settled, once again, back to normal.

As occurred in many of the natural disasters I have observed, the first impact—whether a tsunami, a flood, an earthquake, or a forest fire—is seldom as serious as the disaster's aftermath. In this case, the aftermath was particularly horrible for the survivors. At least ten major volcanoes in the Western Hemisphere—hitherto inactive—erupted within hours of one another, casting a pall of smoke and ash. This cloud darkened the skies and soon encircled the globe. It was this cloak of darkness that was responsible for cutting off the sun's rays and interrupting any hope of photosynthesis in the affected areas. Swathes of grassland and forests in North Africa and Europe were left leafless and dead.

There followed the most serious die-off of human beings and animals the world had seen since the natural disasters of the thirteenth millennium. As the seventh millennium drew to a close, it was as though the survivors of the catastrophes would have to start all over again from square one.

It is this period that is so puzzling for contemporary anthropologists and archaeologists. On the one hand, they say we have early man chipping away with his stone tools, wrapped in animal skins (if he's lucky), and living a short, brutal life; then, on the other, there is the majestic stonework of sites like Göbekli Tepe, which predate the disasters of the seventh millennium.

This period has also led to some confusion among those who are interested in Atlantis and the timing of its eventual demise. I have noted previously how the first of the series of natural disasters to strike Atlantis had occurred in the thirteenth millennium and had devastated the Atlantean civilization. So seriously had the island nation been ravaged that it had taken the survivors nearly two thousand years to repopulate and rebuild their city.

In a sense, those in Atlantis—celebrating the advent of the dragon in the seventh millennium—were at least partially correct. There were sufficient numbers of them left with enough knowledge retained from the time before the disaster to rebuild the Atlantean culture to its previous full strength within a mere seven hundred years.

I have to credit the inhabitants of the island for their resilience and for their remarkable determination to reestablish their civilization. They built their oceangoing boats with the same fervor that they rebuilt their temples and palaces. This permitted the copper trade to restart after a long break that, in turn, contributed to a revival of the manufacture of bronze implements that spread throughout the expanding area of Atlantean influence over the next three millennia.

What of Prince Caligastia and his rebel midwayers during this tumultuous era? What effect did this second dose of calamities have on the very island upon which the Prince had devoted so much attention?

I couldn't help wondering whether the Prince had taken note of the regularity with which his plans were apparently being thwarted. He'd had a few successes, for sure. As an example, I'd heard from Astar that a deconstruction of Prince Caligastia's sabotage of the intraterrestrial mission—and his bringing down of the MA's two magnificent glowing visitors—was already being taught in the Jerusem courses on religious engineering . . . if that could really be regarded as a success.

Yet, over the previous twenty-five thousand years, Prince Caligastia had met with very little obvious success. It must have felt to him as though every time he and his midwayers had thrown their energies behind a specific group or culture, it had ended in a disaster of one sort or another. And the various disasters invariably appeared to occur just before that particular culture developed to a point of becoming an overwhelming threat to planetary integrity.

As a related side note, when one culture or civilization becomes too globally dominant and overbearing, it can stifle innovation as well as deny opportunities for its inhabitants to exercise their free will. I have heard mortals question whether this action itself eliminates the individual's free will by killing them en masse. Let me remind them that the Multiverse is an extremely well-organized place, and these natural disasters are carefully constructed to achieve specific results. Humans might describe these "natural disasters" as arbitrary and subject only to natural processes, but serious events like these are far more intentional than that.

The appropriate approach from which to frame these natural disasters is to appreciate that they are designed to further the overall advancement of the human race. The death of an individual—or even a mass of individuals—is regarded as subordinate to the good of the race in general. There are no rights and wrongs in these assessments, as the ancients used to believe. The Atlanteans were not brought down because they were wicked—or because the devastation was a punishment from the gods—but because the direction in which the Atlanteans were leading the world was out of sync with the true destiny of the planet.

I've already described how the Pleiadian arks lifted off the majority of the population of Lemuria as their islands disappeared beneath the Pacific and how the Sirians rescued the best of Atlantis at the time of their first series of calamities. In both cases, this should demonstrate the depth of caring in the Multiverse—as well as the elegance of the coordination that exists between the celestial realms and beings from more advanced, fifth-density worlds.

It is significant to note that during the entire chaos and damage of this recent Atlantean catastrophe, there was no sign of any rescue or evacuation occurring as a result of Sirian, Orion, or Pleiadian efforts. It appeared there was no need.

I believe one reason for this was the massive infusion of rebel angel incarnates into Atlantean society. When I came to look into the figures—Astar had "telehacked" into the Jerusem registry—we found that 98 percent of those killed in the floods and by subsequent diseases were all rebel angel incarnates. The implication of this is clear: each individual rebel angel would have agreed prior to their mortal incarnation to the fate that awaited them. Upon their being born into mortal form, the shroud of forgetfulness would have fallen over their spiritual vision, as it does to this day for almost every angel incarnate.

I say "almost all" as I've observed during the course of my ward's travels over the past thirty years that a number of the children he encountered—many of those among the so-named Indigo, or Crystal, children—have a remarkable access to their preincarnation memories.

I'm in no position to second-guess the timing of the MA's actions in seeding Atlantis with so many incarnate angels specifically within the generations that took the brunt of the disaster, yet it was obvious it was carefully planned.

It was also obvious that MA's decision to open the opportunity for incarnation to rebel angels was a direct response to Caligastia's autocratic play to manipulate the grid for his own purposes.

So what were Prince Caligastia's plans?

It appeared he had been outfoxed by the MA. The rebel angel incarnates were of very little value to the Prince or his midwayers. Some incarnates were too somnolent to be of use, while others were compelled to rebel against any expression of authority. When the Prince realized that he himself had inadvertently opened a door through which had poured this new kind of being, he effectively lost the opportunity to create his race of reincarnated slaves. Instead, this became the first hint of *Homo angelicus* as a serious prospective symbiosis of angel and mortal.

This event, from what I can infer of the MA's plans, must have represented an early experiment on a large-scale inundation of rebel angel incarnates, all within two or three generations. Many tens of thousands of them. No one had ever seen such a massive influx of incarnates before. One or two here and there over the past few millennia, but nothing like this. Astar recently said that, in her opinion, it was a practice run for the veritable flood of angel incarnates that occurred in the late-twentieth century—and that we are still observing now.

Rebel angels have been used throughout history, but they are generally incarnated in small groups when a culture needs to be stirred up and provoked out of their complacency. These are beings who—when they have advanced into their maturity through a large number of lifetimes on this and a variety of other worlds—become the ones who are unwilling to accept any authority but that of the Living God.

In their most developed form, mature incarnate rebel angels have undergone numerous lifetimes in different physical forms, thus allowing them the fullest range of experience of all that was subject to the profound dislocation caused by the Lucifer revolution. These angels— many of whom are now present on this planet—are being regarded as the highest expression of *Homo angelicus,* the new symbiote.

Such are the times that many of these angelic incarnates have had profound spiritual awakenings that have given their lives meaning and have shown them their true purpose.

My ward is drawing my attention to an essay, "NDE as a Threshold Experience," written by P. M. H. Atwater for *New Dawn* magazine—one of the original researchers on near-death experiences—in which she makes much the same point and draws a significant conclusion. She writes:

> Currently the conservative estimate worldwide for people having had a near-death experience is 4% to 5% of the general population. This estimate does not take into consideration near-death-like

and spiritually transforming experiences that are also intensely life changing. Counting them too could easily double or triple that figure, indicating that a realignment of global consciousness toward a higher order is well on its way to becoming highly charged.

There will be more incursions of rebel angel incarnates in subsequent eras, but I believe Atlantis was one of the prime incubators of *Homo angelicus*. And, as Astar speculated, all these incursions also functioned as preparations for this precise time in the early twenty-first century.

There are many angel incarnates living now on the planet who were also present during the different phases of the Atlantean civilization. Their presence here at this key juncture in the Earth's transformation functions as a form of a fifth column operating under the radar of prevalent belief systems. I've observed that these incarnate angels have been generally—and appropriately—placed within all the people of the world to work most effectively in support of the "realignment of global consciousness" that P. M. H. Atwater writes about in the above quote. I should also note that incarnated *rebel* angels do not necessarily make up all of these so-called starseeds—although they are the vast majority.

We've already met Hilda and Jeanne in Father Jesse's life—both of whom were aligned with Gabriel—and there will be some more out there. There are far more extraterrestrials mixing unnoticeably with the populations of the great cities than is generally supposed, and a small number of extraterrestrial walk-ins are also quietly joining the fray. I have even heard from a reliable source that midwayers from other, more settled worlds have been recently brought here to reinforce the indigenous midwayers, but I have yet to encounter one. And, since I can't be everywhere and know everything, I have no doubt that all manner of beings are finding their way here for what lies ahead.

However, as I've already reiterated, the conditions are notoriously grim and uninviting on this world. While the rebel angels have been long prepared for this lifetime in their previous incarnations and have very specific functions, most extraterrestrials on the planet play relatively secondary, but often vital, roles. (I say "secondary," but I've been made aware that extraterrestrials have quietly intervened to prevent a potentially dangerous escalation of hostilities on at least half a dozen occasions.)

If you, loyal reader, have been following my *Confessions* thus far, I can almost guarantee that if you're not an extraterrestrial, then you are most likely an incarnate rebel angel—if you are not already aware of that.

* * *

It was in the summer of 1976 that the fourth of the angelic interventions occurred in Mein Host's life. This time it came in the form of two very different young women. Neither knew each other, and both used every possible feminine wile in their competition for my ward's attention.

Karen was a slimly built woman who appeared older than her early thirties. To look at her was to feel she'd given up on herself somewhere along the way. She seemed to wear the same dirty jeans and oversize sweater every day and dragged herself limply from place to place. Her long dark hair—parted in the middle and framing her face—was frequently stringy and unwashed, and she'd habitually pull it in front of her eyes as though she was hiding. She had a pretty face when it wasn't drawn into self-concern, with sad, brown eyes and—for an American woman—unusually poor teeth, with some obviously missing. For all that, Karen was an intelligent, well-educated woman, and on the rare occasions she was happy, it was invariably as if it were for the first time. Her eyes would light up, her hair was pushed back, her back straightened, and then—for no apparent reason—her happiness would disappear, overwhelmed by the darkness in which she lived and to which she was accustomed.

Perhaps everybody knows or has known someone like Karen, so it should come as no surprise that she had been sexually abused as a young girl and had never managed to get over it. She'd been so psychologically damaged that she still carried the scar in her posture—her shoulders pulled forward to protect her small, underdeveloped breasts.

Karen played the victim card with such dogged persistence that for all my ward's kindness in responding to the challenge she presented, her problems went far too deep for the minimal amount of time he could afford to spend with her. My ward once remarked to Juliette that Karen possessed "the lowest self-esteem of anyone he'd ever met."

Karen loved my ward with a hopeless, hapless, adoration; the love of a woman who was so accustomed to being used that she'd given her heart to a man who was kind to her without expecting anything in return. In her own shy way, Karen had tried everything she knew to grab Mein Host's attention. When it became obvious he wasn't falling for her tricks, she became slavishly devoted to him.

Let me just interject something I've noticed before about my ward, but that I saw most clearly illustrated in the connection he formed with Karen in the two years he knew her. It would have been obvious to him that Karen was much too damaged to ever make it into the community, however much she might have loved him. She wasn't cut out for it. My ward has said that sooner or later he could get most of the people who were drawn to him to redirect their affection and their attention to the religion and their gods. Not so with Karen.

He was patient and kind with the girl, but he was obviously embarrassed by her doglike devotion. He would actively try to avoid seeing her. Yet knowing how fragile Karen was, he clearly had no desire to throw her into an even deeper depression. He couldn't turn her away. His attempts to discourage her from becoming involved in the community by explaining how much self-discipline and focus would be demanded of her if she ever joined it tended to provoke the opposite response. Karen would dutifully try to make herself attend the various classes and sessions until the water became too hot for her, and—as my ward might have predicted—she would fall back into her victim role and mope around the chapter again. She would then disappear for a few weeks before returning and repeating the pattern all over again.

Karen appeared to be one of those unfortunate souls who simply lacked the capacity for sustained focus and was unable to summon the sufficient determination to overcome her limitations. Yet, from an angelic point of view, she was an excellent choice. She was never meant to join the community; her mission was to lure away my ward's attention through the constant emotional neediness of the perpetual victim.

Jackie—the second of the pair of the angel incarnates—was just as needy, but she manifested the other side of the victim and aggressor equation. My ward would find it a great deal more challenging to handle what the beautiful young Jackie would throw at him.

Not as much was known in the 1970s about the long-term use of stimulant drugs. Karen, as a rebellious young girl, had been prescribed amphetamines and Ritalin, creating an unacknowledged addiction that had pursued her through college and into her late twenties. She had started to struggle to get off drugs a couple of years before she came to the Foundation Center and met my ward. So, in one sense, he would spend the ensuing two years helping Karen finally put the drugs behind her. In that one way he proved successful.

As a rebel angel, Karen was at a relatively early stage in her incarnational journey. Her karmic choice to experience such serious sexual and chemical abuse had, sadly, severely impaired her physical and emotional bodies. Mein Host was sensible enough to know that she was far beyond his capacity, or responsibility, to restore to wholeness and, as he told Juliette, he'd "determined to be resolutely kind and supportive of her—however many times the poor girl fell off the wagon."

There was no refusing people if they wanted to be there. Mein Host would have said—and meant—that it was more a question of finding a way that people like Karen could be helpful to themselves and to the community by discovering what they were good at and what they loved to do.

Mein Host had become aware of the reality of angels in the course of his NDE, although the experience itself was so profound—and the demands on his life at the time were so extreme—that he'd pushed all thought of angels aside. He was unaware that he was himself an incarnate rebel angel; had he known, he wouldn't have understood what it meant.

He certainly would have never guessed that Karen, too, was a rebel angel; a rebel angel who was desperately rebelling against finding herself trapped in a human body. It would have taken a rare psychiatrist—or the most knowing of metaphysicians—to even comprehend her basic issue. My ward was neither.

As is generally the case with incarnate angels, although they may be strangelings among their siblings and to their parents, they will likely have a close relative—an uncle or aunt, a close family friend, or sometimes a grandmother or grandfather—who will also be an incarnate angel. These will be the ones who will reach out and support the younger incarnates as best they can over the course of the young ones' growth into adulthood.

In Karen's case this was a man whom she was keen for my ward to meet because, as she said, she was quite sure they would get on well together. This proved, as with so many of Karen's other judgments, to be a lot more complicated than she could have intended. But, then again, perhaps she did intend to mix it up.

William Maxwell Gaines (Bill Gaines) was Karen's favorite uncle. He was a large and imposing man in his early fifties who'd become infamous for publishing some of the better-crafted horror and science-fiction comics; the comics hated by adults that my ward used to lap up in 1950s England. The days he could get hold of a copy of *Tales from the Crypt*—or a tattered issue of *Weird Science* or a well-thumbed copy of *The Vault of Horror*—would find him hiding them away from his mother and reading them at night by flashlight. I'm sure he recalls his precious pile of horror comics being confiscated by his horrified mother in his eleventh year. (*I hadn't remembered until Georgia brought it up. —TW*)

In 1952, Bill Gaines had launched *Mad* magazine, which he

published until he died in 1992. When Karen took my ward around to meet her uncle in the summer of 1975, *Mad* was reaching its zenith—with more than two million copies of the eight issues a year sold—and had become the most influential of the satirical comics in America.

Bill Gaines was one of those incarnate angels who would have been appalled to learn he was an angel. He was a lifelong confirmed atheist and would have laughed it off as an absurd idea. He might have thought rather differently had he known who the rebel angels actually were. Likewise, if any of Bill's friends had known the truth about incarnated rebel angels, every one of them would have likely said that no one fit the bill—and they'd have chuckled at the pun—more than their good friend, Bill.

It was a curious meeting, with Bill reveling in being known as the most amoral publisher in America and boasting how he'd rubbed the censors' noses in their own hypocrisy. He was proud of his business and how he ran it, and he told stories about the lengths he went to keep *Mad* looking cheap and tatty. He talked about turning down multi-million dollar offers from corporations so he could keep the magazine as creepy and outrageous as he wanted.

There was a feeling that I knew my ward shared. The more that Bill continued to talk, the more it seemed that for some reason the man needed to justify himself to Mein Host. Then he would change and be thrilled with his own irreverence as he rolled out his worst God jokes, hoping to get a rise out of my ward.

Bill Gaines was loud and rude and funny—and he clearly disliked my ward on sight. As an atheist he had every reason to believe he was trying to save his niece from the clutches of a predatory cult. No doubt he would have heard from Karen before the meeting about this well-dressed and charming so-called priest now sitting in his office and had decided to take exception to him. He poked and he probed—abusive and rude one moment, and roaring with laughter the next.

If there was one skill my ward had learned from his years of donat-ing on the streets of the cities of Europe and America—as well as the exercises in communication the group had studied and practiced so assiduously—it was how to respond to verbal abuse with grace and how to defuse aggressive challenges. He remained resolutely positive and kindly disposed toward his host, psychically weaving and dodging the angry, insulting thoughtforms.

Bill softened up after that.

Although the two men could not have been more different in every way save one—the most significant and the most deeply occulted—they started getting on well together for reasons neither would have been able to understand. Evidence of this came when Karen and my ward finally left the *Mad* publisher's office, and Bill showed no sign of continuing to warn his niece of the evils of the church and exuberantly shook Mein Host's hand and waved them off with a great burst of laughter.

Although Jackie, our second angel, had also endured years of childhood sexual abuse, she manifested the scars in quite the opposite manner to Karen.

Jackie was the outgoing and flirtatious extrovert to Karen's guilty introvert. Jackie was tall and willow-slim, with urchin-cut blond hair and a beautiful elfin face, and she was vain about her looks, while Karen projected dark, brooding, and melancholy moodiness. Jackie was bold and provocative and used to successfully seducing whomever she desired, while Karen demonstrated unrequited and calflike devotion.

Jackie was a few years younger than Karen, and because her legs were long, slim, and tanned, her breasts were pert and firm and well-formed, and her face was gaminelike and shone with mischievous sensuality, she appeared to have based her self-esteem entirely on her sexual allure.

It's not surprising given what Jackie had been through as a child—and the fragile beauty she had developed as a young adult—that she would never have much bothered to develop her intelligence. This combination of beauty and simplicity gave her an almost childlike innocence. When something puzzled Jackie, her blue eyes emptied and her finely etched features would wrinkle briefly as if a cloud had passed over the sun.

I believe—of all the young women surrounding my ward—he felt particularly tender toward Jackie. He would later say that it was Jackie with whom he would have chosen to make love if had he been free to do so.

But he also clearly understood that to allow himself the slightest intimacy with Jackie—or with any of the other young women—would break what he thought of as a sacred trust. He knew the women essentially trusted him as a celibate Priest to rise above his carnal desires, even as they did their best and worst to seduce him.

Karen and Jackie had both been betrayed so deeply and so many times by the men in their lives that their need for the kindness of a man who was trustworthy gave an additional meaning and purpose to my ward's decision to be celibate.

It was much to his credit, in my opinion, that my ward stayed true to his vow despite all the temptations.

*　*　*

Watching the Atlantis survivors struggling to start over and pondering the fate of the rebel angel incarnates got me thinking once again about life on the planet Zandana. In the past I have found that my mind often turns to Zandana when I want to avoid some awful calamity on Earth. This time it felt different. I'd seen the worst that Prince Caligastia could inflict on the world, and I hadn't yet been crushed by it.

I confess I was somewhat shocked to observe all those rebel angel incarnates on the island prior to and during the disasters. I still wasn't sure how to interpret their presence—not from the rebel angels' point of view, anyway. I was fairly certain I knew what the MA was up to in sabotaging Caligastia's plans to enslave human beings in his "Reincarnation Express." But the rebel angels themselves? How did they approach this mission? Was it a punishment? Did they volunteer for the incarnation? Was it understood as the MA's gift of redemption? An exercise of karma? A prescient promise? Indeed, would such an influx of rebel angels ever be repeated? And, perhaps more importantly—to me anyway—what did all those angel incarnates mean for my destiny?

At that point, I still hadn't fully grasped what lay ahead for the rebel angels. This Atlantean influx could just have been a one of a kind. I just didn't know. It was that thought—and the questions I was left with—which gave me the sense that I would know more if I took another careful look at the planet of Zandana.

Zandana was similar enough to Earth to permit me to make some reasonable comparisons between the two worlds. Their Planetary Prince's mission had occurred at about the same time as Earth's mission, and—like Caligastia and Daligastia—both of Zandana's Planetary Princes had led their planet into Lucifer's revolution. Their two intra-terrestrial visitors had even arrived at approximately the same time on both planets. However, soon after that, the dissimilarities between the two worlds started to show, and the gap progressively widened over the ensuing millennia.

The most recent time I was on Zandana, I had been privileged to spend some time with Prince Janda-chi—their mission's second-in-command—and learn from him that Caligastia was becoming increasing isolated and despised by his high-level co-revolutionaries. Prince Janda-chi was actually holding Caligastia responsible for ruining the revolution for all of them—for all thirty-seven planets that joined the revolution hoping in good faith for a more independent life for all beings.

As I mulled over the meaning of what Janda-chi had told me, I realized it was more than possible that the thirty-seven worlds were not being treated equably by the MA. For example, I don't believe I ever directly observed any rebel angel activity during my visits to Zandana. As I thought about it, I couldn't recall seeing one . . . not one. I wondered if they were camouflaged in some way that prevented me from recognizing rebel angels. Or, was I being masked off in some manner of which I was unaware?

The more I pondered this the more I realized I needed to return to Zandana to observe for myself, once and for all, whether the rebel angels were incarnating on worlds other than Earth.

I knew I would need to be careful. Although I didn't have a choice to disregard an open edict from a Planetary Prince, I really didn't relish being used as a covert conduit between the princes—a function for which I'd started to suspect Janda-chi was positioning me.

Of course, I couldn't entirely ignore a Planetary Prince's request—although in Janda-chi's case it was scarcely more than a hint—but I'd been around long enough to become more confident in my ability to telepathically mask and dissemble. Not the easiest of tasks. But then again, Planetary Princes usually have a great deal on their minds, so I have generally been able to slide past them without alerting their telepathic tendrils.

Should I take another quick tour of Earth before leaving for Zandana? Is that what Prince Janda-chi would have hoped for? In light of that last meeting with him, I wondered if all I did—or observed—from now on would be part of some covert mission. A mission so covert that even I, as the bearer of the occulted information, would be unaware of it happening!

So many questions!

I am sure you can discern just how uncertain I was at that point in time. It was a level of uncertainty that was becoming progressively insistent. I took this as a sign to stop thinking about Zandana—and worrying whether I was being used as a spy—and simply go there.

I could have used the far closer Seraphic Transport Center (STC) at the eastern end of the Mediterranean, but that STC was close to Caligastia's palace, and I was anxious to avoid any interaction with him.

So instead, I formed the intention that should have taken me directly via dimensional shift to the STC in the redwood forests on the West Coast of North America. Yet, in spite of trying three times—it wasn't a matter of effort, so three times was quite enough—nothing happened. Nothing whatsoever changed. Nothing at all. There was no shivering in the aethers. No instantaneous transport. I was still sitting on the island of Atlantis.

So I had to make the trip myself.

And I decided to take it slowly.

It was as I was passing over the Atlantic that I observed a mass of debris stretching as far as I could see from my elevation. A mess of tree trunks and logs already covered with barnacles were floating on the surface like a great island. A variety of seabirds were already colonizing the tangle of dead branches and fighting happily and noisily among themselves.

In the distance, I could see cormorants—and other even larger diving birds—dropping like small missiles into the ocean, catching the fish drawn by the nutrients and the security of the floating island. Parrots of every color flashed in flocks of four or five between the ragged branches.

Dropping closer I could see the debris had melded into what appeared to be one homogenous mass. The mud from the uprooted trees along with small branches and brambles had congealed and hardened in the tropical sun into what seemed to be solid ground. In some places the mud had been washed away by the seawater below, exposing the mishmash of reeds and branches that were holding the island together beneath the surface.

There were stretches where grass was growing, some of it burned and brown, and yet looking almost like an Alpine meadow. "Almost," because the meadow lifted and dropped with the swell of the ocean beneath it. Recent rain had filled small hollows with fresh water, which was slopping and splashing this way and that with the wash of the waves beneath the meadow. And scampering over rotting branches were lizards and goodness knows what other small creatures whose ancestors had found themselves swept away by the megatsunami, along with the branch on which they had been perched. Somehow in the turmoil a few creatures must have survived and bred, creating this unique ecosystem that would swirl around the ocean for a century or two before finally rotting away, the great trees waterlogged and dragging what remained of the island down to the seabed.

We were shown in our Jerusem training programs how carefully nurtured are the solar systems that support inhabited or soon-to-be-inhabited planets. Potentially serious impacts from asteroids are monitored, and in some cases space rocks have to be pulverized if they threaten the biosphere. We were shown comets whose orbital paths had been gently nudged to avoid inhabited solar systems. We were lectured about the extreme complexity of even the smallest manipulation of a single physical element because any change affected the overall equilibrium and required—or so they told us—endless and rather tiresome calculations.

I can infer from such an assertion of precision that the orbit that brought the comet so close to Earth was clearly intentional, and it would have taken some very careful and, no doubt, tiresome calculation. In light of all this complexity, I'm sure the MA would have thought of the floating island merely as an unanticipated consequence of the megatsunami. And the island's demise? Collateral damage, and of no real concern given the alternatives.

The metaphor quickly depressed me, so I turned back toward the west. After a while the shoreline of the Caribbean islands appeared on the horizon. It had been some millennia since I'd been on this side of the Atlantic, and I was astonished to see how profoundly the landscape had changed. Many of the islands I'd remembered seeing previously had completely disappeared; others had been swept clean of trees and could be mistaken for sandbanks. The Atlantean trading city that was part of a landmass of which only the island of Cuba now remains, had sunk deep beneath the waters.

Vegetation was very slowly returning to the islands. It was in sharp contrast to how rapidly life had taken hold and was flourishing on the floating debris island. It was as though nature itself knew the arc of the island's existence would be a brief one and was wildly accelerating in its joyous dance with death. Compared with that floating terrarium, many of the islands were entirely devoid of animal life. Only the higher slopes of the volcanic islands appeared untouched by the ravages of the tsunami. On one of the mountainous islands I could barely see the form of the land for the enormous flocks of birds that were circling beneath me.

I crossed the Caribbean and made landfall—if it could be called land—over the marshes of the delta of a great river that emptied out into the Gulf of Mexico.

As I followed the wide river upstream I saw the answer to a question that had been worrying me ever since passing over that sunken Atlantean city. I knew the city had developed over the centuries from a simple trading post to one of the main ports on the east from which the copper and other precious metals were shipped across the Atlantic. I was aware that transatlantic shipping had started up again after Atlantis recovered from the recent disasters. It was a sterling tribute to Atlantean organization and ambition that I could now see below me that another less ostentatious trading post had been set up, where the copper was now being warehoused and transferred to the boats.

The building work was far simpler than that of the sunken city, as they knew the new site wasn't likely to be permanent. Yet the builders had maintained the same basic circular pattern established by the singular form of the island of Atlantis itself.

I cut eastward across the endless mangrove swamps to then move up the North American coastline. Like the islands, the coast was unrecognizable with vast swathes reduced now to barren cliffs and the endless dunes left by the receding waters.

When I reached the Carolina coast, I suddenly found myself whisked interdimensionally straight through to the western STC. Afterward, when I had a chance to think about it, I attributed it to my having cleared up my doubts. That is the way it works. Only a pure intention can activate dimensional access and transport.

My friendly Transport Seraph (TS), Eleena, was waiting for me in the transport lounge and didn't appear in the slightest bit surprised when I manifested beside her. I was more used to her offhand manner by now and no longer took it personally.

In fact, it once again left me wondering how subtly we are all interconnected in the fifth dimension. After spending so much time in the density of Earth's astral realms—where the entities are all defined, as they tend to define themselves by their separation one from another—I found it all too easy to forget the inherent closeness of my connection with the Multiverse. And, as for observing the development of human intelligence over the recent millennia, I had noticed a gradual drift toward separation that had been actively encouraged by Caligastia. I have even heard the Prince boast that with some appropriate prodding—and as human beings come to value their progressive individuation and make it a matter of personal pride—this separation can be used to his advantage.

I could feel Eleena listening to my thoughts and clucking in telepathic distaste, so I quickly brought my attention back to her and how, once again, I was marveling that my favorite TS was there.

On a previous occasion, Eleena had tried to explain how she was always at the STC waiting for me—even when it was a last-minute decision on my part. She'd spoken of combining the purity of intention with a multiversal element she had respectfully called "necessity." And the one time that Eleena had not been there waiting for me, I understood what she meant. There'd been no "necessity" for me to travel on that occasion.

Eleena was smiling at me when she gestured to the light over the entrance to the transport chamber flashing blue. I followed her through the door and turned to watch it slide quietly closed behind us. Another, rather more substantial, secondary door then ratcheted down with a deliberate slowness from a receptacle recessed above the door.

"It dissipates the energy," Eleena said quietly in my mind. "The build-up of energy that occurs when we lift off. It's why we don't use the transport chambers immediately after another TS has just taken off. Haven't you noticed there was always a slight delay before the blue light goes on?"

Indeed I had, and I'd met some interesting beings in the transport lounge while I was waiting for that blue light to flash.

"Come," Eleena said, opening her heatshield wide to encompass me. I turned back toward her and, mounting the raised central platform, I backed myself into her welcoming embrace. The two halves of her heatshield unfurled from her back like two magnificent wings, which curled around me and locked in place.

There were a few moments when the material of the shield compressed itself into an impermeable shell—an organic, ceramic-like substance that induced a phase change in the material when subjected to the heat produced by subspace friction.

"Like magic, isn't it!" I could hear Eleena laughing quietly behind me. "If the technology of the future is indistinguishable from magic, what, I wonder, would they make of my very own heatproof wings?"

We were both laughing at the thought when I felt a slight tremor and knew we'd soon be accelerating into subspace. Sometimes we would communicate during the trip, but this time all Eleena whispered was for me to listen to the new composition that she'd been working on since I had last traveled with her.

I've already written about the pride Transport Seraphs place on the music they can make by micromodulating the surface of their heatshields to create and manipulate minute indentations. By skillfully positioning the tiny dents and their relative depth, the TSs could produce chords of melodious and microtonal complexity similar to the sound of the wind blowing over the top of an open bottle.

Eleena's music was not so much an acquired taste as it was an exercise in the depth of listening. As the distance between the point of Zeno's arrow and his target can be divided into ever smaller units, so the gap between any two musical notes can be divided into an almost endless number of microtones. All TSs, so Eleena has told me, are equipped with an extremely highly developed auditory apparatus, which she said was an original gift from the Holy Mother Spirit to accompany them on their long interstellar trips.

Even beings as perfectly created as TSs seek to perfect their creative talents, so over time these beings have become known as the proponents of their own very specialized musical form. Some of the more adept TSs were regarded as exceptionally fine sonic artists and were frequently booked for travel well in advance by a connoisseur of such glorious sounds.

As we picked up speed, Eleena's music began. This time she started simply, a single continuous note that she twisted into a widening spiral of sound. The vibrations were transduced by the heatshield into the sound that turned and twirled through me as it intertwined and danced with every ultimaton in my body.

I became absorbed, at one with the glorious sound.

6

The Unfurling of Wings . . . and of Understanding

Musical Synesthesia, a Transport Seraph's Warning, the Freeze, Life the Teacher, Zandana's Astral Realms, Meeting a Zandanan Watcher

In the stillness of Eleena's embrace, another single note joined the first—looping and braiding around it. Both notes were so distinctly defined that it was as though the sound was starting to gain actual substance.

I believe it was when I had this realization that the notes assumed two different colors—one a deep scarlet, the other a luminous green—that appeared to be snaking up through my body when I closed my eyes.

Now this *was* something new. I'd never seen the colors before.

Then the two color streams become four streams, then eight, then sixteen, and so on, subdividing ever more subtlety until all the sound streams joined to become a single, multicolored membrane. I watched this membrane with amazement as it curled and bent with the slow and rhythmic undulations of the wings of a manta ray. I knew I was being shown something of supreme importance, but it felt just outside my grasp. And yet that was only Eleena's introductory piece!

As though she was demonstrating the basic construction of what was to soon become the most beautifully complex piece—I dare not even call it music, as it soared so far beyond anything I'd ever heard before. Eleena added indentation to indentation, minutely shaping each to produce a precise pitch. Although many I'm sure were well beyond my hearing ability, those soundless notes transduced into flashes of intense color on the rippling surface of the membrane.

I can compare this with nothing else you have ever seen. The membrane, while retaining its undulating form, was scintillating with pinpricks of brilliant color. It was so intense that I opened my eyes . . . and there it still was, the membrane flowing and billowing through my body, so I could even feel the exquisite tingling of the different colors flashing on and off. It was a cloak of many colors made of light falling on dark matter.

There was enough space within a TS's embrace to allow my hands and arms freedom of movement, so I tried an experiment. Using one of my hands as a fin, I lowered it gingerly into the membrane and immediately pulled it back in surprise. I was so excited that I'd forgotten how she was constructing the sound and therefore the colored membrane. I'd come to think of it as a static sheet of color, but when I dipped my fingertips into it I realized it was moving very rapidly, and my fingers opened up a dark hole that left a wake, which closed again behind my hand.

I then slipped my whole hand into the flow, and I found that if I curled my hand—cupping the currents of color—the chroma responded, changing slightly with my movements so that before long I felt that I was actually contributing to the complexity of the melody.

The melody? Contributing to the melody?

Did I really believe I was changing the melody by messing with the color stream? I heard a ripple of light laughter from Eleena behind me.

"Many of my travelers make that mistake," I could hear the lilt in Eleena's tone. "I thought you would enjoy being saturated the first time you felt the music's synesthetic properties. It can be disturbing to begin with. We usually take it more slowly with our travelers, but I know you well enough to feel your developing interest and enjoyment of novelty."

"So you can see the membrane, too?" I asked her in surprise. "I thought it just appeared within your heatshield. Wasn't it *my* synesthetic faculty that was manifesting the membrane? How could *you* have seen it, Eleena?"

"Do you imagine you are the only Seraph who is a synesthete?" I caught the sharpness in Eleena's tone. "Not only can I see the membrane, but it stretches outside me like a diamond-shaped wave on which I'm surfing while I'm simultaneously creating it—*as* I am moving through subspace. I only wish you could see it as I can . . . from the outside!"

I was about to say the membrane was quite impressive enough from the inside when the colors started to change, progressively slowing down and then dimming altogether, until I was once again alone within Eleena's heatshield.

There was never any somatic sense of acceleration or deceleration when traveling with a TS, but—with experience—the changing tone of the music tells you all you need to know. Though this was the first time I had experienced the membrane dissolving back into the ribbons of color that, in turn, dwindled and faded away leaving only the music, as an experienced traveler I was quite familiar with the music itself evaporating, and I knew that within a few moments there'd be a slight click—an almost inaudible hiss of decompression—and the two wings of the heatshield would lift free to swing back and furl behind the TS.

I moved out from within Eleena's embrace and stepped off the platform before turning to thank her for the journey. As she came to join me and the single door of the chamber slid aside behind me, I saw a curious expression flicker across her beautiful face. I hadn't seen this before. Was it concern for me? Had I done something to offend her? Was it a warning? Or had it, in fact, nothing to do with me at all? (The self-concern that is revealed by my questions and suppositions now embarrasses me. In many ways these were new feelings—mortal-type feelings I had never experienced before the revolution started turning sour. At that point, I still hadn't grasped the extent and the depth of the preparation I was receiving for mortal incarnation.)

It wasn't until we parted in the lounge of Zandana's main STC that I had my answer . . . and yet another surprise.

"Be fully attentive, sister," Eleena said to me softly, looking into my eyes. "You will find Zandana much changed."

Just how changed she wouldn't tell me.

More and more I was having to find out the truth for myself.

* * *

I don't want to give the impression that Mein Host thought the community revolved around him. It certainly didn't—even if I sometimes unintentionally make it sound that way. Other members of the community come and go in my narrative as they interact with my ward, yet each has a story as distinct and as strange as my ward's.

His old friend Malachi—who was also at Xtul and with whom he stays in contact—recently commented (after reading my ward's published account of their time in Xtul) that any description of his own experience would be quite different. So it would be the same for the rest of the individuals in the group. In fact, as I was writing this week, my ward found one such book recently published that does exactly that: *Xtul: An Experience of the Process,* written by Sabrina Verney. She was one of the handful of people who would choose to leave Xtul and the Process community in the days before the hurricane.

Yet, if Mein Host was to step back and contemplate the community *as if* it revolved around him, he would have to explain how unusually specific the preparation he received was to how his interests have developed during the thirty-five years since he left the community.

Much of the training was indirect in the sense of pushing him into situations in which he had no choice but to confront his demons. He speaks of the whole process as being one of accelerated evolution. It allowed him to go through a far wider array of experiences, both positive and negative, than ever would have been likely in the outside world—and within a (relatively) safe environment. "This providing a safe space," I've heard him say, "is one of the most valuable functions of a cult. The trick is to know when to get out!"

People instinctively avoid pain—whether physical, mental, or emotional. All animals are wired to avoid pain. To willingly move toward pain, a creature needs a motive more powerful than the imminent prospect of pain. In the animal world, the options are generally clear-cut: a bear risks pain to protect her cubs; a trapped hyena tolerates the pain caused by gnawing off his leg to release himself; and even your little pussy cat risks pain every time he fights to defend his territory.

Mortals are not only subject to the instincts of their animal natures, but they also clearly introduce a far more complex set of variables. A human being might invite physical pain, for example, and cut themselves simply to mask or override the emotional pain. Much of human life in the twenty-first century can be thought of as a continual distraction from the emotional and spiritual pain that people experience as lives of quiet desperation. Xanax, Prozac, Zoloft, Wellbutrin, Celexa, Paxil, Lexapro, Effexor . . . the list of antidepressants grows yearly as more and more people dose themselves to avoid their mental, emotional, or spiritual pain.

In the contemporary world there is little to motivate people to have the courage to face their inner fears and pain. And—because courage is so central to the spiritual journey all mortals are taking—if an inner fear is not confronted and released, it will tend to manifest as an external confrontation until that fear is finally faced and mastered. That is the only way courage can be developed.

Mein Host had a clear example of this process in action over a ten-year period from 1979 to 1989, which revealed itself with angelic precision. He has written about these events in one of his books (*Adventures Among Spiritual Intelligences*), so here I will tell it as I observed it.

I'm jumping ahead to a time about a year and a half after he left the community and was staying with Alma Daniel in her apartment in the Eldorado on Manhattan's Central Park West. Alma would later come to play a central part in his life, but this event occurred early in their friendship.

The Eldorado is an elegantly designed, art deco apartment building that fills the block on Central Park West between West 91st and 92nd Streets, with the nearest subway station at 85th and Central Park West. It was a short walk to the train, and my ward took it frequently as he traveled around the city.

When he left the Foundation Faith in 1977, my ward was not in a good state. I will explore the reasons for this in more detail when I come to address his exit in the next chapters.

Granted, over the course of his thirteen years with the community he had developed self-confidence, leadership skills, and a far deeper understanding of himself—yet there were still many buried fears that continued to lurk untouched.

The first of these incidents occurred one Sunday morning as he was striding down Central Park West toward the subway station on his way to visit his friend Marty Jacobs, a psychiatrist living on Long Island. It was a sunny day, and early enough for the traffic to be light and the sidewalk empty. He was walking fast and about three yards from the corner of West 88th and Central Park West—on the west side of the street—when I could see what he could not: a large black man pursued by two younger white guys about seventy-five yards behind him was running for all his worth toward Central Park West on the north side of 88th Street, and on a collision course with my ward.

Mein Host must have heard the pounding feet and the shouts of the pursuers just as he reached the corner, but to see a large man about ten feet away hurtling full tilt straight at him must have been a nasty shock. But he recovered fast, and, presumably responding to the men's shouts with some idea of stopping him, he turned to move toward the running man.

The running man was built like a football player and was at least three inches taller than Mein Host, who at 6'2" was tall but only half the man's width. I could see their eyes connecting with a visceral shock. Panic. Anger. Fear. Threat. I could perceive the thoughtforms—like daggers and darts—flying between them. My ward later described the man's eyes as "boiling with dark fury."

The man veered slightly to my ward's right to avoid him without breaking his stride, while simultaneously reaching with his left hand under his jacket in a gesture that gangster movies have taught everybody implies the certain presence of a gun. A gun.

Mein Host, mid-stride, froze in his tracks.

Still as a statue.

Motionless.

He describes it as a weird immobility that closed down all his reflexes. He said it struck him out of nowhere, and that it had never happened before. He said he watched in horror as the man ran past him, followed a few moments later by the two pursuers and the further humiliation of their clucking scorn at his apparent cowardice.

Upon reaching Marty's Oyster Bay house and confessing his cowardice to his host, Marty the shrink tried to reassure him that it was for the best—he might have been killed! True, perhaps, but that wasn't at all my ward's concern. What appalled him, he said, was the automaticity with which he'd frozen. He said he'd felt he had no choice, that his body just stopped moving in mid-stride. He said that he'd heard of fight or flight, but never of freeze. Marty's kind, but superficial, reassurances clearly missed the point entirely.

The decade of the 1980s would prove to be a time when my ward would delve as deeply into his inner world as he had plumbed the extremes of the outer world while with the community. It would become a time during which he would begin to actively work with—and for—the angels. To do that, he would have to confront and release—with the angels' help—deeply buried trauma, such as his abandonment at the age of two by his father, George. He was consciously unaware of the emotional insecurity he'd felt as a small child at his father's disappearance.

His mother, Diana, came from old-school thinking, and—on the rare occasion the subject of George's leaving came up—she would resolutely insist that a child of two doesn't have any feelings and certainly has no idea of what's going on.

At some point in the mid-1980s, Diana made this absurd Victorian claim in front of Jenny, one my ward's girlfriends, who was a mature woman with three children of her own. Jenny reacted with derision: "*Of course* a two-year old child has feelings! They have feelings *in utero,* for God's sake!"

Whether or not Diana fully accepted it—and she obviously had her emotional investment for *not* accepting it—Jenny's reaction was so sharp and knowing that suddenly the reality of his father's abandonment hit Mein Host like a train.

By this time, he had been shown by the angels a system they had termed the GRACE process: Grounding, Releasing, Alignment, Contact, Enjoyment (or, as my ward preferred to say, *Experiment*). With some serious inner work, he was able to examine and accept the abandonment, then release the fear-impacted thoughtform. There was much else he needed to face and release—and he would be tested to the limit—but by the end of the decade he was largely free of the fears and the trauma of his childhood.

Thus the situation existed one damp afternoon in the late fall of 1989. Light was fading as Mein Host was walking down Central Park West to the subway. It had been raining earlier in the afternoon, and the cars' dipped headlights flashed in the puddles on the sidewalk. A few of the office workers emerging out of the subway station had turned north on the sidewalk, so there were more people around on the streets than during his encounter with the running man ten years earlier on the very same block.

Mein Host had crossed 89th Street and was halfway down the block when half a dozen young guys started running helter-skelter up the sidewalk in his direction. There were enough people on the sidewalk so that although my ward could hear the commotion ahead of him and the running feet, he was not able to see clearly what was happening.

About ten feet in front of him was an elderly woman also making her way slowly toward the subway and carrying her purse hooked onto her left arm. Mein Host said later that he'd noticed the old lady *because* she was moving so slowly, and he was going to have make it past her.

There was a sudden explosion of violent action as one of the boys barged heavily into the old lady, sending her stumbling. Another grabbed at her handbag, pulling it away from her in the scuffle.

As my ward said later, everything happened extremely fast.

In the moment of confusion the purse slipped out of the second kid's hand and skidded across the wet sidewalk, stopping about four feet away from his grasping hand, and about seven feet in front of where my ward had now fallen into an aggressive half-crouch.

The mugger started to launch himself at the purse, but as he did his eyes locked with my ward's. The other kids were jumping around and screaming at the lad to grab the bag and run. He was reaching out as far as he could with his right hand—scrabbling blindly for the purse—but he couldn't break my ward's stare.

This time Mein Host didn't freeze up.

As he commented later, somewhat dramatically: "I felt I was staring into the guy's soul! He was terrified; I could see that. So, holding his gaze I threw my arms out at him and let go with this god-awful roar that rode into him with the energy I was throwing at him. Now it was *his* turn to freeze!"

Then, forgetting about the handbag, the mugger and his friends were up and racing away, leaving my ward to pick up the purse and return it to the grateful lady.

It wasn't until he had reached the subway station a few minutes later, he says, that it came to him that the two events—though separated by ten years—had happened on the same block and contained so many of the same dynamics: the running footsteps, the shock, the speed of it, the inherent threat; yet this time his reaction was entirely different.

"It was absolutely fluid," he told Alma later, "like a well-oiled machine. There was no break between thought and action. Thought *was* action. I was kinda bent forward with arms out, letting fly with all this energy, and the shout just poured out of me. Geez! I musta looked a sight! It was really, really loud. Everyone on the street jumped halfway out of their skin!"

"Lucky little old lady!" Alma was grinning at the thought.

"It all happened so naturally, so easily, it was like a theater piece," he said. "Like we all knew exactly what to do. And the little old lady? She just smiled up at me. Seriously! She briefly thanked me and tottered off like it was simply one more New York moment!"

It might have been a New York moment for the elderly citizen—though hopefully she hadn't had too many such moments. As it turned out, however, in the twenty-three years my ward lived in Manhattan—and in all the strange encounters and events to occur during that time—nothing quite like this confrontation ever happened again.

Fortunately for Mein Host, by 1989 he had no doubt about the existence of angels and was aware that the obvious synchronicity linking these two events was an ingenious piece of angelic maneuvering. Although he already had a number of such confirmations of angelic involvement, this one sequence of events—and the meaning they carried—appeared to hold a particular significance for him. I believe it was the first time I heard him use the phrase "Life itself is the teacher."

A modest enough recognition, perhaps, under normal circumstances. But during my ward's thirteen years in the community, he, like the others, had been persuaded that important insights and revelations issued forth only from Mary Ann or Robert. Although my ward had exited the Foundation Faith more than eleven years earlier, some echoes of that spiritual dependency had continued to reverberate, below his conscious awareness.

It took these two events and what they signified for him to finally shuck off the last vestiges of Mary Ann's hold on him and to accept that life itself is indeed the teacher.

But it won't be the end of his history with that enigmatic woman who had such a profound influence on him for all those thirteen years.

* * *

Ah! Zandana! Almost a second home to me now.

Zandana has been my restoration, my rejuvenation, and my place of peace, as it has also been a place where I overstepped my position and inadvertently let slip an idea that was then taken up with some enthusiasm by the Planetary Princes.

Fortunately for me, the project, code-named "Love not War"—which I've previously written about in greater detail—turned out to have been remarkably successful. I was more than happy for the princes to take credit for the idea, while I was able to slip away unnoticed.

On my recent trips, the princes and the few most senior members of their staff had been polite enough not to bring it up, but I could see from their eyes that they were masking a more complex range of emotions.

And then there I was, a mere watcher, called into the august presence of Prince Janda-chi and hearing those terrible truths about Caligastia, now being blamed by the other Planetary Princes for dragging down the entire revolution with him.

I moved out from the STC to the promontory overlooking the bay and found the tree I so enjoyed sitting beneath with the city of Zandan wrapped around the far side of the bay. I made sure I was alone and then downstepped my vibrations from the fifth dimension to the lower astral realm of Zandana's third-density reality.

Making myself comfortable with my back against the great tree—its violet-colored leaves strewn around the ground in tones from the lightest lavender all the way through to the deepest blue/violet of the dead leaves—I relaxed for the first time in millennia. At least that's what it felt like. I had no idea how filled with tension I'd become in my long stint on Earth until I was able to relax in the healing clarity of Zandana's astral realm.

Unlike Earth—whose astral realms were as often as not impenetrably thick with the lost and troubled souls of the deceased and filled with the violence, fear, and lust of those asleep and dreaming—Zandana's astral regions encircled the planet, holding it in a more pellucid and loving embrace.

I don't want to exaggerate the condition of either world's astral realms as they can change under certain conditions for better or worse. Zandana's astral realms generally tended to be so much clearer than Earth's because there was far less violence and aggression among the population, even on the less advanced continents. One of the princes, I don't now recall which, had informed me that in the city of Zandan, across the bay from where I was sitting, violent crime—and most other crimes, too—had been left behind and were now almost entirely unknown.

When someone died on this world and passed over to the other side, they were very quickly transferred to the mortal ascension program. There were no lost souls frozen in the lower astral regions, and even the dreamers of Zandana rarely clouded the astral lucidity.

It was therefore a little troubling to remember Eleena's last words to me. A warning, perhaps. The state of affairs on Zandana wasn't quite what it seemed. Wasn't that it? What was it that she was preparing me for?

I'd found myself becoming increasingly liable to slip into a fear-for-self mode, which, like all celestials, I have been by nature largely unaccustomed to. Knowing ourselves to be deathless, we have no reason to fear for ourselves. Even the rebellion changed this little. The MA can sometimes sound a little overly gleeful with its threats of "personality extinction," but the truth of it is that personality extinction is in no beings' interest. It would reflect extremely badly on the Local Universe ethos, because it suggests that the spiritual and social methodology available to beings in that Local Universe was wanting.

If a being like Lucifer—who the MA believed to have transgressed their most fundamental laws—cannot find a path to personal redemption, then it showed the Local Universe in a very poor light. When the tone of the Local Universe is one of mercy and forgiveness—as is the case in this Local Universe—then a personality who is unable to forgive itself surely requires loving compassion and a sufficient time for self-examination, not the horror of personality extinction.

I am left with the distinct feeling that while the threat of personality extinction may not be entirely real, it does—perhaps in the MA's terms and paraphrased by one of your recently deceased writers—"concentrate the mind quite marvelously."

It was thoughts like this that were running through my mind as I sat feeling the grounding strength of the great tree pouring into me. I absorbed the tree's blessing as the tree's deva, in turn, basked in my delight.

Any thought of Eleena's warning—was it a warning?—that Zandana might be presenting me with a false face was almost completely dissolved when, as can happen to watchers, I found myself transported spontaneously to another region of the astral. This area appeared to be separated from the main astral realm by a river of subtle energy that tingled slightly as I moved through it. Inside this enclosure I was able to observe a rather more familiar sight. Here were the shades of those who had passed on from some of the less developed continents on the planet and who were evidently not yet ready for full ascension. There was nothing of the attempts at violence that were so common—and fail so pathetically—in Earth's lower astral. Here the souls were bent over, each in their personal misery, as if no one else existed. I could see spirits moving between the mournful souls and reaching out to them in silent encouragement, but the disconsolate souls appeared almost completely oblivious to their loving ministrations.

Each one in a world of its own.

It was then that I saw a sister watcher moving steadily toward me through the despondent, solitary souls. It was a curious sight. Like myself, the Zandanan watcher—whom I'd not previously encountered— was maintaining a slightly higher frequency that rendered her imperceptible to the somnolent solitary souls. Well, almost imperceptible.

Nothing strange there, you might think, angels do it all the time. Yet we seldom see ourselves as others see us.

I confess that my mood changed there and then, and I burst out laughing.

The watcher was approaching me directly and passing through the bodies of these morose and downcast souls as if they didn't exist. What struck me as so humorous was—while the watcher may have seemed unaware of passing through the astral bodies of those unhappy souls— each individual soul came briefly alive as she moved through them. It was as though I was looking at a line of puppets, each in turn coming momentarily animated with their bodies unfolding—their arms and legs wobbling feebly, before collapsing in on themselves again—when the watcher moved on to the next.

Can you see it in your mind, dear reader? This line of motionless puppets starting in the distance where the watcher must have first observed me. Each downcast astral body suddenly and unaccountably— from their point of view anyway—bobbing up and shaking its limbs before deflating once again, while the next in line bobbed up and jiggled around, and the next, and the next, in a rippling wave of bobbing and wobbling as the watcher drew closer.

"Enjoying the show, eh?" Her tone was deep and vibrant and filled with quiet laughter. She knew exactly what she was doing. I was going to like this one!

We embraced as sisters and moved together back to where my body lay, its back still against the tree. I've no doubt I must have looked every bit as humorous when I slipped back into my vehicle and animated it, because my new friend was shaking with laughter when I came back to full awareness.

Yes, indeed, this watcher was going to be a much-needed friend.

I'm going to call my new friend Clarise, as that is what her name sounded like—although she told me she'd shortened it from a longer name that she would find most irritating if I was to try to repeat it. It was little thoughtfulnesses like this that so endeared me to Clarise—she had nothing of Astar's brusque temperament and seemed to be as interested in me as I was in her.

Two watchers from two very different worlds—each of us deeply affected by the missions and the Planetary Princes to whom we were assigned to serve—and yet whatever it was that linked us ran deeper than any disagreement we might have.

That was my feeling—and I believed it was Clarise's, too—as we sat side by side with the water of the bay stretching out beneath us, gleaming in the shadowless glow of Zandana's two suns.

"We're at the apogee," Clarise murmured reverentially in my mind. "The stars are at their most distant, and you can see how the rays of the two suns coming from the two directions has that curious effect on the landscape . . ."

"Kind of flattens everything out, Clarise. Look, the bay . . . it's standing upright . . . it's like a great green snake!"

"Very fanciful, I'm sure," Clarise's tone was dry. "The natives call it the 'Time of the Wise Twins.' It won't last for long."

I must have looked puzzled. Won't last for long?

"It's the time when the two suns appear to be the same size in the sky, yet you know one of them is larger, but more distant than the smaller one. It's a particular point in the orbital cycle of Zandana . . . How long will you be staying?"

That took me aback. Staying? How long?

Of course I didn't know how long I'd be here! I never knew until it felt like the moment to leave. That's how it was for me. What a strange question!

"Not so strange," Clarise was laughing, and I realized how disorganized I must have sounded. The watchers must run a tighter ship on Zandana.

"If you'll be here for a while," she said, "you'll have a chance to witness a phenomenon I guarantee you won't have seen before. We're not quite there yet, but, as you noticed, you can already see it beginning to happen in the way the bay seems to flatten out."

She was looking up, her head swinging from side to side comparing the two suns. "But soon—very soon—Zandana will swing briefly into a position where the photons streaming from each sun intersect at a ninety-degree angle. Do you know what happens then?"

I could visualize it, but no . . . I'd no idea what happened then.

Clarise was grinning again. She clearly enjoyed surprising me. And I, in turn, thoroughly appreciated her unbearable lightness of being and the humor behind her words.

"Well," she giggled, "I won't spoil it for you by trying to describe the effect. If you stay around, you'll know it when it happens!"

We were quiet for a while, each in our own thoughts and respecting the other's privacy.

It felt very good to be here with Clarise; she was warm and familiar. She was a reminder to me of who I wasn't—I felt like such a "country cousin" by comparison. But, it felt wonderful; I never felt judged by her. What is more, she seemed as intrigued by the developments on Earth as I was in the events happening on her world.

When I heard her again, I realized she had caught the tail end of my thought. "As you think of Zandana"—her tone was generous—"as being in many ways the opposite of your home world, so, too, do I find Earth of great interest for its very differences."

"So, Clarise, have you traveled to Earth?"

"In my time, yes; not recently though . . . not for ages."

Did I see her shudder when she thought about her last visit?

As we were telepathically linked, I caught a brief glimpse of Clarise sinking deeper and deeper into the dense and chaotic emotional turbulence of Earth's lower astral, drawn deeper yet by her fascination with the wanton violence—human against human, man against woman, old against young, tribe against tribe—with which she was so unfamiliar on Zandana. I saw that she only managed to drag herself out at the last moment and had never wanted to return.

"Which is why you interest me so," she said, to my surprise. "I see you are made of sterner stuff. After your Prince Caligastia drove the nations into that atomic war, I couldn't face it."

"But that was more than seventy thousand Earth-years in the past, Clarise. You mean you haven't been back since then?"

"I saw the direction Prince Caligastia was taking the world with his policies of divide and conquer and his complete indifference to those in his charge . . . and that ugly overweening pride of his . . ."

The Prince wasn't really so bad when you got to know him. . . . Holy Mother! Did I just think that? What a stupid knee-jerk reaction— I owed no special fealty to Prince Caligastia.

"I envy you," she broke into my self-concern. "Yes, I envy your toughness. Can I say that? You have had to observe the very worst I could imagine."

"I ran away at least twice, Clarise. Believe me! I couldn't take that terrible atomic slaughter either. I was here on Zandana when that happened; I only saw the aftermath. That was bad enough! More recently, though"—I heard the pride slipping into my tone—"I've been more courageous; I was able to remain present on Earth for the two most recent Atlantean catastrophes."

I paused to allow Clarise to view as much as she could absorb of my stored memories of those terrible disasters.

Now it was my turn to smile, perhaps with a tad too much condescension as her kind and exquisite face transformed, flickering with the harsh and unfamiliar emotions passing through her. When she opened her eyes again I continued. "You are quite right Clarise; it *has* toughened me up to serve the Prince's mission on Earth. But, it takes the contrast of coming here to Zandana to realize it."

I felt her gratitude at my not belittling her for her emotional frailty. I knew what it had taken to bring me to a place where I was able to tolerate the appalling conditions Prince Caligastia and his minions were forcing upon the mortals under their control.

What I didn't know then, but of course became so much clearer in retrospect, was just how much worse it was going to get on Earth over the next six thousand years and just how vital whatever toughening up I'd already received would come to be.

How little did I know!

7

The Setting of a Stage

Radical Discontinuity, the Wise Twins, Cleaning the Calder, the Rainbow Bridge, Lucifer's Drive for Perfection, Le Corbusier the Rebel

It was hard to discern, even for a watcher, exactly when the trouble started at the heart of the Foundation Faith. It might have begun quite innocently, or it just as likely could have been one of Mary Ann's whims. Whenever life was going too smoothly in the community, she seemed to need to stir everything up again.

Unfortunately I wasn't privy to the discussions between Mary Ann and the Four up at Mount Chi, as I was spending all my time with my ward in the New York Chapter while he was attempting to balance his many responsibilities.

Hilda Brown was proving to be a boon and had taken over much of the event planning that had consumed so much of Mein Host's time. She was clearly blossoming under his wing—new haircut, new clothes, new woman—so, as time passed, it became more obvious that her basic attachment was to Mein Host and not to the Foundation Faith's obscure religious cosmology. She had dutifully attended the various religious celebrations for a while, but as she told my ward, "It all seemed harmless enough, but the religious stuff never really clicked with me."

The money was continuing to pour in. A two-day conference titled *Alternate Methods of Treating Cancer* that Mein Host organized with Hilda's invaluable help—as well as the credibility she brought to the operation—packed the house and brought in yet more money. It also gave a number of courageous independent cancer researchers—some of whom had been cruelly persecuted by the American Medical Association—the rare chance to mix with other freethinking scientists and researchers.

Father Dominic's radio shows were building an audience and had become an effective tool for drawing people into the chapter. Dominic's interests, like my ward's, tended to be more wide-ranging and Catholic than the singular focus the Foundation Faith expected of him. As a scientist himself—he had an advanced degree in chemical engineering—Father Dominic frequently invited fellow scientists to his shows, and these people had very different beliefs and opinions from those espoused by the Foundation Faith.

This created a certain tension with those my ward has called the "purist faction." This group wanted to use the radio program—as well as the magazine—to function purely as an outreach and propaganda tool for spreading the community's message—whatever that was. No one really knew for sure anymore.

Since Mary Ann had taken over the reins after getting rid of Robert and Verona, she had started shaping the religion more to her taste. She'd dropped Lucifer and Satan from the community's roster of gods. Having sidelined Christ into a subordinate position, she was left with Jehovah—with whom she identified and, I've no doubt, believed would be an easier sell than Satan or Lucifer.

I thought at the time that Mary Ann's casual exclusion of Lucifer and Satan from the community's self-proclaimed "Game of the Gods" would have some serious repercussions among the rank and file—and I was right. The problems just didn't manifest in the way I thought they would. After all, to radically change a belief system that was carefully built up and experienced by the community over an intense ten-year period appeared to portray no understanding or respect for whatever religious authenticity they may have once been able to claim.

I don't believe this radical discontinuity in their belief system had an immediate and obvious impact, yet there's no doubt in my mind that it gradually ate away at the community's sense of its own integrity. And, of course, their interpretation of Jehovah had very little to do with the Jehovah of the Old Testament—with the singular exception, perhaps, of the old tyrant's autocratic and bullying behavior. Mary Ann had no problem with emulating that!

It was clear to me that not everybody in the group felt entirely comfortable with having to promote Jehovah, and they started to focus less on religion and more on the various ways of bringing in money. And again, the money was certainly coming in. They were paying their bills, and the usual healthy percentage was still going up the line to the central fund, which was—now that Robert was out of the way—solely for Mary Ann's personal use. Aside from that—and the absurdly high forty-thousand-dollar-a-month mortgage for the New York Chapter—there was now the monthly rental of yet another, even smarter, and more expensive New York townhouse for the senior Luminaries.

The owners of 242 East 49th Street, Ruth Gordon and Garson Kanin, had returned from working in Hollywood and reclaimed their house after their two-year contract was over.

I overheard Mein Host joking with Juliette about whether the owners would ever spot the extra barn added to the original Grandma Moses rural snow scene, which was hanging over the mantelpiece in the living room. Adding a barn to the painting had been a running joke among those living in the house. My ward started the rumor, and because the old lady had painted her barns in such a crude and primitive fashion, it was almost impossible to tell what was original and what might have been painted in later.

The barn soon became an apocryphal story so that by the time they were moving out of the house no one was quite sure whether an extra barn had ever really been included on Grandma Moses's erstwhile masterpiece.

My ward will be relieved to know now that nothing had ever been added to the painting.

Although the 49th Street house had served their purposes for the time, it was uncomfortably "chintzy," to use my ward's expression. He told the others that, in his opinion, he didn't feel it right to invite people back there if they wanted to impress them. In fact, it gave exactly the wrong impression—it was just too finicky and kitschy and old-fashioned. Mary Ann had never much liked the place either and, with the rental agreement on the 49th Street house expired, she had insisted that the Luminaries find a more appropriate house.

I saw Mary Ann's insistence for her inner circle to live in fine circumstances as one of the more elusive—and corrupting—aspects of the authoritarian personality. While none of the Luminaries received any personal money—they'd all taken their vows of poverty—I saw it as Mary Ann's way of doing what every tyrant does: using the natural greed of their intimate circle to create a protective and self-reflective shield around themselves.

This strategy is probably more familiar nowadays as news spanning the downfall of various dictators and their coteries, to popular Middle Eastern uprisings, commands the nightly television newscast. They are really just reiterations of Prince Caligastia's pattern rippling down through the millennia.

The new house they rented at 130 East 64th Street—only a few blocks around the corner from the First Avenue chapter—made a point of shouting its self-importance to the street.

The house had been designed and renovated after the war by the eminent, but rather traditionally minded, architect Edward Durell Stone as his Manhattan office. Stone had a monumental style, as can be seen in the heavy-handed, symmetrical facades of the U.S. Embassy in New Delhi and the original marble-fronted Huntington Hartford

Gallery of Modern Art that once dominated Manhattan's Columbus Circle. The man's approach to design was precisely the kind of "architectural egotism" that my ward so disliked.

What might have been valid in the tropical Indian sun, a brise-soleil—an elaborate concrete grill covering the facade of the embassy— becomes a ridiculous affectation in a New York street. In fact, a quick search through images of the Edward Durell Stone buildings that my ward insists on doing for this narrative suggests that the architect could have had a bit of a fetish for brise-soleils. In a surprising number of his buildings, his intention seems to be to keep out the sunlight—even for buildings that didn't need the protective grill.

I couldn't help being amused at the metaphor presented by the brise-soleil that covered the front of the 64th Street house. It was, quite literally, a facade. An artifice. Behind it lay the curtained wall of windows, which was the actual front of the building.

The house stuck out from its neighbors like the proverbial sore thumb, making absolutely no compromise with the rest of the brownstones on the street. Quite the opposite: the house was a visual insult; an immodest taunting of the quieter and less conspicuous buildings around it.

The brise-soleil facade was constructed of uniform-size concrete blocks, painted white and supported on either side like a lattice between the two party walls. This thrust the building a little farther out into the street than its more modest neighbor—as if the house was puffing out its chest in pride. If I was to add that by 1975 this brise-soleil was so long uncared for—with the concrete blocks starting to crumble at their weakest points—then it only serves to bring more local color to my metaphor.

The word *facade,* of course, has an intriguing double meaning: "the front of a building" and—in the figurative sense—"an outward appearance concealing a less appealing reality."

So what was the reality that Edward Durell Stone's brise-soleil was concealing? A blandly minimal interior, all white walls and marble-tile floors, hardwood fixtures, stainless-steel surfaces, and—upstairs—acres of expensive carpet.

Hanging from the double-height living room ceiling was a large mobile by Alexander Calder, its many painted metal plates cunningly balanced to sway at the slightest breeze.

The Calder mobile was the only article remaining in the enormous space—the double-height room stretched the entire depth of the plot—and although it looked magnificent in the setting, there was also a sad quality to it.

The owners had left the Calder behind.

It was either too large, too ungainly, or simply too complicated to dismantle with the risk of never being able to put it back together in its original form. Perhaps the mobile was never much liked and was accepted only because the artist was a friend of the owner, because the sculpture did have something of the abandoned orphan about it.

It remained this way until Brother Joshua, who was more enthusiastic about cleaning dirty surfaces than he was familiar with modern art, took it apart one day to give it a good scrubbing. The mobile was a large affair with a span of about ten feet and some fifteen or twenty metal plates hanging from ¼"-horizontal metal rods—all of which pivoted around the single main hanging bar.

So keen was Joshua to clean the Calder that he didn't photograph it or make any notes prior to dismantling the mobile. So of course he had no idea of how to put it back together.

It is perhaps a curious commentary on the artistic integrity of Mr. Calder's sculpture that when it was finally put together—though shinier and perhaps somewhat droopier—Joshua's new arrangement seemed to make no difference at all.

To give Durell Stone his due, he had designed the place as his office and not as a domestic home. He may not have taken into account just how much of the interior would be revealed through the wall of windows when the house was lit at night from within and barely concealed by the suddenly transparent brise-soleil.

Does my metaphor still hold, I wonder? Am I throwing any light on what went on behind the self-important and decaying facade of the Foundation Faith? Is it really any surprise the community would be drawn to this house, all crumbling pomposity on the outside and slick, shiny surfaces on the inside?

* * *

I wasn't aware of the passage of time on Zandana while Clarise and I rested on the soft, green grass, shaded by the massive old trees growing on the promontory overlooking the bay. It must have been far longer than either of us imagined, because we were drawn out of our reveries by a gradual and very subtle change in the atmosphere. But before I go into what happened that day on Zandana as the atmosphere built up in intensity, I just want to note how both Clarise and I, as watchers, can so easily slip back into the timelessness of the fourth dimension.

I have written previously of a watcher's discomfort—as would hold true for any celestial being—when we have to lower our vibrations to interpenetrate the astral realms of a third-density world. The lower astral regions of Earth are by far the most ugly and challenging—especially when compared to Zandana—and yet, for all the clarity, both of us needed to use a certain amount of energy simply to maintain our presence in Zandana's lower astral realms.

It was during the steady and gradual depletion of this psychic energy—which was starting to tire us both, dragging us back to the comfort and familiarity of the fourth dimension—when Clarise suddenly brought me up with a start.

"It's beginning to happen," she said in my mind, "sooner than I'd expected. Can you feel it?"

"The exhaustion, you mean?" I asked, misunderstanding her.

"The suns . . . the two suns, or the Wise Twins, are moving into the position I told you about when their rays intersect at a ninety-degree angle."

"It's going on now? Is that what you mean, Clarise? Right now?" I could hear the anxiety in my tone.

"Be silent and observe. You will not have had this opportunity before, and I guarantee it will interest you."

I was silent and observant, although little was happening that I could see apart from the intensifying psychic pressure, until I heard her again.

"Come with me," she said, and moments later we were standing together on a gentle grassy slope in the foothills above and behind the glorious city of Zandan, which lay beneath us, stretching all the way to the coastline.

"Be patient," I heard her murmur, as she gestured for us to settle down. "Soon you will understand."

Something was happening to the light, to the way it was starting to reflect on the distant waters of the bay; and in the manner the shadows were changing on the buildings in the city below us. Yet that still wasn't what grabbed my attention.

How can I describe this without it sounding impossibly weird? Or having you dismiss what I was observing as a hallucination—as I might have myself if I hadn't been fortunate enough to have Clarise alongside me.

Oh yes! It was happening alright.

Right in front of us.

My first thought was "a crack is opening between the worlds!" It's what it looked like—a livid scratch across the landscape that, bit by bit, deepened and then gradually opened and widened as we watched.

The precise position of the Wise Twins in relationship to the position of Zandana seemed to be dictating the manner that the crevasse appeared to be stretching away from us out across the ocean—gradually spreading open and up as if the planet's skin were peeling back. And yet beneath this long opening wound, the planet itself remained completely untouched. I couldn't make out what was happening.

I was frankly horrified at first until I felt the calming influence of Clarise, who had evidently observed this unusual scene occurring before.

"Each time it happens, it changes slightly," her tone was confident. "But this is new . . . I've never seen it quite like this before . . . it's what the Zandanans call the 'Moment of Unity.'"

As she was reassuring me, the light completely changed . . . no, more than that! Reality—what you might call Zandana's consensus reality—folded back to reveal the curving and defined form of a prodigious rainbow set against a dark sky.

But, of course, it couldn't be a *real* rainbow, could it? There was no rain. No clouds. Just a starry sky and this Rainbow Bridge. Is this what occurred when the Wise Twins came together?

"Quiet your mind and watch," Clarise said, her tone soft and almost affectionate.

I'd barely heard her advice when I sensed a gentle breeze flowing over the city. With it I saw the light-bodies of Zandanans—first only a few, then more and more—until a whole stream of light-bodies were spiraling up to and across the Rainbow Bridge in a magnificent procession-like myriad of sparks of light coursing up to a new world.

I was too astonished to make a sound.

The brilliant sparks of light all moving steadily over the Rainbow Bridge was a sight too beautiful for words.

Yet, whatever the effect was, it didn't last very long. The stellar geometry behind the phenomenon must have been extremely precise, because as soon as the light-bodies slowed down to a trickle—and then ceased entirely as all the sparks had safely traversed the bridge—the light seemed to change yet again.

The Rainbow Bridge faded first—before the lips of the chasm folded together. Life for the citizens of Zandana picked up again, and they went about their business completely oblivious to rainbows and bridges—as though nothing strange or untoward had ever occurred.

I knew I'd been privileged to observe a rare and precious event—one that I had never witnessed or even heard rumor of back on Earth.

I wondered whether it was merely a solar-determined phenomenon, dependent and precipitated solely by the exact position of the two Zandana suns or . . .

Clarise interrupted my thoughts: "In time you will observe this on Earth. What you saw, in actuality, were two different events happening simultaneously. Why this was, I cannot tell you, as I myself have only seen the Rainbow Bridge once before.

"Yes, yes," she said to my unasked question. "The time of the Wise Twins, *that* I have seen before, a number of times, as the twins swing on their looping orbits, at once clinging to one another's embrace and flinging themselves away into great sweeping curves until they are once again drawn irresistibly back into each other's orbital embrace."

I thought aloud, "Only to start the dance all over again," to show I'd understood. "But the Rainbow Bridge?"

"The bridge? That I have only seen once before. It was relatively recently, and what's more, it *didn't* occur at the Moment of Unity."

"And that's why you infer that there are two separate events and they're not dependent on one another?"

"That is why I say with confidence that you will witness such a Rainbow Bridge on Earth when the time comes . . . when the mortals are ready."

"But what's actually happening, Clarise?"

"These are the first signs that Zandana herself is preparing to move from third to fourth density . . . the planet is ready, the mortals are ready."

"And the light-bodies? Those bright sparks crossing the bridge?" That's what I still didn't grasp.

"Those are the mortal souls who have been prepared in the planet's dreamtime for the tasks ahead within the fourth-density reality. We think of them as the explorers of the new world who will help fashion the consensus reality to welcome all those who are able to maintain their loving hearts."

I must have been depressed at this thought because Earth seemed so far away from these illustrious events.

Clarise kindly cut me short: "There'll come a time when you will observe such events occurring on Earth. But much has to happen first, and given the manner in which your Prince Caligastia is said to be behaving, it could take an extremely long time!"

I'm not sure what came over me, or where my protest or my confidence came from—or even why I assured Clarise with such certainty that for all Prince Caligastia's many faults, I felt sure we were all going to be surprised at Earth's true destiny.

Yes, that's what I thought aloud.

I don't know where the thought came from. But there was a quality I'd observed in my vision of the Rainbow Bridge that touched me deeply, and it also encouraged me to think of my home planet, Earth, in a new way, too.

It would be many millennia indeed before I would start to understand the truth of what I'd glimpsed.

Clarise turned out to be very open and free with what she knew. When the extraordinary event we'd just witnessed was over and life returned to normal I had a chance to ask her more about what we'd just observed. I told her I thought that Zandana was about six to eight thousand Earth-years in advance of life on my home world. As we discussed what this meant I learned the answers to some of the questions that had been evading me on Earth.

"The MA's programs for advancing intelligent life," Clarise told me, "may have seemed glacially slow, but do you see now how the emotional, spiritual, and technological state of the mortal population needs to be matched with the natural development of the planet itself?"

"So it's like everyone has to grow up at the same time?"

"That's the ideal, yes," she said smiling. "It's what happens on normal worlds. As a normal planet moves naturally from third to fourth density, its mortal population is expected to be sufficiently emotionally and spiritually prepared to move into the fourth density along with their planet."

Now that was news to me!

In a way it was blindingly obvious, but it took being on another world with a remarkably open and astute sister watcher to fully absorb the impact of this. Why didn't I know it, if it was so obvious? Why hadn't Lucifer and Caligastia spoken to us about this natural deadline? Did *they* know about it, I wondered? Would they have rebelled against the MA's accepted and time-tested natural rhythms had they known their attempts to artificially accelerate mortal advancement would have ultimately thrown the planetary population out of synchrony with their planet?

Clarise—who had put more thought into this than I had—believed that the rebel princes either didn't know or had been convinced that it wouldn't make any difference in the long run whether a population was prepared for the dimensional shift.

"And Lucifer?" I'd asked her. "As a System Sovereign, surely he must have known of the dire consequences of throwing a population out of sync with their planet?"

"He must have taken it into account," Clarise's tone took on a conspiratorial note. "I think his original intention was always to secede, to carve himself out his very own piece of territory. He didn't really care that much about the mortals; he knew they'd all make it through eventually. There'd always be some mortals who'd make the transition along with the planet. I suspect that was good enough for him. He was always more interested in territory than in mortals."

I couldn't help snorting derisively: "Lucifer may not care much for mortals, but Caligastia's brutal indifference to mortal welfare is becoming a scandal."

"That's very different," Clarise reminded me. "I can't answer for Prince Caligastia, but Lucifer, I know, was always after perfection. He wanted to achieve a level of perfection far greater than anything the MA could attain."

Now that filled in one of the gaps in my understanding of Lucifer's enigmatic personality. A desire for perfection hadn't been the first characteristic I would have associated with Lucifer. Yet I could see it fitted the lengths he went to . . .

Clarise interrupted my thoughts: "Remember this?"

She conjured up the pictures for me. "Lucifer used to say that if only a few tens of thousands out of a much larger mortal population made the transition along with their planet, then he'd have the opportunity to start with a clean slate on the fourth-density world, along with the best and the brightest of that particular race. I don't think he much cared about the mortals he left behind on the third-density world."

Could this drive for perfection at all costs have been behind Lucifer's stated accusation that the MA had been placing far too much importance on mortal ascension? Too much importance on mortals in general? Mortals were always bound to cause trouble—to mess up his perfection.

Perhaps it wasn't so much that Lucifer was fomenting rebellion so as to gain greater freedoms for mortals and celestials but perhaps that he was always intending to skim off the finest specimens to nurture his perfect worlds. He had no interest in who or what remained within the third-density after the planet had made its successful transition to the fourth.

It was when I had this thought that the strangest sense came over me of almost stumbling on a profound truth about Lucifer . . . something he'd told me in confidence . . . the key to it all . . .

And that was it. A blank. A discontinuity of memory.

I was so close to knowing the truth, but it slipped away from my grasp, leaving me none the wiser. If there was some reality to this odd sense of knowingness—and to a truth that was suddenly snatched away from me before I'd ever been able to absorb it—then I realized it could only have been that Lucifer had dropped an amnesia veil over whatever he'd told me.

However, just having the strange feeling that somewhere deep inside me I knew the key to the whole revolution—and to what was really happening on planets like Earth—encouraged me deeply. I'm not quite sure why having this feeling so buoyed me up, because it should have felt unpleasantly irritating; it could have been as annoying and persistent as an itch on a phantom limb.

Yet, it wasn't like that at all. I felt revitalized.

Then, on top of this renewed sense of confidence, came the subtlest insistence to return to Earth. What I'd witnessed on Zandana had both puzzled and encouraged me. Clarise had given me a lot to think about, and I was hoping I could discuss with Eleena some of what I'd heard from the watcher—if I was blessed enough to be picked up by my friendly TS this time.

I really did feel like I was on the edge of knowing a great truth.

* * *

The implacable drive for perfection that Clarise identified as one of Lucifer's dominant features is a quality shared by many rebel angel incarnates. Yet, perfection is a deceptive word that can mean many things to many people. It can be open-ended in that one person's perfection is not necessarily another's.

"Perfection is impossible," an angel once told my ward in another context. "Perfection is an impossibility in a relative field."

As an aspiration to be free of flaws or defects, or for making things as complete as possible, the goal of perfection is a noble and desirable one. Yet perfection itself is merely an abstract concept, a word, and those who strive for perfection without knowing this can easily turn into monsters.

Language itself is inherently metaphoric. Nothing new in that. However well turned or onomatopoeical they are, the words will never actually *be* what they describe. The map is never the actual territory.

A simple enough truism, you would think. Yet, wait until you become immersed in simulated environments that are so superbly constructed as to be indistinguishable from reality! In those cases, if the artificial reality is properly seamless and affects the participant's all five senses, the simulated reality will be both map and territory! On the *Starship Enterprise*'s Holodeck—not an entirely improbable device—it will only be a person's somatic memory of reality that will be able to discern the difference. Try living in a simulated environment long enough and *it* will become the reality.

Architectural style, too, is a language; didn't someone call architecture "frozen music?" And music is another form of language. Yet music is transient, it passes through; in its evanescence it is instantly forgettable. Not so a building; it stands making its statement, however odious, for as long as people can tolerate the point it's making.

In a long work such as this, additional information and insights will frequently flow in on the spiritual or electronic circuits from kindred spirits. When their insights contribute directly to what we are writing on that particular day, my collaborator insists such synchronicities should not be overlooked.

Jason Barenholtz is one such example. He's a man whom my collaborator has never met—save over the internet—who may or may not be aware of the angelic assistance he brings to his research. But as Jason later wrote, he could have sent the information on the French architect Le Corbusier a week earlier—yet he felt the time wasn't right until the very day he sent it. As I'm currently using architecture as a metaphor—and Jason's contribution throws some light on the lesser-known aspects of one of the world-class architects of the twentieth century—it seems fitting to include a short digression on Le Corbusier.

Jason turned out to be a keen reader of my collaborator's books. He had read what my collaborator had to say about incarnate rebel angels in his 2011 book, *The Return of the Rebel Angels,* and he had written to ask whether my ward reckoned that Le Corbusier might have been one of them. Jason became even more curious when he learned about my ward's mother, Diana, and her brief fling with the French architect whom he had previously studied.

Le Corbusier was never one of my collaborator's most favored architects, but the man's influence on modern architecture was profound and undeniable. As an architectural student my ward had traveled out of his way to visit Le Corbusier's buildings. When he was in India he had admired the architect's magnificent government buildings in Chandigarh, the capital city of the Punjab. He was fortunate to have the chance to see the buildings during the monsoon season, when great curving waterfalls gushed from the brutally oversized concrete spouts. On one visit to the south of France, he'd paid his formal respects to the architect's influential revolutionary apartment block in Marseilles, the Unité d'Habitation, and said he disliked the regimentation imposed on the occupants.

Yet all that fell away when he visited and then fell in love with the Chapelle Notre Dame du Haut, Le Corbusier's masterpiece in Ronchamp, France. I've heard him say that if Le Corbusier had only designed and completed that one single building, the Ronchamp chapel, he would still be hailed as one of the greatest architects of the twentieth century.

Without knowing very much about the man himself, my collaborator answered Jason by saying that yes, he intuitively felt the architect was most likely among a small wave of rebel angels that included the better-known George Gurdjieff, Aleister Crowley, and Jean Cocteau—whom I had indicated came into incarnation toward the close of the nineteenth century.

When he asked me for my input on this, I, too, agreed with his intuition. On hearing this, Jason evidently felt prompted to research Le Corbusier's life in more depth to see if there were any clues the architect left behind hinting that he might have been an incarnate rebel angel.

I should make it clear that most incarnate angels, rebel or otherwise, live relatively unremarkable lives. They are, in a manner of speaking, preconditioned to keep their heads down and avoid attracting unnecessary attention to themselves as they continue their regular mortal lives.

This is the incarnate rebel angel's challenge (one among many): how to rise above their self-imposed limitations without "alarming the locals," as my ward puts it. He reminds me of a concept he picked up in Australia called the "tall poppy syndrome." It is what those Down Under say is the process by which anyone who becomes exceptional—who sticks their head up too high above the others—gets quickly cut down to size. This treatment isn't restricted to Australia, of course—as it applies to all mortals, whether they be incarnate angels or first-timers.

Yet in the reincarnate's case, they are hiding so much from themselves that they require great courage to emerge as who they are. And because most of them are not yet aware of their angelic heritage, it is impossible to predict whether they will awaken in this lifetime or a later one.

However, there will always be exceptions: reincarnates who brave the taunts of the skeptics and refuse to be cut down like an over-tall poppy, or who find an expression of their true self in a manner that doesn't draw destruction on their own heads. As my ward likes to say: "We've all had enough of being burned at the stake!"

If I'm belaboring this issue it is only because there will be progressively more of these awakened individuals expressing their true selves as time passes and as the generations born over the previous thirty years grow into maturity.

Charles-Édouard Jeanneret was born in Switzerland in 1887 and took the name Le Corbusier in the 1920s. Over the course of his life—he died in 1965 at the age of seventy-seven—he became one of the six most important architects of the twentieth century. Many would say *the* most preeminent architect of the modern movement.

Le Corbusier was always extremely controversial in both his opinions and his approach to design. He always appeared to be completely certain of himself; he would have been unlikely to press his cause so effectively without a Machiavellian side to his personality. He was intensely disliked by some for what they felt was his autocratic style and what his critics believed was his careless indifference to the fate of those sacrificed on the altar of his architectural ideology. They've pointed out his apparent willingness to work with the Vichy government in occupied France during the first half of World War II.

Here is a caustic comment about one of Le Corbusier's most

distinguished works, the Unité d'Habitation from, of all people, author Ian Fleming in his book *Thrilling Cities:* "Having taken a quick and shuddering look at Corbusier's flattened human ants' nest in Marseilles some years ago . . . I had already decided that he and I did not see eye to eye in architectural matters." And Fleming goes on to add that the Germans also rejected Le Corbusier's approach to design when they were rebuilding after the war and that they had christened the architect the "Devil with Thick Spectacles."

That's a bit harsh. The Devil? Really? *The Devil?*

Not necessarily an unknown label for an iconoclast, but in Le Corbusier's case it would have had a deeper resonance that might well have amused him. Although he may have had a different reaction to finding—posthumously—a section heading in a 2001 thesis submitted by Deborah White to the School of Architecture in Adelaide, Australia, which reads "Le Corbusier as Lucifer!"

I'm not, of course, suggesting that Le Corbusier was in any way the actual Lucifer, nor do I intend to make a detailed analysis of the architect's work or his influence on his contemporaries, but only to reveal some of the hints that Jason's digging revealed about the man.

In *The Return of the Rebel Angels* my collaborator had written that the Cathars represented an early wave of rebel angels who incarnated in eleventh-, twelfth-, and thirteenth-century France. I won't go into his understanding of this here except to say he is correct in his intuition. Le Corbusier, throughout his life, showed a strong interest and sympathy for the Cathars; even his pseudonym—derived, so he claimed, from an ancient ancestor named Lecorbésier—clearly relates to the Cathar town of Béziers. The chapel at Ronchamp can be thought of as the architect's tribute to the Cathars.

However, there was also the darker side to Le Corbusier's personality, and in it can be found some clues to probable rebel angel characteristics. Following is Jason Barenholtz with an example that turned up in his research.

Next I came across Corbusier's plan for Algiers. On the cover of the book that contains the plan, there is a picture Corbusier drew of the Angel of Death. I think this is how he viewed himself. He was moving in to wipe out the past, to clear out the debris, and to make a new world.

After World War I this might have sounded like a noble intention, yet trying to wipe out the past will inevitably result in some unfortunate consequences. If there is no past to remember, there's no way to avoid repeating it.

While incarnate rebel angels aren't the only mortals who create with the best of intentions—only to find the opposite reaction is the result—they are the most likely to fall afoul of this particular dynamic, whether it's because they tend to overreach in their ambitions to be found worthy, or their talents are unrecognized and dismissed by their peers, or perhaps the ideology they have passionately espoused is later found wanting. Rebel angels, in general, incarnate to learn from their failures . . . and not necessarily from their accomplishments.

I've no doubt that the handful of leaders of the modernist movement—those who threw out all the old rules to reconceive architecture for the technological age—had no idea their coldhearted fantasies would blow back less than fifty years later and that they would find themselves accused of all the impositions of the worst kind of architectural colonialism. Le Corbusier—perhaps more than any other leading architect in the movement—invited the sort of critical observation as the one voiced by Michael W. Mehaffy and Nikos A. Salingaros in a January 9, 2002, article ominously titled "The End of the Modern World" and published in the online journal Planetizen:

The twin towers were the grand expression of Le Corbusier's early twentieth-century modernist vision: rigidly geometrical towers, floating above a superblock, erasing the "clutter" and complexity of the street and replacing it with a breathtakingly "pure" and rational geometry. That was the modernist program in its essence: an art of geometrical fundamentalism, a chilling echo of the terrorists' own religious fundamentalism.

The two authors continue to develop this line of thought drawing not unreasonable conclusions that would appall Le Corbusier were he to look back over the fifty-plus years since he died in 1965 with an openhearted caring for others.

Even before he passed away, trouble was starting to stir in the many apartment blocks thrown up all over the world in crude emulation of their model in Marseilles. By clearing up the debris of the past and taking families out of their houses, no matter how modest or decrepit, and then stuffing them by the hundreds into uniform modular boxes—which were themselves slotted into multistory slabs of concrete—he was merely imposing his own sort of hell on the occupants. It was, after all, Le Corbusier who coined the revealing phrase "A house is a machine for living," and the hell of the technological age was that people had to adapt and fit into their machines.

It was this coldhearted approach that my ward found so unpleasantly off-putting and yet so entirely absent in the chapel at Ronchamp.

Here are Mehaffy and Salingaros from "The End of the Modern World" again, this time taking Le Corbusier's metaphor to its logical and unfortunate conclusion. They write that Mohammed Atta—not a name easily forgotten—gets to play out the darker side of Le Corbusier's modernist fantasies, and that he

hated the West's hegemony in the third world, and he hated the western modernist buildings that he saw wiping out the traditional vitality of its cities. The thesis Atta wrote to get his master's degree at University was on the preservation of the ancient Syrian city of Aleppo, against the onslaught of western modernism.

Mehaffy and Salingaros then get to the heart of the consequences of Le Corbusier's severe metaphor for living.

It may seem odd to call Le Corbusier a fundamentalist, but the term is apt. He was a utopian visionary with the most grandiose aspirations, willing to destroy almost anything in his way to build a new doctrinaire regime. Le Corbusier proposed to bulldoze the streets and buildings of Paris and replace them with soldier-like rows of modern towers.

Parisians didn't let him, thank goodness. But other cities weren't so fortunate. Le Corbusier tried to convince successive French governments, including the collaborationist Vichy regime, to implement his plan of razing Algiers, the capital of Algeria and then a French colony. The plan's eventual realization after the war coincided with the anti-French resentment that precipitated Algerian independence—a movement that continues to fuel terrorism to this day.

If only in the mind of a fevered terrorist, this is *not* a legacy anyone would want to leave, let alone an architect with a consuming intention to bring order to the chaos that he may well have felt subconsciously to be of his own making.

More than one person has associated Le Corbusier with Lucifer and not, as I said, because he was an incarnation of Lucifer, but because there was something—albeit consciously unrecognized—of the Luciferian rebel angel in his imperious and uncompromising determination to get his way.

Le Corbusier was also one of the most metaphysical of architects with a deep and abiding interest in the occult. His choice of pseudonym contains a variety of hidden meanings in addition to the Cathar reference to Béziers. *Corbusier* is a variation of the French word *corbeau,* meaning "raven," which was a symbol of alchemy and to which some have likened the architect's facial profile.

Jason Barenholtz directed me to an article that noted that

the raven—the *avis hermetis*—was closely associated with the original primal blackness, a state of putrefaction, dissolution or death out of which all matter must pass as it tended toward the quintessential white . . . it is the raven that transforms matter into spirit. (Andrew Childs, "The Fearful Mirror of Apollo," *Interstices* 4:1–7)

Jason completed his exegesis with the following article's observations on Le Corbusier's esoteric interests.

There are many excellent studies on Le Corbusier but although these illuminate his life, ideas, and theories, and many aspects of his work, few do real justice to his extraordinary powers of synthesis as a designer; to his attention to the nuances of function (despite lapses too) and how his buildings suggest these; and to the multiple layers of allusion to be found in seemingly abstract works. In part this lack of understanding—and controversies about, say, how much his architecture was shaped by his interest in astrology, alchemy and religious heresies—is because, although he was a prolific author, there was much he chose not to write about. These matters he felt should remain esoteric, intended only to be noticed and understood by initiates and the deserving—those who had cultivated their perceptions. (Peter Buchanan, "The Big Rethink Part 6: Learning from Four Modern Masters," *The Architectural Review*, May 28, 2012)

But even to the majority unaware of such matters, the compelling qualities of his work that so many respond to arise from the many levels at which he engaged architecture and from how much of himself he invested in his explorations (much of it in the privacy of his painting studio) and, equally important, his patient distillation and the depth of his synthesis.

I include these short analyses of different well-known rebel angel incarnates to alert a person to any resonance they might feel when reading about them. From those few I have included so far, it is evident that while rebel angels might incarnate in a variety of manifest forms—with different talents and missions—there is a great deal under the surface that they all share.

I trust my examples are helpful to those who seek their own true identities.

8

Behind the Curtain

Zandana's Inspired Art, a Restoration Center,
the Oracle's Fury, Shared Tenderness, Heart
of the Matter, the Fourth Dimension

I knew by this time to pay closer attention to my unexpected inner impulses, however subtle they may be. This is not as simple as it sounds for a watcher. It had taken me a long time to achieve the equanimity required to discern and cherish my own impulses.

Does that sound strange? An angel not taking notice of her inner promptings? Surely that is what angels do. We obey our inner callings.

And that, of course, is true. But this impulse to cut short my visit to Zandana was a quite different feeling. I knew it came from me. It was mine. But what made it so immediately unrecognizable was that I was having an *emotional* reaction to it, to my *own* impulse; that was why I was so disconcerted at first.

Of course I was quite familiar with the psychic circuits by which I normally took in the guidance I received from the Seraphic Overgovernment, but that had been infrequent enough since the revolution. I think they washed their hands of us rebels.

I knew all too well the experience of being taken over by Prince Caligastia's brutally telekinetic commands. These were the impulses that overwhelmed me to such an extent that I would have no alternative but to obey. These experiences are the reason I make it my business to keep as far as possible out of the Prince's way as I also try to make sure any thought of my presence stays out of his mind. Whenever I was back in Caligastia's domain, falling under the Prince's telekinetic thrall was what I most disliked. I suppose it could be likened to what mortals describe as being "possessed."

Yet for a watcher it is, sadly, much more unpleasant than that.

In a mortal's situation the possession is either total—in which case the possessed person is unaware of what they are doing when possessed—or the possession reflects or amplifies the person's own agenda. The latter ones may have even invited the possession to occur. In that situation, the person will be aware of what is happening to them and may well participate willingly in acting out whatever the possession appears to command.

A watcher, however, has neither of these advantages. A watcher will be aware of Prince Caligastia moving into her, commanding her movements as if she were an animatronic robot or—worse—becoming Caligastia's "hand puppet," as I once heard Astar referring to the Prince's invasive telekinesis.

Am I getting across something of the difficulties we experience when our bodies are taken over by the Prince and used for his purposes? We have no choice but to observe what we're being made to do! And, sometimes, what we had to do under those circumstances was horrifying.

What was still very new to me was finding myself having an emotional reaction to my own impulses; impulses that were generated, as far as I could make out, by how I felt about what I'd seen on Zandana and the information—sparse though it was—Clarise had told me about the Rainbow Bridge.

It was with this ambivalence overshadowing me that I discovered Eleena once again waiting for me in the STC on Zandana. I was no longer particularly surprised to find her there—even though my decision to leave was made by me on the fly. I had long since stopped second-guessing just how interconnected we all are and accepted that Eleena's presence there was beyond my current comprehension.

I had traveled with Eleena numerous times over the millennia and had come to think of her as something of a mentor. You'll recall that it took me some time to befriend her, but over my recent trips we've been greeting one another as old friends. I've come to look forward to hearing all the gossip she picks up on her travels.

When she scanned me this time, Eleena's kind, welcoming smile quickly turned to concern. Taking my arm, she guided me toward a section of the STC that I'd never had cause to visit before. Doors slid silently open and then hissed closed behind us as we moved along a well-lit, curving corridor. We came to a halt in front of a pair of large, ornately sculpted, double doors. Before Eleena could push them open, I stopped her so I could more carefully examine their carved surface.

Needless to say, the elaborate biomorphic forms were superbly crafted—as had been all the art I'd seen on Zandana—which in itself was intriguing. We were in the fifth dimension, after all, which doesn't have a great deal to do with the third density. I was left wondering which was the source—or reflection—of which.

Those doors represented a rather different dynamic from anything I'd seen before. STCs are always located within the fifth dimension, and on most worlds with which I'm familiar there is limited artistic congruity among the levels. I thought it was unusual to find such a subtle aesthetic symmetry reflected between a third-density artistic sensibility and how that aesthetic was being represented here. There were the same interlocking tangles of biomorphic forms I'd seen sculpted into some of the walls of the buildings in the city of Zandan; there were even many of the same elaborate and incomprehensible symbols entwined with some of the simple floral motifs I'd observed printed on fabrics worn by the women of Zandana.

"We emulate the inspired art of the natives," said Eleena as she gently traced one of the spiral forms with her hand. "As this is one of the first things a Zandanan native will notice after she or he passes over, we use the art as a symbol of familiarity and reassurance." And then with a wink, "Although you may find we've made a few improvements!"

Eleena was patient with me when I asked her to wait while I studied those splendid doors and wondered at their idiosyncratic carvings. I stood back so I could take in the design as a whole, and, as I did, the oddest thing happened. It was as though the entire carved bas-relief stretching over both doors . . . well, it seemed to *shiver*. Yes, it actually trembled for a moment. Then the whole elaborate construction fluidly and almost imperceptibly metamorphosed, shifting into another imponderable tableau.

As I gazed bewildered at this new permutation, I felt a delicious warmth starting to spread through my body. This culminated in an unexpected surge of renewed self-confidence, which felt like a starry cape falling over me.

I turned sharply to Eleena—still taken aback by what I had just seen and felt—to see her smiling knowingly down at me.

"You will understand more when we enter," she softly said and pushed the heavy double doors slowly open.

I had no idea of what to expect, and I was still tingling all over from the charge I'd received from the sculpted doors of what I came to learn was called the Restoration Chamber.

At first, all I could see through the slowly opening doors was a fountain in the middle of a lawn with the lavender-colored grass glowing in the bright sunlight. Following Eleena through the doors, I was in a small, cloistered courtyard with the lawn and fountain open to the sky—a surprisingly modest sight to be hidden behind such elaborately ornate doors.

There was a tangible stillness in the air as we turned to the right— along one of the cloistered passages—and passed the fountain burbling joyfully in the golden sunlight. I suppose it was the sound of the water murmuring like a distant crowd that reminded me that, with the exception of Eleena, I hadn't seen another living being since I had entered the

STC; and Eleena had been so uncharacteristically quiet that she might not have been there.

Reaching the far end of the cloisters, we turned to the left and Eleena gestured to the first of maybe a dozen doors set in the masonry wall that enclosed the courtyard. Before we had a chance to enter the room, however, I saw another door—four or five down—beyond where Eleena was waiting for me to catch up with her, and this door was being opened by someone or something inside. I motioned surreptitiously for Eleena to slow down so I could observe who or what would come out of the door.

First came a tall, humanoid light-body, who I assumed was a citizen of Zandana in an out-of-body state. He looked briefly in my direction (I thought, without seeing me). He was followed by a TS whom I'd not met before, but who nodded a friendly greeting to Eleena. We watched them as they made their way slowly around the courtyard. The TS appeared to be quietly encouraging her ward as they left together from the same magnificent doors through which we had so recently entered.

The doors closed behind the pair with a hermetic hiss that I could hear above the burble of the fountain; then Eleena and I turned to enter the Restoration Chamber.

I was disorientated immediately, for there at the other end of the chamber, instead of the fourth wall, was the glorious ocean—the very bay Clarise and I had been admiring only a short time earlier. And yet I knew perfectly well we must be far back from the coast. Moving closer, I could see far away in the misty distance a small flitter-boat returning (I imagined) to the port city of Zandan after a long day's fishing.

Once again I heard the amused voice of Eleena inviting me to sit with her in the shape-adjusting chairs common to most of the STCs I'd visited.

"The simulation's just been upgraded," she purred in my mind. "Convincing isn't it?"

Such simulations are familiar to watchers from the intense training we all receive on Jerusem, so possibly I wasn't as impressed as Eleena might have hoped I would be. I relaxed back into the chair while it arranged itself around me. I didn't feel a reply was required, although the simulation was unusually good. For some reason I found I really didn't want to admit to Eleena that despite my familiarity with Jerusem simulators, I had, in fact, been taken in momentarily by the ocean view.

"There's your answer," Eleena said smoothly, moving right to the point. So far I had no idea what I was doing here, and if I was in a Restoration Chamber, then I wasn't at all sure who or what needed to be restored!

Eleena said, "These chambers are generally used for the more troubled deceased Zandanan souls before we transport them to Jerusem. You saw my colleague with his ward in the cloisters . . ." she let the thought drift.

Of course I picked up her meaning. I knew I was feeling somewhat ambivalent after what I had just experienced with Clarise, but I hadn't realized my concern had risen to the point at which Eleena might be unwilling to transport me.

It's true. I do spend most of my time on my own. Being an observer is a solitary task. I have my various colleagues—both in the Earth realms and in the handful of worlds I have visited—but these encounters have been rare enough. Without having the opportunity to view my reflection in one of those I know and trust, it can be hard to gauge the state of my conflicting emotions.

"You were more shaken up than you knew," Eleena said soothingly.

"I saw the Rainbow Bridge, Eleena. I saw Zandana open up . . . the souls, I saw them ascending . . . I never knew, Eleena. Forgive me, I never knew."

I think it was then that I had a worrying thought about Lucifer. Hadn't he railed against the excessive importance that the MA continued to bestow on mortal ascension? Or, was that just the MA's propaganda? Had Lucifer ever witnessed such a magnificent sight? And if he had, would he have ever been able to proclaim such indifference?

What I had seen when the world cracked open was so mysteriously and deeply fulfilling, so infinitely beautiful and so unexpectedly moving, that it seemed hard to imagine that a System Sovereign could ever be openly dismissive about such an inspiring vision.

Eleena said, "Emergency procedures, that's what I call them. It's what they don't include in the Jerusem lectures, and it's probably why you've never known about it. I've heard of the bridge being used rarely and only on worlds subject to the rebellion."

"I've never witnessed anything like that Rainbow Bridge back on Earth," I said, still not really understanding what was going on.

"There's not been the need. Not on Earth; it's still too backward compared to Zandana. Didn't you tell Clarise you thought there was a six- to eight-thousand year difference? That's a modest estimate in my opinion. Since the arrival of the Magisterial Son, life for all mortals on Zandana has experienced a tremendous burst of advancement."

"I saw it, Eleena. I felt something like that during my previous visit. It seemed that everyone on Zandana had a chance to observe what was firmly lodged in their hearts. I did sense that something significant had occurred; I could feel it. But, as I told you, I was hustled off to see Prince Janda-chi and, I imagine . . ."—I felt sheepish to admit this— "I think because he'd not said a word about the radical change in the planet's psychosphere . . . he never even commented on it; and then he went on to fill my mind with his contempt for Caligastia, so I didn't think much more of it . . ." I ended weakly.

It wasn't a very good excuse, I admit.

I am a watcher, an observer; yet I knew I needed to have more confidence in my observations, and not let them be brushed away so easily by the distractions of a more powerful personality.

"Very good, young watcher," Eleena said with a genuine new warmth in her tone. "But there is more that you should know. It will help relieve the inner conflict that brought you here to the Restoration Chamber."

Eleena paused, and I imagined she was putting her thoughts together before continuing. "There is an important truth that we of the Transport Guild have agreed to impart to the watchers on the rebel-held planets, trusting you will communicate it to others of your kind."

I thought admiringly that from the dawn of time it has always been those who transport us who seem to be the first to discern the hidden patterns of life.

"What you were so fortunate to observe on Zandana—that emergency procedure—has also been seen on other advanced rebel worlds. This has allowed us—those of the guild—to make an educated calculation. We can now state with some certainty that a far greater focus of the MA's attention is being placed on your planet Earth than on any of the other rebel-held worlds. We do not yet know the reasons for this recent intensification of interest but what is occurring is undeniable and completely unprecedented in this Local Universe."

This came as a confirmation of what I'd been feeling, but without the wide-ranging data-collecting ability of the guild—with a membership ranging throughout the Local Universe—I couldn't be sure a pattern was emerging.

"And you've no clues as to why this might be happening?" I asked Eleena, pushing her a little.

"The guild isn't saying—even if they know," Eleena shrugged delicately. "For myself, I think Lanaforge and the Council may be preparing to make a move on Caligastia."

"You really believe the MA's going to intervene?"

I hadn't even considered the possibility. I thought that an intervention like that wasn't permitted.

"Think about it," Eleena said. "Zandana received a Magisterial Son, when . . . about two or two-and-a-half millennia ago, and after that, well, it was as if the whole world took off. Everything blossomed: the arts, the sciences, the spirit, the good nature and morale of the people of Zandana—it was a renaissance to top any renaissance I've ever heard about."

"And you think that's what's going to happen to Earth?" I wanted to hear if Eleena was prepared to commit herself.

"That's why you were blessed to see the Rainbow Bridge. Zandana was preparing herself for her own transformation . . . and it's why you have never observed it occurring on Earth."

"So, you believe Earth is soon to receive a Magisterial mission?" I asked again, but Eleena wasn't budging. I had the sense she might have felt she'd said too much already.

"How are you feeling now?" She leaned forward in concern. "Are you feeling more settled?"

Now that was interesting! I checked out my emotional state and indeed I *was* feeling an unexpected sense of peace. More than that, it was a deep feeling of exhilaration—an excitement tempered with a lucidity I am quite unaccustomed to experiencing. I thought it must have been hearing what Eleena had to say about Earth, about an intervention of some sort. Then again, perhaps it wasn't going to be a Magisterial mission; maybe they are just planning to replace the errant Princes Caligastia and Daligastia.

"The Restoration Chamber played its part, too," she reminded me. "It's why I needed to bring you here. All the chambers have resonating generators. They'll balance your conflicting energies, and then they'll recalibrate you to your optimum state."

I must have looked startled because she quickly assured me with a grin that the euphoria wouldn't last long, just long enough for her to get me back to Earth without sullying herself with my emotional conflicts.

"Ready to travel now?" Eleena rose gracefully to her feet, stretched, and briefly unfurled her heat shield, softly shaking the two wings as a bird might on awakening, before retracting them and guiding me to the door.

I turned for one last look at the chamber. The original flitter-boat had long passed, to be followed now by a score of the small, fast fishing boats, bent for port before darkness fell. I could see the closer and smaller of Zandana's two suns low on the horizon beyond the bay.

Forgetting for a moment that I was staring entranced at a simulated seascape, I wondered with longing whether I'd ever witness such an extravagantly peaceful scene unfold on my sad and suffering home world.

"Come on, come on," Eleena was gently pulling on my arm. "We have some traveling to do, and I have a new piece I'd like you to hear."

Soon, I was enclosed again within my TS's embrace and basking in her glorious sounds as we accelerated through subspace.

Whether it was Eleena's new piece I was hearing in my euphoria, I was, I'm sorry to say, quite unable to tell.

* * *

There is only so much money that can be made by about thirty-five people each month—however hard they work at it. And, of course, it was never quite enough.

Toward the end of 1976, the income of the New York Chapter of the Foundation Faith had flattened out. It seemed there was nothing anyone in the community could come up with to push the finances upward any farther. Over the previous year this struggle had become increasingly frustrating, as the income of the chapters was expected to rise steadily month by month as it once did.

Mary Ann had clearly been impressed with my ward's leadership in pulling the finances of the New York Chapter out of the doldrums and achieving the unprecedentedly high—but never high enough—income that was now appearing to have hit a ceiling. As a result of this, word came down to Mein Host that Mary Ann had charged him with producing a detailed financial analysis of the community, together with his recommendations as to how to free up the flow and move the income up to the next level.

As my ward studied the problem, his desk covered with flow diagrams and a variety of graphs and columns of figures, the answer soon became all too obvious. A rigid hierarchical structure—through which all power devolves from a single source—can work to the benefit of religious/spiritual organizations, especially when they are establishing themselves and need a strong leader. Few, if any, religions have ever been started by committees.

However, when a hierarchical religion such as the Foundation Faith becomes obsessed with making money, all decisions from on high can become counterproductive. People beneath the top can easily become robots; they don't bother to use their own creative imaginations and become dependent on the decisions coming down from above. Middle management—in this case the junior Luminaries and Priests—were not being used as productively or efficiently as they might be. To achieve more optimal results it would be necessary to break down the strict pyramidical structure and redistribute the everyday decision-making to those on the spot, to those immediately responsible for that specific result. To create, in a sense, a series of lesser pyramids, each devoted to a single activity.

He pointed out that this was already starting to occur as a natural process. Already, there were the Radio Ministry, the Healing Ministry, and the Angel Ministry. The other activities, he suggested, could be broken down in the same way and decentralized. This would allow the Luminaries or the Priests heading up the different ministries to have the ultimate responsibility for their domains—to win their own successes and make their own mistakes.

This was the essential thrust of Mein Host's analysis.

In my humble opinion it was an accurate assessment—though not one any professional business consultant would consider particularly original. My ward was obviously proud of his evaluation. It made sense; decentralization was already occurring as a natural response to the pressure for money, so he was sure Mary Ann and the Four would appreciate the many advantages of his proposed recommendations.

I watched him as he tapped out his report. Because it was intended for Mary Ann's eyes only, he had to pick laboriously away at one of his secretary's aging IBM Selectric typewriters to type it out himself. He was neither a trained nor a natural typist (*He still isn't! —TW*), so it took many hours of concentrated, tongue-biting work to complete it—together with an accompanying waste bin piled full of botched and rejected pages.

All of which is to say, he put a considerable amount of time, thought, work, and devotion into compiling his report and was probably somewhat blinded by his enthusiasm as to the reception his analysis might provoke.

Nothing occurred immediately.

My ward heard via the grapevine that his report had been received and was, presumably, being poured over by Mary Ann and the Four.

Ah, yes! The Four. The four Luminaries who lived in the Westchester house with the Oracle; the ones who had tried unsuccessfully, one after another, to head up the New York Chapter prior to my ward taking over. Four people at the top of the pile—directly under their Oracle—who really didn't appreciate being shown up by someone they considered below them in the hierarchy. Four people, each of whom may have liked my ward—and whom he certainly liked as individuals—but when falling so completely under Mary Ann's thrall, the same four people who would speak with her voice.

What Mein Host was completely unaware of was what was actually happening up at Mount Chi. He had no idea of the terrible fury his report sparked when the Oracle read it.

Weeks passed, and still he heard nothing from Mount Chi. He seemed to be quite oblivious to the fact that while his ideas and recommendations may have made perfect business sense, they would be running in total opposition to what Mary Ann might have anticipated finding in his analysis.

Whatever solution to all their financial woes she might have hoped to discover in my ward's report, the last truth Mary Ann ever wanted to hear was that for the next stage to be successful, she would have to give up her absolute hold on power. No, that wasn't what she wanted to hear at all!

Yet, still there was silence from above as life continued much as it always had in the New York Chapter. There were some small changes. For example, the strict rules around alcohol for the IPs had been relaxed somewhat, although only for thoroughly containable situations: on the Oracle's birthday, on Christmas Day, and on Thanksgiving—not a day the English celebrate with any patriotic pride but which was added for the sake of the American members. On those special occasions, the evenings were spent together feasting and drinking.

These were the only times they were permitted alcohol and—predictably enough—many of the IPs, having been denied any sort of normal intake, tended to make the most of the evening. It wasn't particularly pretty.

Back at Balfour Place in London, where it all started, the community would hold weekly "knees-ups," at which they were able to let off steam to screamingly loud rock and roll. They all knew each other so well by that time—and were so uninhibited—that without any alcohol they were able to throw off the chains of civilization and dance with the wildest abandon. Mary Ann and Robert never deigned to come to the Balfour Place knees-ups, so it had been an opportunity for the rest of them to really let their hair down—and they had a great deal of hair to let down.

Now, only eleven years later—still with no Mary Ann present; Robert, of course, long gone; and their being plied this time with drink—the IPs of the New York Chapter would take that one evening to behave badly.

Introducing alcohol into a celibate community for even a single evening, let alone twice (or three times) a year, might be considered rash. Surely, it couldn't fail to stir up unfulfilled—or unrequited—desires and passions among the faithful. And, as I've come to know the way Mary Ann works, I've no doubt this was—at least in part—her intention.

The rule affirming celibacy remained the same, of course, but after a merry feast and with a few stiff drinks lowering their inhibitions, a number of them would pair off and find a quiet corner of the chapter to enjoy the tender intimacies of kisses and cuddles. It was not in my purview to know or report on the behavior of other people, but I very much doubt any of those intimacies extended to exclusively sexual contact. They certainly didn't in my ward's case with his choice of a young woman.

Sister Judith had always been an enigma—as much to herself as to other people. She was in her early thirties and had a beautiful face with well-balanced and delicate features. Her light-brown hair was cut in a pageboy style, which framed her heart-shaped face. The lips of her small mouth would tighten and the lines on her forehead wrinkle whenever she felt self-conscious—which was much of the time.

A librarian by profession, Sister Judith was an extremely serious-minded, well-educated young woman who had—in her terms—the misfortune of being beautiful. She would have been utterly appalled had anyone told her what a beauty she could make of herself.

She had the body of a fashion model—long-legged, thin as a rail, flat-chested, and almost six feet tall—and could well have been an accomplished one were she not so withdrawn and awkward by nature. I heard Mein Host once describe Sister Judith as a "magnetic mix of the Ice Princess and Bambi" as she seemed both unapproachable and adorably coltlike with those long, slim legs. Like many tall girls who are self-effacing and shy about their undeveloped bodies, Judith pulled her shoulders forward and stooped slightly as she must have once spent her days leaning over a counter signing out books in the library where she'd worked.

I'd observed that Mein Host, celibate or not, always appreciated a slightly eccentric type of beauty—as well as enjoying the challenge presented by emotionally unavailable women. I could see he'd always had a soft spot for Judith ever since she joined back in Paris, but they had rarely been in the same chapter together and had never known each other well. His interest in her appeared to be more erotic than sexual—a desire to discover if her frozen heart could be melted, or to put it in his words, "to soften those tight little lips with my kisses."

It was clearly much to his surprise to find, after one of the New York Chapter's special evenings of feasting and drinking, that Sister Judith appeared, while not wildly enthusiastic—given her nature—but at least gently responsive to the kindness of his touch.

Although it was never to be repeated, they were able to cuddle and caress each other that evening without any need to sexualize their contact. They clearly thoroughly enjoyed the sensual experience of each other's long, thin, and remarkably similar bodies.

I believe my ward when he says that single brief physical closeness with the beautiful Sister Judith, as innocent as it was, softened some of his brittle edges at a time when he was in danger of becoming hard-hearted and cut off from his innate gentleness.

Whether their shared tenderness softened up the lovely—and quite possibly virginal—Sister Judith in the same way might be revealed by what my ward subsequently learned after he left the community a year later. The coolly alluring Sister Judith had formed a liaison, so he'd heard, with an equally attractive young woman in the community who had a known preference for lesbian lovers.

In retrospect, my ward believes it is quite possible that Judith might either have previously enjoyed some lesbian experience—or possibly she'd been so hurt by a man (or men) in her life before the community—that she'd turned to the safety of women.

What he couldn't have known until this moment was that Sister Judith was also an incarnate rebel angel of a particular type we haven't yet met. While most of the angel incarnates I've described briefly in this narrative have chosen the arts as a context within which to seek their redemption, Judith was an example of a rebel incarnate who was desperately trying to hide the truth from herself. In her case, this repression was precipitated by a terrible shock she had received in an earlier incarnation of which she was barely conscious. As she had yet to bring to full consciousness the horror of being burned at the stake, she continued to carry the pain of the fire in the rigidity of her body as she portrayed the terror she had lived within her stultified emotional body.

Judith had originally joined the community, for the most part, to avoid the danger of the sexual and emotional entanglements that could bring up the pain of the past and—in lesser part—in the hope of discovering what was causing her such unaccountable psychic pain. Sadly enough for Judith, community life proved to be far more effective at protecting her while putting her to work—she was one of the most accomplished donators—than it had been at helping her resolve her troubling issues.

It appeared that Sister Judith chose to remain in the group after they finally left New York City at the end of the 1970s. So, in the unlikely possibility that she will ever read these words, I, as my ward, would like to believe she will find what I have revealed to be of value—either as a confirmation of what she has since learned about herself, or as a sincere gift of revelation for her to make of as she will.

I echo my ward in assuring Sister Judith, wherever she is, and whatever she's currently calling herself—and whether she is alive or passed over—that the words are written with love and with the fond memories of those tender moments he was able to spend with her thirty-six years ago.

* * *

I thought I would be psychologically prepared for returning to Earth from Zandana. Sadly, I was not. Eleena—without even asking me— had thoughtfully left me off at the North American STC rather than dropping me off in the Middle East (right in the middle of Prince Caligastia's domain). It was kind of her to take my wavering state of mind into account, but this time it made little difference.

Okay. So I knew it wasn't going to be easy. I hadn't been entirely blind to the direction that Caligastia was propelling conditions on the planet. But once again, I simply wasn't prepared for the increased emotional density that was now permeating even more of the astral than I last remembered. It became progressively more painful while I was down-stepping from the fifth-dimensional STC to where I could observe activity better in the third-density astral realms.

One of the less-obvious consequences of an increasingly confused and barbaric way of life for a mortal population is the manner in which people meet their death. Many who die fighting on a battlefield, for example, will frequently continue their fighting in the astral, seemingly unaware that they are physically dead. Others who are chronically addicted to the physical pleasures of the body—or unhealthily obsessed with a particular living person or perhaps entangled in a specifically earthbound ideology—will quite likely spend some time lurking in the lower astral regions after their physical death.

It won't necessarily be a very long time—and it certainly won't be an eternity—because all souls find their way to the Light or are guided there sooner or later. And as far as I have observed, it was most often sooner rather than later.

I believe it was Astar who first noted the exceptional level of compassion shown to mortals who pass over on rebel-held planets. While humans are expected, as all are, to learn from the mistakes they made when living in the flesh, considerable allowance is made for human ignorance. This is also why the inverse of this—a human being who can live an authentic and worthwhile life despite the continuing confusion created by the rebellion, which has rippled down through time to shape human history—has always been so highly thought of by celestials on the mortal's passing over.

As the population of Earth increased following the natural disasters of the seventh millennium, so also had the intertribal violence and other forms of degraded or depraved behavior been on the rise. This, in turn, further seeded the astral realms with emotional confusion.

I could see the spirits moving between the gray astral forms, ministering to the ones who could rise momentarily from their depressions or who could be persuaded to put down their weapons and move toward the Light. Mixed among all this useless activity—whether violent or engulfed in gloom, grandiose or self-pitying, remorseful or berserk—was the mighty multitude of dissolving astral shades of the long-dead, drifting in various stages of disintegration among the melancholia and frenzy of the more recently deceased.

As I sank lower into the murk I could see the occasional flashing form of a sister watcher, yet not one of them showed any desire to slow down and make contact—if they even saw me. The atmosphere was unpleasantly thick and soupy, far worse than I'd remembered. Soon I simply couldn't tolerate it any longer and had to flick back into the fourth dimension to clear my mind. (I'm aware that I may risk sounding self-indulgent with my constant references to my varying states of mind—even my collaborator can get impatient with me—but the state of my mind, after all, is what I'm really trying to understand. It's not only what I have observed that interests me but also the state of the observer.)

Have I previously described the subjective experience of being in the fourth dimension? My collaborator thinks not, and I can feel his interest rising. He is familiar with the fourth dimension as it equates to his fourth chakra and how that relates to his heart—and the "Heart of the Matter," as he likes to call it.

The fourth dimension from a watchers' viewpoint is somewhat more elaborate, although of all the dimensions it is probably the most difficult to describe because of its constant fluidity. Yes, it is indeed the dimension of the heart, but more than that, it is the dimension of *heartful thought*. It contains all that manifests in a third-density world, but in a state of potential.

This is where it gets so difficult to find the appropriate words to describe, not the ineffable this time, but the innate indescribability of a reality that exists purely in a state of potential. Think of it as a dimensional reality that is totally subject to heartful thought—you could say that is what protects the dimension from being sullied by thoughts of dominion and savagery. Those are the thoughts generally held by thinking creatures of the third dimension, inherited from the instinctual behavior of the lower animals, as those instincts are derived from the reflexive motions of the simpler life-forms.

Thus, if an entity, mortal or watcher, possesses the heart to enter the fourth dimension, the reality will immediately reconfigure itself to reflect or fulfill the heart's desire of that entity. And because in a relative field no heart can be entirely pure—as no heart can be totally evil—the fourth dimension can be a most confusing domain for the uninitiated who venture there.

My ward has been guided by his companion angels over the course of his life to become familiar with the many regions of the fourth dimension—both the dark and the light. Here are the afterlife realms of the heavens and hells, the bardo realms of Tibetan Buddhists, the happy hunting ground of the Native Americans. Almost all religions and most established spiritual paths have their own versions and their own words for the fourth dimension, many of which confuse the dimension with the end of the journey. A devout Christian, for example, might pass over and find themselves "sitting on the right side of the Father," without realizing that she has entered into the fourth dimension, and the reality has reconfigured to reflect her heart's desires and expectations. At some point, her celestial guides will gently show the soul that there is far more to go, that there is a great journey awaiting her in which she will rise toward the Godhead.

The fourth dimension can be entered by mortals when alive and conscious, but generally only under exceptional conditions: a mystic entering Nirvana; those moments in sport (so my ward tells me) when everything is operating at optimum; certain shamanic or entheogenic journeys; and NDEs. However, for most people their experiences in the fourth dimension will only occur during dreams. That is where human beings are able to achieve some familiarity with the idiosyncratic nature of the fourth dimension.

My ward has been shown that the heart chakra can be best thought of as a many-petaled flower—the thousand-petaled lotus of the Vedic tradition—and that the petals will open and close separately or together as necessity requires. This is intended to illustrate that while someone's heart chakra can be loosely described as being open or closed, there are a large number of incremental states between the two extremes.

If I describe my own experience on retreating to the fourth dimension that time I had just returned from Zandana, perhaps it will better illustrate my point.

The moment I entered the fourth dimension I focused my mind on my desire for peace and a restful place to collect myself. There was no discernible pause, and I found myself on the bank of a small stream burbling over polished pebbles; willows wept on the opposite bank, and the long grass that tickled my feet was scented sweet in the summer heat. A pair of kingfishers flashed past me to settle on a smooth, black rock somewhat upstream from where I stood. The fluorescent blues and greens of their feathers flared out against the shiny darkness of the rock, and the two birds were now fixated on the water running beneath them and the possibility of a fishy feast.

If I was to say this scene seemed so authentic that I could even see the birds' claws scrabbling for purchase on the smooth surface of the rock, would that get across just how real a self-created reality can appear in the fourth dimension?

Well, of course you can imagine it. You dream yourself there almost every night!

I relaxed with my back against a young willow tree, deeply breathing in the succulent scent of the wildflowers that were blossoming all around my reclining body, listening to the excited chattering of the stream, and reflecting on the curious situation I was in.

I must have lost myself in my thoughts because when I emerged I could see that clouds heavy with rain seemed to have darkened the summer sky. A new, bitterly cold wind had picked up and was swirling through the long, drooping branches of the weeping willows, sending the leafy fronds gyrating in dances with one another. Tiny bright-green leaves were being blown free from the willows and were billowing in spiraling eddies, and I could see that they were turning brown and dying before dropping into the water. The kingfishers had vanished, and the wildflowers that had previously filled my head with their sweet scents were now wilted and dead.

Lightning split the sky, and the rumble of thunder grew closer before I started to realize what was happening to me. It wasn't that I hadn't experienced this phenomenon before but that I forget it after each time. In this I believe I am subject to the same dynamic as human beings who visit the fourth dimension and on returning have only the most fleeting memory of what occurred when they were there.

If I relax my conscious intention on creating the scenario I desired and slip off into my thoughts—which is what must have just occurred—then the fears that I harbor can overcome my conscious desires and start distorting my reality.

It was then I heard a loud, sharp bark followed by the growl of what sounded like a large animal somewhere close behind me. Next I found myself enveloped in a swarm of tiny midges that whirled around me, settling for a moment on my arms and legs and signaling their landings with their sharp little bites.

When a fourth-dimensional reality becomes even more intolerable than the third, it's time to move.

Which is what I did.

The first thing I noticed on returning to Earth's third-density astral realm was how much warmer and more humid the environment seemed to be since I was last here.

I was in the mountains to the east of the region where the STC was located in the great redwood forests that ranged inland from the western coastline of the American continent. I could see how much farther the glaciers had retreated north, leaving their terminal moraines and their long valleys scraped barren, each with its rushing river carrying torrents of glacial meltwater that cut deeper into the ravaged landscape. New-growth trees were already starting to poke their heads above the rubble on the valley's scarred sides.

I turned south, thinking to myself that it had been many millennia since I last traveled down the western coast of this continent and even longer since I had surveyed South America and the land across the Pacific Ocean. It came to me then that I must have been unaware that I was avoiding traveling west across the great ocean as I once did so frequently when observing the peerless Lemurian culture.

This insight surprised me.

Was I so deeply affected by the final disappearance of the last truly shining civilization the world has ever seen that I would shun the whole region? Was this another manifestation of my temerity? Was it an unacknowledged sadness that I had sentimentalized? Or was it possibly some deeply buried sense of guilt for the absence of those glorious islands?

This was a necessary introspection I'd learned I needed to do ever since the revolution started imploding on itself. I was still trying to make sense of all these novel feelings to which I was unaccustomed. Suspicion? Guilt? Shame? I barely recognized the feelings, least of all name them.

I was saved from my navel-gazing by observing what I'd witnessed only once before on this continent—and never this far west.

I have mentioned previously the natives who had migrated their way across the land bridge from Asia, and who were working their way south and east across North America. They had traveled from Asia across the Bering Strait in small familial clans that had expanded and then fractured into various tribes that, in turn, had chosen to maintain their nomadic ways as they spread over their vast new home.

What I was now observing, however, were the natives who had been migrating north from their original Lemurian settlements in South and Central America. They had been moving steadily up into the American Southwest for the previous three thousand to four thousand years to a region centered around the Four Corners, spreading out into the surrounding states. These were the peoples whom even the Anasazi referred to as the "Old Ones."

There were always likely to be conflicts between a tribe or a people who prefer to settle and farm in one place and those tribes that choose to live a nomadic life. The word *Anasazi* is derived from the Navajo word *Anaasází*—which has the double meaning of "Ancient Ones" and "Ancient Enemy"—and portrays both the respect and the enmity felt by a vigorous nomadic tribe for an ancient Pueblo people.

My collaborator, who likes to research these points I bring up, has found that David Roberts—the author of *In Search of the Old Ones: Exploring the Anasazi World of the Southwest*—says that he chooses to use the term *Anasazi* over *Puebloan* (a term often used by younger archaeologists and some Pueblo people) because, as he explains, the latter word "derives from the language of an oppressor who treated the indigenes of the Southwest far more brutally than the Navajo ever did."

This is a clear reference to the hostility that existed between the marauding nomadic bands and the ancient cliff-dwelling people that preceded the Pueblo tribes. This mixture of a respect amounting almost to ancestor worship and the deep fear embedded in the name Anasazi itself is exemplary of how a lesser-developed culture can frame its relationship to a more advanced one.

The Old Ones—the predecessors of the Anasazi—were both more advanced and peace-loving than any of the tribes that roamed the Southwest. Their continuing peaceful existence depended more on their intelligence than on their fighting skills, and it was for this that they were resented and labeled the aggressors *by* the aggressors.

I had an opportunity to observe this dynamic in action when I broke my journey south in a broad canyon bordered to the north by precipitous cliffs and great wind-sculpted rock chimneys a thousand feet high. The floor of the canyon, which will later be named Canyon de Chelly—with its broad, fast-moving river running down the center—was green and fertile, the long grass currently being appreciated by several hundred buffalo (or more accurately, *Bison*).

At the junction of this canyon and an adjacent one, a single rock chimney rose vertically from the canyon floor almost a thousand feet high. This spire would later be called Spider Rock, and it would be known by the Navajo as the abode of Spider Woman. Think me childish, but I couldn't resist finding a perch right on the top of the spire from where I could see the full length and breadth of the main canyon before it disappeared together with the river behind the high rock walls.

As I peered down, the long shadow the spire cast on the canyon floor looked like a massive sundial. I amused myself by standing right on the summit and waving my arms in the air, just to see them moving around at the very end of the long shadow. Of course, no arms appeared below; there was just the gargantuan sundial. It was easy to forget that I cast no shadow.

I soon got bored with this silly game and settled down with my back to the sun. I was idly counting the buffalo spread out on the valley floor beneath me like a casual throw of chocolate sprinkles, when I noticed a slight movement among the trees bordering the river. (*Note: I have tried previously to question Georgia's use of such similes as the buffalo appearing like "chocolate sprinkles," but she assures me that she gets far more fun picking through my own lexicon for her similes and metaphors; and besides, what is sometimes a cliché to me, she says, will often be the first time she has ever used the phrase, so it's no cliché to her. How can I argue with that? —TW*)

As I looked more closely I could see a small band of natives—a hunting party I assumed—perhaps there were twenty of them, maybe more that I couldn't see for the trees. Each of them was moving surreptitiously from shadow to shadow, from tree to tree, ducking and crawling between the flowering bushes. I watched in fascination, thinking they were most probably stalking the buffalo, or perhaps they had spotted some prey in among the trees that I couldn't see.

The mature buffalo, their massive heads bowed and clearly savoring the long, succulent grass, seemed unaware of the hunters creeping past them along the bank of the river. Some of the cows lifted their heads and sniffed the air before returning to nursing last year's calves; others had evidently recently given birth as I could see scores of tiny calves cavorting happily among the sturdy legs of the cows.

There was also a certain amount of mating going on, which—as I remembered Astar once informing me—occurred only in the late summer months before winter set in, and it was time for the creatures to head for the forests. She explained how the buffalo cow's gestation period of about nine-and-a-half months—so close to a human pregnancy and yet in a creature ten times as heavy—allowed the calves to be born in the midsummer months of the following year.

At first I thought it was just a white limestone boulder surrounded by the massive bodies and legs of the grazing beasts. Then, the boulder unaccountably moved. It started scampering. It pranced, it gamboled, and it frolicked. The little white form, a white buffalo calf—the only one in the entire herd, and startlingly white against the dark mass of the reddish-brown coats of the adults—was scampering around like the proud little prince he was.

It seemed to me to be the most tranquil and pastoral of scenes. The buffalo were apparently quite unperturbed by the hunters passing so close by. Even the number of large males guarding the perimeter of the herd seemed more preoccupied with grazing than with keeping, what I considered, a sensibly alert eye open for predators.

This puzzled me, so I asked Astar about it when I next saw her. She said she'd noticed how buffalo invariably seemed to know if a predator was hostile or not. She said she'd once seen a pack of male wolves actually loping through—*through* mind you—a small herd of buffalo, and the enormous creatures remained completely unruffled because they knew instinctively that the wolves weren't hungry.

Astar had called this phenomenon "the interconnected matrix of all biological life." It was the first time I'd heard that phrase used, and it was a concept probably more intuitively familiar to earlier peoples than to many of a more contemporary scientific mind.

I watched as the warriors slipped unnoticed through the trees, leaving the buffalo to themselves.

What were those hunters up to?

9

Simpler Time

The Anasazi, Ancient Enemies, the Five Angels, Jehovian Dogma, Traitor and Betrayers, Canyon de Chelly, a Levitating Shaman

I scanned the canyon more carefully and saw what I had not previously noticed. About a quarter of the way up the cliff face—on the opposite side of the canyon—there was a series of cave openings . . . and yes, some of them even had signs of human habitation. I could see rock walls that had been built across some of the cave entrances and ledges that had been cut into the cliff.

Now I could discern a dozen or so tiny figures moving around close to the base of the cliff. They were bending down and picking a plant—one that I couldn't see from my faraway perch—that they put in baskets carried on their backs. A few men were moving quietly among the bent figures. All of them appeared entirely unaware of the hunting party about half a mile away from them and creeping slowly closer.

All of a sudden I saw the bent figures mysteriously straighten up as one person, each of them now on full alert. This was followed almost instantaneously by a high trilling sound drifting up to me on the afternoon breeze. Then I saw the source of the whistle, a sound so close to the call of an eagle that the hunting party appeared to have taken no notice and maintained their furtive advance. The man stood high on one of the pinnacles overlooking the canyon, barely discernible against the cliffside. He was blowing lightly into what could have been a horn or a shell. I was too far away to see clearly what he was using to make the sound, so natural and innocent. Yet it was clearly a warning.

My view from the top of Spider Rock made it hard to gauge whether either party had actually seen the other for the thicket of trees between them. It came to me as I watched this macabre drama from on high that the hunting party had tried their hand at this before. I could feel the warriors' excitement matched by an angry frustration at their previous failures . . . they wanted the women—yes, that was it: the women. They would have enjoyed killing the men, I've no doubt, but it was those women collecting herbs at the base of the cliff that they really wanted to take.

Then, all my conjecturing ceases to matter anymore. There occurs a sudden explosion of action in which a number of elements unfold with much of the elegance of a long-practiced tradition.

Men appear at the mouths of several of the caves and throw down what I can see are crudely made rope ladders to the women who are now gathering together at the base. Some are looking above them in antici-pation of escaping up the ladders to safety; others are throwing quick glances over their shoulders to where members of the hunting party have now broken from the trees and are running fast toward them. I can feel the women's fear from where I perch.

The few men I'd seen earlier wending their way among the grazing buffalo seem to have magically vanished.

The fastest among the hunters who are racing toward the women are only fifty yards away when the last of the women clambers nimbly up the first few rungs of the ladder. The men above start to haul on the ladder to pull it up out of the warriors reach when a spear hurled by a hunter chances to slice through one of the ropes about ten feet above where the woman still labors upward.

There is a moment of absolute stillness during which the woman's destiny hangs in the balance.

As if in slow motion the ladder above her collapses, so now she hangs on a single piece of rope. The ladder seems to fold in on itself—the wooden rungs flipping down like a series of dominos, the clacking sound echoing up to me as if the ladder itself is clapping its excited approval of the woman, who is hanging beneath the clatter, perilously clinging to the one remaining strand.

A raucous cheer rumbles up from the hunters who have all reached the bottom of the cliff. Some are jumping up, trying to grab the bottom of the ladder—which is some three feet above their grasping fingers. Evidently it is more a display of machismo among the warriors, but it further terrifies the woman. Other spears are being thrown, but I see one of the hunters gesturing for them to stop. I imagine they don't want to risk killing the woman if they might still be able to grab her.

She is still clinging fast to the rope despite being struck regularly in the head by the flapping rungs just above her. The men are very gingerly pulling her upward and, remarkably, the rope appears to be holding. When I was later able to examine the rope I found it to be made of at least half a dozen thin strands of leather that had been carefully braided into a single, tough rope. The wood rungs were pushed through the braided leather rope and were secured in place with a crisscross hatching of thin leather strips. I could see the rope was a great deal stronger than I'd imagined when the drama was unfolding.

Now the woman is slowly nearing the ledge on which the men are perched, hauling her up hand over hand. They're being extremely careful, and even from here I can almost feel those looking on holding their breath while the woman lurches inches upward. Spears are still clattering against the rock face, but now they are striking well below her.

The woman is wisely not struggling, for fear she will dislodge her precarious hold as she allows herself to be slowly scraped up the rock face. I can hear her quiet mewling and the panting breath of the men as they take care to pull as gently and evenly as possible.

The basket the woman had been carrying had long since clattered to the ground to be promptly pounced on by some of the younger hunters who fought among themselves to cram the contents into their mouths.

The woman is finally being helped up over the edge into the arms of the men, and the broken ladder is hauled up after her. A ululating howl of triumph issues from the victors, shriller than the grumbling taunts of the disappointed warriors, who are milling around, not sure what to do next.

So the situation stood, taunts and insults flying back and forth, until one of the warriors—evidently their leader—started making gestures that I interpreted as the formation of a plan.

I watched with renewed amusement. Did I just say *amusement*? Of course, I meant *interest*. I watched with a renewed interest as the warriors settled down directly beneath the cave entrances high above them, breaking into small groups of four or five, sitting and sprawling on the ground. Are they settling down for the long haul? They'll know the cliff dwellers will need to come down at some point. Were they intending to lay siege? Did they really have the patience and self-control to wait them out?

Darkness fell quickly in the depths of the valley. The high canyon walls blotted out the sun yet still left me on my pinnacle, basking in rays that left no shadow behind me. I could no longer see the warriors gathered at the base of the cliff, and the cave dwellers had long since disappeared into the depths of their subterranean dwellings.

Mother Earth rotated to finally block out the last of the rays of the sun, smearing the western sky with pastel colors of every hue and shade.

Silence fell with the gathering gloom. I could just discern the dark lumps of the buffalo, who were either standing very still or had settled down for the night. I couldn't tell which from my vantage point.

Later, on this moonless night—when I was looking deep into the darkness at the bottom of the cliff—it seemed to me the canyon itself was a river of stygian blackness that was cutting its way through the starlit gloaming above.

I was settling in myself for the night when I saw the glow of an ember in the depth of this river of pitch blackness and then a flare as the dried grass caught flame. A guttural singsong muttering drifted up to me from the depths of the canyon, while the fire flickered into such a blaze that I thought briefly they might be trying to smoke the cliff dwellers out of their caves.

But no. As the flames took further hold and erupted into a fire that silhouetted the figures of the warriors dancing around it, I realized it must be some form of ritual. The singing assumed a new and different tone as the dancers found the trance rhythm they were seeking.

This performance continued until daybreak, when the fire was smothered and the warriors retired in small groups to the river to bathe and drink, always making sure one group was left to guard the base of the cliff.

The next two days and nights passed much as the first, the cliff dwellers coming to the cave mouths once or twice a day to peer over the edge at the increasingly angry and frustrated warriors below them. If one of the warriors happened to see heads poking out of the cliffside far above him he would set up a caterwauling howl, and all the others would soon join in. The heads would then quickly jerk back and disappear back into the caves. Yet the terrifying caterwauling continued unabated until exhaustion must have set in. Over and over this happened, three or four times each day.

When the sun was directly overhead on the third day I sensed a change in the atmosphere of the action being played out beneath me. Yes, I was still at the top of Spider Rock, and by this time I realized I'd been sharing the spot with a loyalist midwayer. She wasn't there when I first chose the spot but arrived on the second day. Since she was unaware of my presence in a slightly different frequency domain, I decided to remain silent and continue my observations.

It was then—on the third day and with the sun high in the

sky—that I saw one of the reasons why the cliff dwellers deserved their reputation for cunning intelligence. The warriors had clearly reached a pitch of frustration and exhaustion, and I could see them arguing among themselves. A couple of men were emerging from a cave above the quarreling hunters. They carried an object I couldn't make out, but I could see that it was balanced on two poles. The object was a dark-colored, uneven lump, about the size of a tumbleweed, but the men were obviously handling it with a great deal of care.

I could see the two of them pausing at the lip of the cliff. The lump between them continued to be balanced carefully on the two poles until—in one graceful movement—they upended the poles, sending the dark enigmatic mass falling directly on the heads of the warriors below.

It fell more slowly than I might have imagined had it been a solid mass. As the lump turned in the air it seemed to change its shape, almost as though it were alive.

None of the warriors appeared aware of this falling chunk of trouble until it struck one of them lightly on the side of the head. This was followed in rapid succession by two more of these objects hitting the ground in their midst with dull "thunks." By this time, there wasn't one warrior who had any doubt what was falling out of the sky.

The wasp nests barely hit the ground before the furious insects were in the air covering the bodies of the screaming hunters and stinging them by the thousands. This sent the warriors howling and running— each man surrounded and almost obscured by an aura of angry movement—back down to the river, where they threw themselves into icy water, wildly trying to bat the wasps off their naked bodies.

It was a rather more subdued hunting party who pulled themselves painfully out of the water sometime later, their bodies covered with bites—only to be set on once again by the wasps who hadn't been drowned in the river. Back into the river the warriors plunged, this time to stay there, continually having to duck down into the water as the wasps spotted their bobbing heads and dive-bombed them.

Dusk was falling before the hunters were finally able to drag themselves out of the river and limp painfully back along the river's bank from whence they came.

I very much doubt if the warriors ever returned to seek their revenge—or in the hope of grabbing some of the women—but a vivid account of the Old Ones cunning and savagery circulated among the nomadic tribes, to be told and retold as a warning to the children of the tribe.

In this way—and along with many other remarkable attributes—the cliff-dwelling people from the south, the ancestors of the Anasazi, earned their reputation as "Ancient Enemies."

* * *

It was 1977—and another sweltering midsummer in Manhattan—when Mein Host was faced with Mary Ann and the Four's response to his report on the managerial and financial changes that would be necessary for the Foundation Faith to reach the next stage of development.

It had been some four months since he'd submitted his report, and in those four months neither he nor anyone else in the New York Chapter had heard anything from the Omega. I listened to him talking to Juliette about his frustration a few weeks before the Omega's response finally arrived.

"I can't imagine what's taking so long," he was saying while they were taking a break in J's Place. "I don't even know if they ever got the thing . . . not a word . . . you'd have thought . . ."

"You'd have thought . . . what?" Juliette retorted, as she had obviously heard this sentiment before. "They'd be falling all over themselves to agree with you? You think they'll change the whole structure of the place just on your say-so? Some hope."

"Sure," he said, ignoring Juliette's pessimism, "it'd be nice, but the longer this great silence goes on . . . I dunno, but it's starting to make me a little nervous."

They drank their coffees and smoked their cigarettes, tucked away in the corner of the mezzanine of J's Place.

"Why did you do it?" Juliette asked after a long pause.

"Do what?"

"Write that report."

"Mary Ann instructed me to do it, Juliette." A touch of impatience in his tone.

"No, no, no, I mean why did you pitch it in a way that was sure to challenge them?" It was clear Juliette hadn't voiced this before.

"You think I did that on purpose?" I could see the genuine surprise on my ward's face. "That I just wanted to challenge them? You think that?"

"What I think," Mother Juliette said firmly, "is that you are stirring up a wasp's nest. You just wait and see!"

And wait and see they did.

For another three weeks.

I should interject an observation here because I'm not trying to write a mystery. You, my patient reader, should know what I knew at the time. I hold nothing back.

It will be clear from the above conversation that my ward appeared completely unaware of the possible impact his report might have on an authoritarian personality.

With the rise and fall of so many authoritarian regimes in the recent planetary history, much more is generally known and understood about the chronic incapacity of the authoritarian personality to hand over control in the face of a challenge to its grip on power.

But if Mein Host knew no better when he was penning his report, whatever or whoever was guiding his pen certainly did. I can't be sure of this—as I wasn't there to witness the act—but I have a feeling that my ward's companion angels had a voice in the way he framed his argument.

In retrospect, I am more sure of this because all that occurred subsequently can be traced back to his report. He certainly wasn't consciously aware of what an impact it would have on Mary Ann and the Four as it never occurred to him that they would respond in the way they did. Had he thought to view his report through the eyes of a paranoid personality, he might well have pulled his punches. It's for that reason I feel sure his companion angel Joy played her part in what was to become a pivotal event in Mein Host's life.

The response from the Omega, when it finally arrived, came in the form of an elaborate questionnaire. On the surface the questions appeared to be designed to discover who would like to work in which specific subchapter—just as my ward had recommended—and who wanted to continue with the community's structure much as it was.

I could see that my ward was most encouraged that (at least) Mary Ann and the Four had read his analysis—even if the questionnaire seemed an odd way to go about taking action. There'd never been anything like it before; the Omega wasn't known for asking the members what *they* wanted to do. It wasn't a democracy! Was Mary Ann really loosening her hold? Perhaps the structure really *was* changing.

I know from what my ward told Juliette later that he decided to answer the questions completely openly and honestly and not try to work out the "right" response—the answer expected or hoped for. He said that—having suggested such a radical decentralization in his report—he was determined to maintain that viewpoint while answering the many questions.

Everybody in the community filled in the questionnaire and returned it the next day. They had been told not to talk about their answers or compare them with other people.

This led to another long silence in which nothing was heard from the Omega for days and then weeks. This period appeared to be an even more nail-biting affair than the first long lack of response. This time—because each person in the chapter was on tenterhooks—the anxiety was building beneath the surface and heightened daily by the need to keep their answers and ideas to themselves.

While this long process—initiated originally by my ward's report—was playing itself out, he continued to be the director of the

New York Chapter, the person who had ultimate responsibility for bringing in the money. He had largely delegated the art direction of the magazine and the newsletter to the magazine's photographer and was spending progressively more time doing serious fundraising. In this way he was able to raise nearly thirty thousand dollars in direct donations and interest-free loans—a pittance when compared to what was required month after month. Yet it's a sum that will make its reappearance in quite another, surprisingly ugly, little drama some months later.

One of the people who was continually generous—and who would press a hundred dollar bill into my ward's hand after spending some time with him—was the first of the five incarnate angels I have previously mentioned as being introduced into his life: the kind and beautiful Doctor Eva K.

Eva K., you'll recall, was the young woman who'd slipped on her bathroom floor, catching her nose on the edge of the sink. She'd reported driving the bone up into her brain and yet had somehow survived with merely a bruise.

Eva was one of those people who could never bring themselves to join a community like the Foundation Faith and yet admired enough what they were doing to support them financially. At least that appeared to be the unspoken agreement been them. Eva had seldom come to the chapter unless she was giving a talk or a workshop, so she would call up and invite Father Jesse to meet her at her apartment only a few blocks away on the Upper East Side.

They would meet for an hour or two every couple of weeks over a cup of coffee and talk. Eva was highly intelligent—with an interest in many of the same subjects as my ward—and because of her extensive training as a psychologist, there was always a lot to talk about. And yet, because Eva came from an extremely straight Midwestern background, she presented something of an anomaly for Mein Host. I don't believe he had met anyone quite like her. She was invariably and beautifully turned out: her clothes were expensive but modestly styled, her golden hair would have been brushed a hundred times that morning as her mother taught her, and many of her attitudes were of the most conventional sort.

She respected Mein Host's celibacy with an almost nunlike deference and avoided the subject of sex so assiduously that it must have been obvious to my ward she was repressing her true desires. This created an electrifying sexual charge around them whenever they met that carried something of the resonance of a fourteenth-century troubadour with his lady. With no promise of sexual consummation—and with both of them, each for their own reasons, apparently happy with the formality of their arrangement—this allowed them to form a deep and loving friendship without any need to sexualize it.

However, there would be others in the chapter who would find it hard to believe that Mein Host's relationship with Eva could be so entirely innocent. This was all too obvious, because if they'd been in a similar situation with a beautiful and loving woman, they wouldn't have trusted themselves to master their sexual impulses. But then again, those particular people were not of an angelic heritage, so I'd suggest that their suspicions were merely those of normal mortals struggling with their own sexuality.

It was not long before the skeptics' suspicions reached the ears of the Four up at Mount Chi. They evidently believed they could assuage their envy of my ward's success by building a case against him on what they'd convinced themselves was his flouting of their vows.

It was when the Four told Mary Ann of their convictions about my ward's presumed affair with Eva that—unbeknown to all concerned—the next tumbler fell open in the lock on the cell in which he'd imprisoned himself.

This "scandal" wouldn't come out for a couple of months, yet when it did it would yield the final insight he needed to release himself from Mary Ann's web. A web, I might add, of such adhesive potency that almost all his colleagues in Mary Ann's inner circle would remain in the community long after her death, until they themselves died—as a few already have.

When Mein Host and the New York Chapter finally received a response to the questionnaire they'd all filled in, a shock wave went through the place. It was the last thing my ward had expected. The recommendations in his report were being used in exactly the opposite way to how he'd intended or even would have anticipated. But he was unaware of just how much he was resented by the Four and how the situation was being manipulated to expose those who didn't subscribe to the strict Jehovian dogma, those who were not considered pure enough.

Not considered *pure* enough!

Well, here we are again! Echoes of Xtul, right? Not letting the poor stragglers into the estate if they weren't sufficiently pure. This is no less than the insistence of the authoritarian personality on absolute loyalty, total obedience, and complete "purity"—racial, sexual, national, bodily, etc. The list can be as endless as a dictator's whims and seems to be a preoccupation of the authoritarian mind.

I believe from my observations that this insistence on "purity" can be reduced to a profound spiritual and emotional insecurity that lies beneath the autocratic mind as much as making such accusations of "impurity" have become useful arrows in every tyrant's armory.

Let me address this particular quirk of the authoritarian mind-set because it is a prime example of how deceptive appearances can be. Why is it, for example, the authoritarian personality so frequently chooses to focus on purity? Why is this personality type so convinced in its own rightness? Why does it brook no opposition or appear so incapable of compromising its opinions? How can it so easily ignore the facts in favor of its own certainty?

These questions are particularly pertinent as the social situation in the modern world becomes increasingly confused. It's an unfortunate truism that human beings tend to turn to strong leaders with a sense of their own certainty in times of social unrest. No doubt it was a survival tactic in early times, when the group—or, earlier still, the pack—needed to react quickly to a crisis. In almost every case that strong leader will be an authoritarian personality. In a more mature and self-governing society the authoritarian personality can become troublesome because it tends to stir up trouble among others simply to create a situation in which it can step forward and take control.

I'm sure this is a familiar personality type to my readers, so I feel no need to further describe how it manifests. The questions I posed earlier sought more to address the internal dynamics: the emotional, mental, and spiritual aspects of the authoritarian mind-set.

I offer the simple observation that the expectations or demands autocrats place on other people are frequently the demands those autocrats fail to apply to themselves. The demand for purity in others, for example, will most likely stem from an unconscious—or sometimes conscious—and unacknowledged sense of personal impurity. An example would be the fundamentalist preacher who is caught in a motel with a male prostitute.

The authoritarian personality needs to be absolutely right. Any chink in that rightness will cause the absolute certainty that sustains the autocrat to start to crumble, which is what makes it so hard for the authoritarian to compromise. To even allow the possibility of another opinion is to risk a breaking down of the illusory sense of certainty. This is the bully who collapses into emotional self-pity when confronted and also the person who flares up uncontrollably when opposed.

The truth is that there can be no absolute certainty in an uncertain, unpredictable, and relative field. Moral certainties are clearly arbitrary—the moral conviction of one culture or age may well be considered beyond the pale by another age or people. This surely must be self-evident to anyone not trapped in a fundamentalist *belief system*. And please note that I stress "belief system" because it is only in the arena of belief that any moral certainty can be claimed.

And that brings us back to the arbitrary nature of belief. Whereas the killing of a person is *believed* in most cultures to be wrong and immoral, the killing of an enemy in war—or in self-defense or in legal retribution—is generally *believed* to be justifiable.

A society's laws might codify what that particular society views as moral or immoral behavior, but ultimately that behavior—whether moral or immoral—is the sole responsibility of the individual concerned. When a society becomes overregulated with laws covering every aspect of human behavior, it infantilizes the individual and focuses the attention on the behavior's legality and not on the commonsense morality or immorality of the behavior. As an example, think of the traders who vastly enrich themselves by looting the pockets of the poor then justifying their predatory behavior by claiming it's all perfectly legal—while giving no thought at all to the harm caused to others by their actions.

A society that prides itself on being a nation of laws will inevitably become a nation of lawbreakers. This holds particularly true for incarnate rebel angels who appear to have an innate sense of justice and, I've observed, would rather learn by following the Universal Law (also known as "The Golden Rule")—behave toward others as you wish them to behave toward you—than merely subscribing to the arbitrary moral standards of the day.

This is as it is intended to be, because it's in making their own moral choices—both the good and bad ones—and by experiencing the consequences of those choices that intelligent beings can achieve wisdom and their own moral clarity appropriate to their culture and age.

Understanding this may not necessarily enlighten or change an authoritarian mind-set, but I hope it may encourage those who are subject to another person's autocratic demands to reexamine their allegiance in light of their own needs and choices.

In the case of their answers to the questionnaires, all the members of the chapter discovered they were being judged on their worthiness . . . on their purity. Each person whose answers were considered loyal and true to church dogma was an "A," while someone whose answers were interpreted as being in support of decentralization was called a "B."

At first this must have seemed reasonable to the Four. After all, they must have argued, those given the B status were going to be awarded what they wanted. They were going to be able to focus on whichever ministry—Healing, Radio, Angel, Psychic Sessions and Fairs, or Conferences and Lectures—would best mobilize their talents.

But that wasn't what shook everybody up.

What the Omega had done was to essentially say, "Sure you can have your subchapters, but they won't be housed in the same building as the Foundation Faith!" Each ministry was going to have to find alternative places in which to live and work; they had to be self-supporting as they wouldn't receive any financial help from the Foundation Faith. They were no longer permitted to wear the uniform, and they were required to tithe 10 percent of their overall income to the main New York Chapter.

Although this might appear a logical extension of my ward's recommendation to decentralize, it was not at all what he had envisioned. It was also painfully obvious that the Bs were being regarded as second-class citizens, and they were soon being treated as "traitors and betrayers of the cause" by the increasingly arrogant and dismissive group of As.

The Four came down from Mount Chi to hold meetings and deliver their edicts. No one knew quite how to respond—although they were being assured that the changes were all being done with the best of intentions. But the usually calm general meetings—especially on those occasions when the Four were present—quickly broke down into anger and confusion when the details and demands placed on the Bs were presented to the community.

A couple of days later, when Father John—one of the Four—took Mein Host aside, the impulse behind the new changes became a lot more obvious.

Father John made it very clear that Mary Ann—as well as the Four—had been appalled and infuriated to find Mein Host in the B faction. John told him that the idea behind the questionnaire was to root out the weaker elements, that it was intended to isolate these junior members so their feet could be held to the fire. Whether or not Father John said this in so many words, he made his meaning all too obvious. Only two senior members emerged as part of the group classified as a B, and both of them were Luminaries: Father Dominic of the Radio Ministry and Mein Host. The other fourteen or so IPs who fell into the B column—apart from three or four of the Priest rank— were all relatively junior members.

Father John was furious, barely containing his anger when he told my ward he should never have answered the questions in that way. The man didn't seem to understand that my ward was bound to support his own advice and that it was this absurd division into As and Bs that was poisoning the whole atmosphere in the chapter, turning brother against brother. Father John would have nothing of that, and when he found he couldn't induce my ward to change his mind, he became even more irate and set out to belittle and insult Mein Host for leading this rebellion.

So, it was a rebellion now, was it?

That was the way the event was evidently being viewed and promoted by Mary Ann and the Four. So that was going to be the nature of their propaganda!

Yet leading a rebellion was the last thing in Mein Host's conscious mind. In talking to Dominic, it became obvious that they'd been put in an impossible situation. They reckoned they'd been thrown to the lions. They'd have to find the money to rent an apartment in Manhattan, to come up with the security payment, to feed and support themselves, and to pay the Foundation Faith 10 percent for the privilege. And to do it right off the top with no help from the main group.

It was, in fact, such a ridiculous demand that both of them realized it had to be a ploy intended to make setting up subchapters so impossible that the Bs would want to change their opinion. If both Luminaries elected to become an A, Father John had said, then the other junior members could be more easily shown the error of their ways.

The "error of their ways," the talk of a "rebellion," being accused as "traitors and betrayers"—the list of insults and dismissals only became more unpleasant as the days passed.

Yet, for all the difficulties presented by moving out and setting up a subchapter under the impossible conditions set by the Omega, for all the humiliation heaped on the "rebels," and for the disparaging and ultimately futile attempts to persuade them otherwise, Dominic and Mein Host resolved to push through all the confusion and actually make a subchapter work.

So, rather than being manipulated to bring the junior rebels back into the fold, Dominic and my ward's determined enthusiasm actually fired up the junior IPs to remain true to their intentions. It was as though they were being forced into an authentic rebellion by the Omega's unreasonable demands.

The failure of the Omega and the Four's plan to tighten the noose and slap everybody back in line had blown back on them in a way they were foolish not to predict. It simply made no sense at all to create the subchapters in a series of other locations. Not only would the Foundation Faith receive only 10 percent of the subchapter's income, but they would also be deprived of all the money that would be required to support these separate establishments. Then add to that the fact that many of the first-rate donators were among the rebel faction. If the Four knowingly intended to push ahead with their plan they must have been aware they were ringing the death knell on the community's finances.

The new regime was either an act of self-sabotage on the part of the Omega, or it was an arrogant error of judgment on the part of Mary Ann and the Four to believe they could threaten someone of such an innately rebellious nature as my ward to toe the line.

After all, this wasn't unfamiliar territory for him. It had been his housemaster, Jock Reith, who—when the lad was leaving Charterhouse—had dismissed him in front of his mother at their final meeting with the advice: "Put him in a bank. It's all he's good for."

I've heard him comment more than once that Jock Reith's casual dismissal of him as only good bank clerk material had so infuriated him that he had used it as a spur to complete his long architectural training. "Just to show the old fool!" (*Note: I never saw Jock Reith again, so disgusted was I with the school in general. —TW*).

Regardless of all the melodrama, all the manipulation and misunderstandings, and all the futile persuasion and spiteful comments—the next tumbler clicked open in the lock on Mein Host's self-imposed prison.

Only two more tumblers to fall!

* * *

I chose not to linger too long observing the lives of the Old Ones—the cliff dwellers of Canyon de Chelly—after the hunting party had limped off down the river to boast of their glorious fight and how their enemies only defeated them by using their wily underhanded methods.

Having become weary of watching the buffalo slowly moving down the canyon in the early morning mist, I decided to leave my perch on the top of Spider Rock. I went without the loyalist midwayer with whom I'd been sharing the summit knowing that I'd been there or, indeed, that I'd just slipped away.

As I traveled south, the landscape changed from barren desert broken up by richly forested mountains and deep valleys to an arid region of flatlands, striated only by dry riverbeds and split by a deep gorge that snaked its way across the parched landscape. The river must have once been a massive torrent to have cut so deep into the rock, but now—as late summer was turning to fall—the river was running low and forming its own snaking path along the base of the gorge.

There was something comical about this sight—as though an immense serpent had swallowed a much smaller snake that was still wriggling within it.

Moving along I saw the occasional hunting party, and at one point I came across a small encampment on the top of one of the larger mesas. I had seen a great many mesas in this area—some large and some small. I knew they were geologic relics, if you like, of a time when the entire landscape was covered by the ocean.

Plate 1. *Father Earth*. Portrait of Timothy Wyllie by June Atkin.
Prismacolor Pencil.

Plate 2. *NDE Healing.* Timothy Wyllie. Prismacolor Pencil.

Plate 3. *Bardo Ascent*. Timothy Wyllie. Prismacolor Pencil.

Plate 4. *Rising In Balance*. Timothy Wyllie.
Prismacolor Pencil.

Plate 5. *Cherubim*. Timothy Wyllie.
Prismacolor Pencil.

Plate 6. *An Unlikely Truth*. Timothy Wyllie.
Prismacolor Pencil.

Plate 7. *Rebirth*. Timothy Wyllie.
Prismacolor Pencil.

Plate 8. *Mechanics of Faith*. Timothy Wyllie. Prismacolor Pencil.

Then, as the land was thrust up and the waters emptied out into the great north–south rivers of the North American continent, the mesas were created by the detritus that was swept along by the flood and aggregated around solid rock protrusions as the waters receded. By this time I had become familiar with the angle of incidence that seemed a common feature to most of the smaller mesas. From the height I was viewing them they looked like the flaring skirts of dancers all frozen in place.

I could see how the curious flat tops of the mesas must have been the result of weathering and erosion on horizontal rock layers. Some of the larger mesas were great lumps of solid basalt thrust up by tectonic forces from the surrounding plain. These mesas often sported sheer cliffs rather than the dainty dilated skirts of dancers.

I descended for a better look at the small encampment I'd seen on top of one of the larger mesas. The mesa in this case rose up out of a flat and sandy plain—a massive stand of sedimentary limestone with a single narrow trail winding up to the caprock.

It appeared there was a ceremony going on in the central square, so I descended even lower to see what was happening. At first it seemed like a crude affair. The men of the tribe were dancing—if you could call it that—in a wide circle, with their naked bodies painted in different earth colors and the many-colored feathers of birds stuck willy-nilly into their long, black, braided hair. Around the perimeter sat the women, their backs against a low wall. Some were clapping, while others sat quite still with their faces turned upward and their eyes closed and their mouths wide open. There were about a dozen children of different ages, all paying rapt attention to the dancers, and there were about six babies quietly suckling at their mothers' breasts while the ceremony continued.

As you know, I'm unable to penetrate a mortal's mind unless invited, so I was unable to discern the purpose of this ritual until I'd watched the dancers' steps more carefully. Bowing their bodies almost double, they stamped hard once with their right feet; then straightening up, they bent their subtle bodies in a backward arc as if saluting the sky, before repeating the process with another stamp of their feet.

Then it became clearer to me. At least I believed that I now understood the ritual.

The dancers bent back to honor Father Sky, forward to bow to Mother Earth, and then stamped their feet to make their point. I could see that the dancers had tied together small shells and seed husks, which were separated by turquoise beads and—yes—a few flattened pieces of gold, all fastened with a thin strip of leather around the ankles of their right feet, which rattled and jingled with every stamp. It was as if they were conscripting all of nature in their prayers, and—when they stamped their feet—all nature would be stamping along with them, reinforcing their prayers.

During all this time the dancers were chanting a circular and repetitive phrase—an incantation, I was sure—with their hoarse, guttural voices joined sometimes by the shrill piping singing of the women.

A man, taller than the others, had moved into the center of the circle. Unlike the others, he wore a skirt of long eagle feathers. Around both knees were bound the white fluffy feathers from the birds' breast. The man's back was painted elaborately in patterns that were vaguely familiar to me; in fact, the whole performance seemed resonant of ceremonies I'd seen taking place on a far larger scale back in the days of Lemuria. Could it be that something of that fine culture had percolated down the thousands of years to appear in this somewhat cruder form on a high mesa in the American Southwest?

The shaman—for that is who the tall man must surely have been—had started with his back to me and was now turning almost imperceptibly in a circle where he stood. I was therefore finally able to see his profile. It wasn't the profile of a man but rather that of a predatory bird. When he'd turned full circle, he raised both arms to a horizontal position to reveal his "wings"—more eagle feathers hanging from leather straps winding around his arms.

The moment the shaman spread his wings the chanting ceased, and a gasp went up from the dancers and the women of the tribe. This loud intake of tribal breath sent the shaman spinning on the spot—this time turning faster and faster in a counterclockwise direction—the feathers streaming from his arms in a blur of movement.

Then, to another gasp of astonishment from the tribe—although they must have seen it done before—the shaman, still a blur of swirling feathers, slowly lifted off the ground to the height of a tall man. He remained spinning at this unlikely elevation for long enough—four or five minutes I thought—to show it wasn't a trick and, more importantly, to demonstrate his power of the natural elements. The speed of his rotations gradually slowed as he descended to the ground until, like a spinning top, he tipped off his central axis and spun off in a wild swirling mass of flesh and feathers among the dancers, who were now standing quite still. Like the women, they all had their heads turned to the sky with their eyes firmly closed.

Something happened then, which—although I like to think I'm au fait with most of the human rituals I have seen in my time—I had never observed before. And what's more, at first glance it seemed completely out of place in a ritual that, by this time, I'd realized was a prayer for the rain to fall.

The shaman, continuing his wild spinning, was now starting to crash into the dancers, who were standing statue still. Colliding with one dancer spun the shaman into another dancer, each one allowing himself to be thrown to the ground by the impact. This odd-seeming "massacre" continued until all the dancers were lying prone, facedown, on the ground.

Now it was the women's turn.

The shaman's gyrations had slowed down so he struck the women and children much more gently, and with a lot of happy squealing from the kids. When the entire tribe was lying flat on the ground—some of the smallest children still bobbed around—the shaman simply disappeared. No, I don't mean he magically vanished—though having seen the man levitate I wouldn't have put it past him—but one moment he was there, the next he was nowhere to be seen.

I was probably distracted momentarily because a most intriguing thought had just struck me. Although I knew by this time that it must have been a rain dance, it was only then that I understood what the shaman was doing.

While the initial dancing by the men as well as the prayers of the womenfolk were obviously directed at asking for the rain, the actions of the shaman seemed to be in direct opposition to this. It looked to me as though he was canceling out the prayers of the tribe by knocking the people over like bowling pins.

It was then the thought hit me. The shaman was acting out the tribe's counter-intention! He was bringing it up to the tribe's collective consciousness in the most dramatically real way possible. He was giving the tribe a psychodrama, showing his elemental power by levitating and then proceeding to demonstrate his power over the tribe. One shaman equals everyone else.

His actions—and the behavior of the tribe who cooperated in acting out the ritual—were so counterintuitive that I realized, there and then, that it must have been inherited from the wisdom Vanu and Amadon were able to impart to the priest-scientists of Lemuria.

How could I advance this idea? Such a sophisticated ploy could only have come from a higher order of intelligence; one who had a far deeper understanding of the physics of matter. Grasping that the observed reality of physical matter is maintained in a state of dynamic equilibrium by the extremely rapid oscillation of subatomic particles between states of matter and antimatter is a little beyond the knowledge base of a sixth-millennium tribe of Native Americans. To understand that mesons dance happily to and fro three million times every second was of very limited value to the well-being of the tribe, whereas the same principle when applied to such activities as rainmaking ceremonies invariably produced the results desired by the tribe.

As though to demonstrate once again the efficacy of this technique, storm clouds were gathering in the northern skies, and by that very evening the rain was teeming down: great sheets of water falling as though a solid mass—more like a waterfall than a rainstorm. Water was bouncing up off the ground, forming puddles in which the children splashed and played, and filling the cisterns and the upturned open mouths of the grateful dancers and womenfolk before running off the mesa in gathering rivulets.

The storm didn't last long, but I could tell from the joy of the tribespeople that the cisterns must have been filled, and the tribe wouldn't have to descend to the plain to find—and relocate to—a more readily available source of water.

When darkness fell, the sky was clear of clouds and glowing bright with stars. There were a few people still on the central plaza quietly talking among themselves. Some small children were playing tag, with one shouting so loudly that it took a sharp look from one of the grandmothers to quiet him down. I could hear someone playing a flute on the far side of the mesa. It sounded surprisingly doleful to me, and I wondered what the flautist had to be sad about. But, of course—rain or no rain, water or no water—the emotional trials and tribulations of the young men and women of the tribe would have continued unabated.

All the dancers had retired exhausted to their simple shelters, followed by the women, and now I could see the flicker of flames coming from the mound of small buildings at the other end of the mesa. Soon, the smell of roasting venison was drifting over the plaza, further crinkling wrinkled noses, ending conversations, and sending the few remaining stragglers scuttling back to their womenfolk for their evening of feasting.

As my collaborator invariably wants to know something of the structural details of the buildings I encounter—once an architect, he says, always an architect!—he would be surprised to know how carefully these simple shelters were constructed. There was such loving attention given to the stonework that the whole complex of buildings exuded what I can only call a sense of the sacred.

These were a fine people, I thought, and for a fleeting moment I felt oddly sullied in their presence—despite their being unaware of me. I suppose this is an example of the difference I was trying to explain earlier between the northern nomadic tribes on the one hand, and the distant descendants of Lemurian colonies in South America on the other.

Both groups had long formed a deep identification with the land. In spite of their many different traditions, both of these groups revered the land as Mother Earth—even if they differed in other ways of worship and principle.

The clans that had been migrating across the Bering land bridge from the Asian continent—starting with a trickle some ten thousand to twelve thousand years earlier and swelling to a flood during the previous four millennia—was now back to a trickle as warmer temperatures and the rising sea levels had been steadily submerging the land bridge.

Many of these tribes had remained on the land bridge even during times when the glaciers were gathering and the temperature was dropping all around them. They had been protected by the warmer temperatures of the land bridge—an area, at its largest, at least one thousand miles deep from north to south—as well as finding the seemingly endless, ideal hunting grounds within forests of spruce, birch, and poplar trees.

It was invariably far colder and more barren at the Asian end of the land bridge than in the eastern regions, which prodded the tribes to move farther southeast to Yukon and Alaska and then progressively farther south into the body of the continent. They were master hunters, and their nomadic ways had allowed them to spread across the land as far east as the Mississippi by the sixth millennium.

As the various clans developed into larger tribes—and as those tribes grew in size—tribal identity became increasingly important, and this frequently resulted in intertribal conflicts when the tribes' paths would cross. A number of these tribes became known for their aggression and their pleasure in fighting. As the nomadic life discouraged the accumulation of possessions, the men of the tribes found their self-worth not in material riches but in the more refined values of the warrior. It would be some eight millennia before there was any attempt made by the tribes of North America to come together as one nation.

But, by then, it was far too late. The Europeans had arrived.

10

Reality and Intent

The Great Secret, Pueblo Tribe on the Mesa,
a Kachina's Family, the Lex Hixon Fiasco,
an Unfortunate Inquisition

It has been my observation that in their appearance first as Compulsions Analysis, then the Process Church, and now as the Foundation Faith, the community invariably had an unrealistic assessment of their own significance in the outside world. They certainly had an exaggerated impression of their own importance, but self-importance is rather different from significance.

In terms of public exposure, Compulsions Analysis had resulted in some scathing articles and national headlines like "THE MIND-BENDERS OF MAYFAIR." The Process Church's main claim to fame—in most peoples' minds—was their assumed association with Charles Manson. Now it was going to be the turn of the Foundation Faith, and yet the community was as blinkered—and as unaware as ever—of what was rustling in the wings.

I don't want to give the impression in this narrative that the young people of the community were inept or foolish as perhaps suggested in the previous paragraph. Each member might have had their moments of foolishness, but they were not inept, and they were not fools. They may have subsumed their identities to that of the community, yet the demands and challenges of the community required strong personalities.

In fact, as individuals, they were a singularly bright and attractive lot, and it was as individuals that they'd been making their mark in what was becoming the New York spiritual scene. Their conferences, the lecture series, their psychic fairs and sessions, their cool avant-garde magazines, the healthy yet delicious snacks in J's Place, and their progressively more-visible presence donating on the streets of Manhattan were starting to create waves.

They were undeniably among the primary progenitors of the New Age movement, especially in New York City. Yet the cloak of mystery with which the community deliberately surrounded themselves—as per Mary Ann's instructions—was sure to attract more attention over time than it was designed to hide.

The wisdom of following this path of secrecy was arguable. Because the community had elements of a mystery school, a certain secrecy was to be expected. It has never been wise or responsible to speak of sacred truths to the unprepared. As a mystery school, much was made in the community of the secrets held among the levels of the hierarchy; it was how individual advancement could be measured. A Priest knew more secrets than a Messenger; a Master, more than a Priest; and a Luminary had more of a grasp of the overall "game" than a Master. A Luminary might be part of the Omega's privileged inner circle—as were the Four—and orbiting close to Mary Ann, or be like Mother Juliette (or Mein Host), whose function brought them intermittently into Mary Ann's presence. Then there were some like Father Lucius—my ward's friend Richard, with whom he'd studied architecture and traveled to India—who, despite being a Luminary, preferred not be too close to the sun.

On top of this pyramid sat Mary Ann, who, if I follow the logic of the hierarchical ladder, knew far more than anyone else. Those who believed she was the incarnate Goddess, of course, will have thought she knew everything.

In the face of that grandiose expectation—one that she had placed on herself as much as she believed that the demands of others were being projected on her—it was not surprising that she chose to appear enigmatic and mysterious. Ever since my ward first met Mary Ann back in the early 1960s, the aura of mystery with which she surrounded herself had fascinated him. Even when he so intensely disliked her for those years before his revelation of her divinity, he was unable to deny his obsessive fascination with the woman.

Secrecy and mystery had always been part of Mary Ann's modus operandi. Her former profession involved mixing with the rich and famous and would have demanded discretion—of which she honored by rarely mentioning details of her life as a courtesan, and then only to the most favored of her inner circle.

Mary Ann was a woman who had re-created herself at least three times that I was aware of, so she had to know the value of mystery; and as a dominatrix—even a retired one—she would have known how efficiently secrets can bind people together, as much as separate them.

There was one great secret. It was the central mystery of the Foundation Faith, as it was of the Process before it: the one name never to be spoken to anyone outside the community was that of Mary Ann de Grimston.

In the fall of 1977, during the upheaval resulting from my ward's report and the subsequent and painful separation of the As and Bs—and while all the uncertainty and anger and frustration this caused was roiling away in the atmosphere of the New York Chapter—Mein Host received a phone call from a man calling himself Lex Hixon.

The outcome of their conversation would further shake Mein Host's faith in the literal foundations of the Foundation Faith, and it would also be the next of the tumblers to drop.

Lex Hixon was a well-known figure in the loose-knit New York spiritual community until he died in 1995 at the early age of fifty-three. He broadcast a weekly radio show, *In the Spirit,* on WBAI, as well as

edited the main New Age paper in the city. He was well educated—
with a doctorate in comparative religion from Columbia University—
and became a disciple of a remarkable number of different gurus and
teachers. From studying meditation with a Lakota Sioux elder; to
praying with an Episcopal priest; to becoming a disciple of Swami
Nikhilananda, Swami Prabhavananda, and Sri Chinmoy, he eventually
studied Zen and Tibetan Buddhism. In short, Lex Hixon thought of
himself as the real thing—an authentic spiritual person.

I have no wish to single out Lex Hixon for unnecessarily harsh criti-
cism, but when he telephoned Mein Host that afternoon his intentions
were neither honorable nor spiritual. Although his radio program had
been broadcast weekly for more than two years, my ward had never
heard the name Lex Hixon before when he took the call.

He joked with Juliette afterward that when he heard the name Lex
Hixon for the first time he burst out laughing. He thought it was "a
prank call from some horrible hybrid cross of Lex Luthor, Dick Nixon,
and Dixon of the Yard."

After introducing himself over the phone, Hixon sounded friendly
and interested in the Foundation Faith, praising their good works and
saying how he'd heard all these good things about the community. He
suggested that rather than interviewing Mein Host on the radio or for
his newspaper—and because the Foundation Faith possessed the elegant
theater—why not do a face-to-face interview, right there in the theater
in front of a live audience?

I doubt if Mein Host thought twice before accepting. He clearly
believed it would be good for everybody. Hixon would bring in new
people and be promoting the event on his show, and my ward considered himself adequately trained to handle anything Lex Hixon might
throw at him.

I knew Mein Host enjoyed a good strong argument with an intelligent opponent, so he agreed on a time and a date during the next week,
and I could see he was looking forward to a spirited discussion.

Here is what my ward didn't know (and had no reason to suspect):

Lex Hixon was no friend of the Foundation Faith. He actually despised the community. He resented the group for its success, and he viewed them as competition to his own self-proclaimed position as the mainspring of the city's New Age movement.

Hixon sincerely believed he had good reasons for his censorious attitudes toward the community. He was incensed that a religious group like the Foundation Faith could just "swan into town"—*his* town—and take over. He didn't approve of the Foundation Faith's religion—though he knew nothing of it save the rumors he'd heard—and it certainly didn't fit into his idea of a spiritual path.

I discovered the man had spent many weeks preparing for the confrontation, digging up any negative material he could find—and there was no shortage of that! He showed no interest in separating fact from fiction, believing—or so it appeared—every unpleasant rumor and outright lie that had been spread about the community over the years. He had made no previous effort to contact the community to check out the facts or hear the other points of view.

In fact, as Lex Hixon was heard to say to a friend before he set out that afternoon, he was interested in doing one thing and one thing only: exposing the Foundation Faith of the Millennium as a fraud and bringing them down. He wanted to destroy them.

In the Spirit had been broadcast on WBAI for a mere two years, and programming on that wildly left-leaning station was notoriously precarious. He believed that if he could stir up a popular scandal it would be sure to mean more listeners, strengthening his position on the station. In addition, Hixon had only received his prestigious Ph.D. the previous year. He made no bones to his friends about wanting to demonstrate his religious chops by destroying the credibility of a spiritual community he had never visited and knew nothing of the worst he could conjure.

There was a revealing contradiction in what Lex Hixon was setting out to do—an irony that he missed in his self-righteous resentment. My collaborator discovered on doing the customary research I require of him that Lex Hixon had based his entire spiritual journey on the life and teachings of Sri Ramakrishna, which had apparently inspired him all through his life.

One of Sri Ramakrishna's most radical approaches was his belief in immersing himself in different religions. He was said to have achieved sainthood—or its equivalent—in at least three of the great religions. He was known for his loving and openhearted acceptance of the Creator wherever She/He manifested. It's my hunch that Sri Ramakrishna would have respected the Foundation Faith and would have applauded the intensity and enthusiasm with which members like my ward were living their lives. I think Sri Ramakrishna would have recognized the purity of the love my ward, for example, felt for the Goddess.

My ward later told me that he hoped that Lex Hixon would pause later in his life to reconsider his resentful attitudes in light of Sri Ramakrishna's openhearted and loving acceptance of the Goddess.

Perhaps when Lex Hixon matured—he was only thirty-six at the time of this confrontation—and had learned more about his own nature and his chosen path, he would have a deeper esoteric understanding of an unconventional, yet perfectly authentic (in its own terms) left-hand path.

Mein Host, as I said, knew nothing of this at the time.

He went about his business in the days before the public discussion at ease with his decision to accept Lex Hixon's invitation. He had been giving interviews on radio and TV as the PR officer for the community and knew how distorted his words could become in newspaper articles. I therefore believe he welcomed a live, face-to-face confrontation with someone holding a spiritual interest.

As was occurring more frequently in his life since his NDE four years earlier, he was creating situations—or involving himself in events—without undue concern for the consequences. I could see something had changed in both his emotional and spiritual bodies. He'd become more confident that if he acted with a full heart and good intentions, the consequences would be positive—even if they didn't immediately appear so.

The coming event would test my ward and his confidence to the limit.

* * *

In the case of the small tribe I'd been observing on top of the mesa, it was evident their recent ancestors had traveled north from Mesoamerica within the past two hundred to three hundred years. They had settled on the mesa clearly believing themselves blessed by their gods to have found such an impregnable fortress. However, there was no spring on the top of the mesa, so there would always be the issue of water.

Although the American Southwest wasn't as dry then as it is in the twenty-first century, the rains were still unpredictable, and long droughts were not unheard of in the oral records of the tribe. I'd overheard some of the elders talking together of a time when they had to leave their mesa, and of the suspicion and blame they still harbored toward the unfortunate shaman who'd been incapable of drawing down the waters.

There was also a lot of happy laughter, which I thought curious—until I learned that the shaman calling down the rain was in fact a test. From what I gathered—amid all the laughter—they knew they had more than enough water now. However, it seemed that each generation of shaman still had to show the tribe they were capable of "calling the rains." That was why they were so jovial. Their shaman had passed the test.

What had happened was that when the tribe had returned to the mesa—sometime after having to leave it—they had made it their first business to dig out cisterns in the rock beneath them. In doing this, the tribe had found that they had broken into a series of interconnected small caverns and galleries hollowed out of the limestone by erosion. Many of these contained water, and they were constantly replenished by rainwater seeping through the limestone. So now they had their cisterns and enough fresh drinking water in the caverns beneath them to survive the worst of droughts.

Knowing that water was readily available had encouraged the tribe to settle there, and the small houses they built for themselves became a symbol to them of their permanence. Using a flat, stratified rock quarried from a deposit at one end of the mesa allowed them to build small, unevenly circular rooms, roofed in buffalo skins stretched over wooden poles that—in turn—were tied together and supported by a central column. Fires burned in some of the hearths, filling the rooms with smoke, coughing children, and what must have been an overwhelming stink of roasting meat.

It was a night of celebration for the tribe, and yet by dawn the next morning I could see a hunting party descending the winding path in single file to the plain below. Women were moving around their huts, some sweeping the dirt floors, others waking the children. I saw flatbread being baked in small domed ovens, old men struggling to get up from their cots, and a group of grandmothers gathering to gossip about the night's happenings as a young woman with a long braid down to her waist set up a simple loom for a day's weaving.

The sun's rays bathed the top of the mesa first, while the plain below was still in darkness. Then—as though it was a theatrical piece—the rim of light crept down the side of the mesa until it stood out, floodlit, against the surrounding darkness. The illusion only lasted a few moments before the world was flooded again with the warmth of the sun.

Another day, much like any other day, had started.

It was time to take my leave.

Leave I did, and as I traveled farther south, I had the opportunity to reflect on what I had just observed. How was the shaman able to levitate? How did he manage to call in the rain so effectively? What was it that had raised my spirits while I was observing the folk on the mesa?

Then I recalled the loyalist midwayer with whom I had shared the pinnacle of Spider Rock, and I realized what I'd been seeing—and why it had taken me so long to realize it.

They were living life as it was meant to be lived!

Is that too strong a statement? Living life as it's meant to be lived? But it was that strong a feeling!

A purist might argue that because the Earth was still a rebel-held planet, life could never be lived "as it was meant to be lived"; at least not on such a corrupted world. I suppose our purist would be correct in an ideal sense, but if he—and it would most likely be a male—had seen the brutality and humiliation I have witnessed in my time on this world, then I'm sure he, too, would have had his spirits lifted.

Here were a people, simple perhaps—certainly when compared to some of the exotic extravagance I had seen displayed under rebel mid-wayer tutelage—and yet there was this palpable sense (I could feel it in the astral) of purpose and meaning to the men and women's lives.

As I'd watched them going about their daily business, it came to me that each person—man, woman, and child—all knew exactly what to do; they were carrying out their duties to the very best of their abilities. I could see how much pride every one of them took in fulfilling their appointed tasks, however menial. They each understood their position in the tribe, and thus their place in the world and cosmos. From a quick review of their emotional bodies, they seemed to be at peace with their lives.

The feeling I had from them may have been palpable to a sensitive, but I could see it was not readily discernible to the men and women of the tribe on the mesa. They were like fish in water, unaware of the spiritual glow within which they went about their daily chores. They didn't know how fortunate they were.

The men and women of the tribe also seemed to have a natural and familiar relationship with the loyalist midwayers I had observed during the previous day's ritual, moving like violet shadows within their own frequency domain. These were the beings, of course, with whom the shaman had performed his magic . . . the beings who, though they have many names in many cultures, will become known to the Native American tribes as the kachina.

I was high over the Gulf of Mexico when once again the aether trembled beside me and there was Astar, drawn in, I imagined, by my thoughts about the loyalist midwayers . . . by the kachina. After greeting one another, Astar picked up on my line of thought.

"Perhaps you didn't know, but these . . . these kachina are among some of those midwayers who originally served very closely with Vanu and Amadon." Frankly, her tone started off irritatingly didactic—how she loved to lecture me! But I had to admit *that* was interesting. These kachina were evidently more important than I'd originally imagined.

Ignoring my reaction, Astar continued, "When Vanu was recalled back to Jerusem, and then the islands of Mu sank beneath the waves, a number of the primary midwayers chose to reassemble on the South American mainland."

That I knew. Those must have been the midwayers I had seen when I was observing that Lemurian settlement on Lake Titicaca.

"Then, did you know that Vanu left instructions for those particular midwayers to follow after he and Amadon had departed?"

I was surprised. "Instructions? After Vanu left?"

"No, I didn't think so." Astar always enjoyed her small triumphs. Why *was* it she always seemed to be competing with me? Did I invite her condescension? Surely I knew things she didn't—she'd never been to Zandana, for example—but I didn't try to lord it over her as a result, did I?

"I observed it happening," she continued, overlooking my pettiness. "Vanu had never intended to allow all he'd built up to just sink back into the ocean. You recall he'd been sending teachers and missionaries around the world. Well, that practice ceased within five generations of his departure. It was then that the midwayers were required to take up the slack; when their instructions started taking effect. It was the midwayers who made sure adequate preparations were being made to transfer as much as possible of the Lemurian culture over to the South American mainland."

After a long pause she continued—with a new sadness in her tone. "And you must be aware of how much was lost at that point! There's been a steady degeneration ever since. That settlement on Lake Titicaca you just thought about . . . when you were there, didn't you notice that it was already a shadow of Lemuria?"

No, I really hadn't noticed—or possibly it was simply that I hadn't expected more. I believe I was just unused to seeing a settlement that *hadn't* fallen under Caligastia's influence, and I was surprised then how at ease it made me feel.

"Vanu's instructions," Astar elaborated, "included sending a select group of midwayers—he even specified the clan—to accompany the peoples' northward migration and encourage them to spread as far as possible throughout the northern continent. They were able to establish their settlements as far north as Colorado and Utah. They were great builders, these Pueblo people . . . you saw how cleverly they'd built into those caves in the canyon wall and the well-constructed houses where they were living on the mesa . . ."

"And you believe the kachina were behind this?" I asked.

"Put it this way," Astar said, her tone becoming surprisingly firm and making me wonder if, as a rebel, she should be quite so impressed by loyalist midwayers. "It had to have been the kachina . . . of course, a lot more have now joined the original ones. Who else would have been able to preserve anything of true essence of Vanu's teachings? Left to the natives alone, the teachings would have been lost within a few generations."

She paused, and I assumed she was weighing her feelings. "I know they're loyalists, yet I really have to admire how the kachina have helped shape and sustain these particular Pueblo tribes. They're peace-loving and they're industrious and—do you know—I've never seen them initiate a fight. Not in all the time . . . yes, yes, they defend themselves perfectly adequately, but they never start the conflict."

I retorted, "They didn't seem all that advanced to me! At least not compared to what I've seen on Atlantis!" I found that I wanted to prick the bubble of Astar's enthusiasm about these loyalist kachina she was praising so highly.

"And the shaman's levitation wasn't advanced? Have you ever seen anybody levitating?" Astar's tone was grating. "And the rainmaking? Have you ever seen *that* on Atlantis?"

Of course she knew I hadn't.

I had to agree there *was* something very unusual and quietly touching about these simple people and the closeness of the relationship they'd established with their kachina. As Astar pointed out, the tribe accepted their kachina as real beings whom they respected, even venerated—but they never worshipped them.

Astar again: "That was important! They *didn't* worship their kachina. In fact, the people believed their kachina lived out their lives in families much as they, the people, did, except that the kachina were imperceptible and, of course, far more powerful."

"So, the people *trusted* them," I thought loudly, surprised at my own certainty. It had come to me suddenly. I was thinking of how suspicious and wary the people in Prince Caligastia's dominions were of the rebel midwayers, as well as all the demands their faux divinities made on them. They may have worshipped their gods and goddesses, but they certainly didn't trust them.

"That sense you had of watching life as it was meant to be lived," Astar reminded me, "well, that was largely the result of the relationship the midwayers have been able to establish with the natives. That's what gave you the feeling that all was in its place, that things were as they were meant to be."

It was true. I hadn't seen or felt that sort of ease and mutual respect between mortal and midwayer since the early millennia of the Lemurian civilization. The natives of Lemuria had Vanu and Amadon as their exemplary models, and both of them had always worked hand in hand with the midwayers. I am sure Vanu and Amadon would have set the standard for the optimum contact between the species. Vanu, especially, would certainly have been aware of the dangers of deifying the midwayers.

Astar broke into my thoughts: "That's what made it so challenging. We both know how most natives have an almost instinctual urge to worship whoever or whatever's more powerful and mysterious than them!"

"All too well!" I agreed. I've often wondered if that wasn't one of the most irritating weaknesses of human psychology.

Astar's tone turned more thoughtful: "But it works both ways. Think about it from the midwayers' point of view. The midwayers must have their temptations, too. They're good, but they're not perfect. Look at the rebels . . . what happens to them. They luxuriate in playing at being gods and goddesses, don't they? They drink in all that worship. They're vampires. Worship gives them energy . . . too much energy! It makes them feel powerful . . . then, of course they all start competing with one another. Humans get to be pawns in their games. They lose track of their mission here, and they become proud and careless. It's a downward spiral."

I had a sudden insight: "The toy dolls! Yes, of course! And all that business about kachina families . . . as if they really have aunts and uncles and grandmothers and everything!" We were both laughing as I completed my thought. "So this was a way the midwayers were making it safe for the natives. They'd seem less awesome. That must be it! They've deliberately allowed themselves to be perceived as less threatening, as more normal, with their kachina families and their little kachina children . . ."

That had Astar laughing again at the image of those "little kachina children." In human terms, those kachina—those midwayers—had been on the planet for thousands of years, many of them were hundreds of thousands of years old. Hardly little children!

Another insight: I suddenly understood the midwayers' dilemma. They were authentically powerful beings who were faced with responsibilities directed toward the well-being of another race of beings; a race far less immediately powerful, who were mostly fearful, belligerent, or emotionally confused—and almost all of them were prone to self-delusion.

Astar broke in: "You see their problem. Under normal circumstances they can't openly intervene. Even that ritual you observed with the shaman levitating and then calling down the rain, even that was seen—*had* to be seen by the tribe—as the work of the shaman."

"Which of course it was . . . in a way," I interjected. "Wasn't it the shaman who was working with the kachina to make it happen?"

"That's just the point!" Astar's impatience had returned. "Don't you understand? The power had to be seen as sourced by a human being . . . like the shaman, for example; of course the tribe would have known he was working with a kachina, yet it'll be to the shaman they will give the credit.

"Didn't you see this when you were observing them on the mesa?" Astar continued. "They encourage their children to make little kachina dolls. They say this gives the children an early sense of familiarity and friendship with a kachina, and because they're dolls, the children grow up feeling they have a certain amount of power over a kachina. Whether or not that is actually true doesn't matter, so they say; each child will find its own natural relationship with its kachina . . ."

". . . and without bringing any of their normal fears and their lack of self-confidence along with them," I finished Astar's thought for her.

I confess it was something of a revelation to me. The ease of the relationship was so entirely different from what I'd been observing elsewhere that I was shocked to find it occurring, even as I was unexpectedly encouraged by the sight of those happy, confident natives, living at ease with another species.

In those brief moments of confusion I didn't notice Astar slipping back into the aether. I was alone in the astral, the mesa still glowing in the late evening sunlight far below me.

I could feel it was one of those occasions in which I was being confronted with the consequences of my choice to follow Lord Lucifer. This wasn't my normal horror at the actions of a brutal tyrant, or the careless actions of a resentful goddess—this was far more subtle. It was a glimpse of what might have been. No. It was more than that, and this is what pierced my heart.

Had the midwayers and mortals been able to form in all situations *from the start* the easy and benign relationship I had just been observing on the mesa . . . I could only imagine how advanced this world might have become had we just left it alone.

Perhaps you can understand the depth of the feelings that were tearing at me; feelings that I was still unaccustomed to and to which I was desperately struggling to keep under my control. You might think of it as something like a feeling of extreme and persistent poignancy, but not mere sadness or regret. It felt a lot more complicated than that.

It's hard not to be wise after an event such as this, but I believe it was around this time that I felt I was starting to get glimpses of the larger picture. I've made my reactions to Caligastia's depredations clear in this narrative, and yet I was still sure there was an essential authenticity to the revolution of which I was unaware.

Whatever an authority might claim, a revolution never occurs in a vacuum. There have to be charges and grievances against that authority that are substantial enough to arouse an otherwise placid population to take action, be they mortals or angels. To expect any administration that functions in a relative field to be free of error—however highly it might think of itself—is a dangerous delusion.

So, while I fully accepted the necessity for the revolution and continued to support Lucifer, I was horrified with how I saw it unfolding on Earth. I was profoundly moved by the courage and openhearted ease of the little tribe on the top of the mesa, yet that was mixed with an intense remorse and sorrow for all the suffering caused by our revolution—and my regret for what might have been had it never occurred.

In my more rational moments I thought I perceived an underlying bifurcation taking place beneath my immediate understanding. Another way of being was starting to open up for both mortals and angels, whereby the emphasis was now steadily shifting toward the individual—and the choices and decisions made by individuals.

I knew this meant something significant was taking place, that we were all being singled out for some future event or task. But I was still too emotionally confused to see any deeper. However, if I thought for one moment that these times were as emotionally distraught as I was ever going to experience, I had no idea just how much more challenging my existence was going to get.

* * *

Lex Hixon had evidently done his best to make sure he had a good audience for his proposed demolition of the Foundation Faith and its teachings that he so despised. The Alpha—the theater that the chapter shared with an increasingly neurotic Gene Frankel—was becoming crowded with people.

These were people whom Hixon had provoked to attend by using his radio show to galvanize their interest. They could have been coming to the Place de la Revolution to watch the French aristocracy being guillotined. I could all but hear the clickety-clacking of the knitting needles of the *tricoteuses,* lusting for the blade to fall.

I'm sure Mein Host agrees in retrospect that it might have been wiser to know more about whom he was up against in Lex Hixon, but—as he would have said at the time—he was far too busy to bother with what he felt was going to be a fairly trivial affair. Just another interview, one of many.

I could see this cavalier attitude of his change rather suddenly when it came time for Mein Host to enter the Alpha and take his seat opposite Lex Hixon. Between the door and his chair I watched the blood draining from his face as the full blast of the hostile atmosphere hit his emotional body.

Out of a sea of more than a hundred people—wrapped in three sides around the stage—were the two or three friendly faces of the only IPs senior enough to attend the event without feeling guilty at wasting their time. They seemed to be beaming a terrifying mix of anxiety and encouragement—with a rather discouraging emphasis on the anxiety.

Gene Frankel's professional theatrical lighting system had been adjusted to throw an ellipse of brilliant light on the two protagonists. The audience, hovering on the edge of rowdiness, was buzzing with fierce anticipation.

After the crowd had quieted down, there were some short introductions, and Mein Host gave a very brief outline of the church's teachings. I could see Hixon sitting impatiently, not really listening but shuffling the pile of paper on his lap, preoccupied, presumably, with planning his assault. Then—although my ward was quite obviously expecting a more thoughtful and respectful opening sally—Lex Hixon, local spiritual would-be guru, came at him, as my ward said later, "with both barrels blazing."

It was frankly painful to watch, so I'll let my ward explain what he went through for himself. However, before that, here are a few paragraphs he wrote in one of his previous books *Love, Sex, Fear, Death,* which well summarizes the position he was in prior to his confrontation with Mr. Hixon.

> The Process, like all such quasi-secret societies, liked to keep a firm grasp on all the inner doings of the community. Our secrets, as well as the chaos and turmoil we were frequently experiencing, were held close to the chest and seldom if ever revealed to those outside the group.
>
> We always tried to ensure that our public face was that of a well-ordered community with a theologically dense but provocative belief system and psychologically well-adjusted and dedicated members.
>
> For that illusion to be upheld the group needed people (like me) to bury our doubts and close our eyes to the contradictions we witnessed among the highest echelons. When the authentic spiritual juice was starting to run dry, it became more and more demanding

to pretend to myself, let alone to the general public, that we had anything of substance to offer them. (122–23)

You can tell from the words above that Mein Host was feeling somewhat more unsure of himself than I'd allowed. I should have known better, but his facade of cool detachment was most convincing. He was also clearly aware that the "authentic spiritual juice" had been running dry for some time, and there's a sense of the specter of hypocrisy looming close—if not already with a spectral foot in the door.

Hypocrisy, if I may diverge for a moment, requires either a cold-hearted indifference to authenticity, an overwhelming greed, or—to use Ronald Laing's term—a *divided self.* All three of these essential requirements for self-betrayal—I've no doubt there are more—ran so entirely antithetical to Mein Host's character that, had he been more farseeing, he might have been grateful to Lex Hixon for exposing the mystery at the very center of the community's world. The secret of secrets, or as my ward has written, "The very person around whom we had gathered—the incarnate Goddess who had been revealed to us, the One we were all serving knowingly, or unknowingly—was the one being we were not permitted to speak about."

The confrontation was not a pleasant experience for him, but to continue my intermittent metaphor of the lock, the event will result in the penultimate tumbler falling open.

Here is how Mein Host experienced the event as he previously described it in his own words:

"Isn't it true, Father Jesse, [Lex Hixon's voice was loud, and I could hear the nervous tremor in it, even if my ward couldn't] that there's a secret leader of your church, a woman called Mary Ann de Grimston?"

What was I to say? No one was supposed to know this. And before I had time to think of a decent reply the questions started again.

"Isn't it so, Father Jesse, that she lives in a luxurious Westchester estate paid for out of church funds?"

Then I had no time for thought at all. The questions just kept on coming.

"And isn't it also true, Father Jesse, that this woman then known as Mary Ann MacLean had numerous convictions in London for prostitution?"

"And how do you account, Father Jesse, for the fact that this woman, with all her prior convictions, has been able to travel freely in and out of this country?"

I was screaming inside for him to stop, to let me out of this hellish position, but the relentless questions continued, heavy with their implicit answers.

"Has it occurred to you, Father Jesse, that the only way Mary Ann MacLean, or de Grimston, or whatever name she used, could only have done this is with the complicity of the American and British intelligence agencies?

"Are you able to assure me, Father Jesse, that you and your church haven't been used as a tool of MI5 or the CIA?"

I was hopelessly flustered. I knew if I admitted to Mary Ann's presence and her leadership of the group—something no one was supposed to know—it would open the door to having to deal with all the other questions. I was sweating through my expensive hand-tailored blue uniform (paid for by an adoring follower), and must have stuttered out some sort of wholly unsatisfactory reply. There was no point in denying the reality of Mary Ann; the man had a stack of documents on his lap.

I now recall this inquisition as an endless humiliation before everyone filed out in silence. (*Love, Sex, Fear, Death*)

I, of course, was in a better position to observe what happened. I'll say in advance that my ward's performance was more dignified than he'd painted, although the situation was just as unpleasant as he intimated.

In a sense, you could say that Mein Host was actually saved from ultimate humiliation by Lex Hixon's odious manner.

At the first question, there was a loud gasp and a "gotcha" roar from the crowd. But as each question inexorably followed each question, never allowing my ward a moment to respond, two things changed simultaneously over the course of the inquisition. Lex Hixon's voice grew steadily louder and more demanding, and the crowd became progressively quieter. It was as if I was watching two interconnected glass beakers: one of which was initially almost full of bright blue liquid, and the other almost empty. As Hixon's questions became harsher—and a sadistic edge started coloring his tone—the level of liquid fell in the first beaker as it rose in the second.

It seemed that Lex Hixon may not have chosen too wisely when he invited an audience of his supporters. These were not bad or cruel people; they had spiritual aspirations—otherwise they wouldn't have been listening or reading Hixon, let alone coming in to support him. I'm sure they would have preferred some healthy intelligent jousting between two differing spiritual paths, because they seemed increasingly awkward and embarrassed while Hixon was ratcheting up the tension. The audience may have hoped for a lively debate, but it didn't appear that they were prepared for a display of such sadistic self-satisfaction—and from a man proclaiming so publicly his spiritual aspirations.

It is possible they may not have been aware of the true depth of Lex Hixon's resentment of the Foundation Faith; most of them would have known nothing about the church except for what they'd heard from Hixon himself. Yet it was hard not to conclude that the unaccountable anger with which the man was spitting out his questions was starting to reveal more about himself and less about the church, or Father Jesse—who couldn't help at least to outwardly appear coolly elegant, even if he was frazzled inside.

It was certainly no triumph for Mein Host. In fact, until I wrote the above—casting a broader perspective on the event—he has claimed it was one of the most humiliating situations in a life by no means free of humiliating situations.

It is not in my brief to comment on whether Lex Hixon learned what he needed to—or could have—from his cruel performance. He certainly scored his points, and he may have been carried away with his triumph, which did nothing but further polish his ego. I would like to believe that his master Sri Ramakrishna might have reminded him to approach another religion with an open heart and set out to experience the divinity within it, just as he did. To deliberately sabotage other people's religion—whether or not it's believed fraudulent—and to do it from motives of resentment and personal advancement was most unlikely to impress the Masters.

However, for Mein Host, it was an awakening. Although he was confused about it, I can assure him that he never revealed anything about Mary Ann, or even admitted she existed. He described the audience as filing out in silence, implying, I suspect, that their silence was an empathic resonance with his disgrace and humiliation.

He may be somewhat encouraged to know, even at this late date, that the audience shuffled out in silence not because my ward had disgraced himself—although there was some of that, too—but because they had witnessed the savage dissection of a man who seemed harmless and pleasant enough and the vilification of a church and a woman that meant little to them. They left in silence because they were kindhearted people who were rightly embarrassed by Hixon's cruelty and disappointed not to have learned more about the beliefs of the church. Mein Host had walked out with as much dignity as he could muster when he'd had enough of the abuse, and when he must have realized there would be no discussion.

However, his humiliation wasn't entirely over. This is how he described the following day:

When Mary Ann found out about the calamity the next day she was predictably in a rage about it, saying I never should have arranged the meeting in the first place and accusing me of not being prepared for the sort of questions that might be asked. Not unreasonable in principle, I supposed, but we'd never had to face that level of anger and intense inquiry before. After all, Mary Ann's name had never come up in our dealings with press or public. (*Love, Sex, Fear, Death*)

Mary Ann may well have been furious at being exposed under such harsh and crude circumstances, but there was not much she could do about it without attracting more attention to questions that she likely had no wish to address.

It might seem curious to the reader, but in all the time I was observing my ward and his colleagues in the community, I never once heard any talk from anyone of Mary Ann having anything to do with MI5 or the CIA. Nor did I hear anyone speculating on how Mary Ann moved across borders so freely.

Those in her inner circle were aware of Mary Ann's former life as a classy call girl because she seemed to be proud of it. Yet she seldom talked about her life in any detail, and my ward didn't discover her prostitution convictions until after he'd left the community.

Mein Host's ignorance of these facts, of course, added another layer of complexity to an already complicated situation. Had the accusations been fabricated—had they merely been wicked lies made up by Lex Hixon to drag down the church—they would never have carried the weight they did. Lies would have been easier to dismiss, but—as I've pointed out in earlier volumes—Mary Ann had been contacted by British intelligence well before Compulsions Analysis.

This is not to say that either MI5 or the CIA were in any way behind the community; they didn't initiate the community, nor did they have anything to do with its teachings or beliefs. The community would have been exactly the same, and it would have functioned in precisely the same way had Mary Ann never been contacted by British intelligence.

But the problem with the contact—since that's what Hixon was hammering away at—was that the accusation was true . . . just not in the way Hixon might have imagined.

11

Bounds of Complacency

The Profumo Scandal, Tactical Insults,
Contact with MI5, Bored with Goodness,
Serving Lord Lucifer, the Prince's Plan

The British intelligence agencies throughout the 1950s and early '60s—as is now more generally known—were in a state of near collapse. If an officer wasn't a Soviet mole, then he was likely suspected of being one—or he was combing the files attempting to dislodge a mole. It was a time when the CIA's James Jesus Angleton was driving himself mad trying to find a Soviet agent he was convinced had infiltrated British intelligence—and all the while he was lunching weekly with Kim Philby in Washington.

It was during these uncertain times, in early 1962, that the Profumo scandal erupted in the national press, further humiliating the intelligence community and exposing the political class to yet more ridicule.

To briefly recap the incident: Christine Keeler—a high-class London call girl—was found to be mistress of John Profumo, Britain's Secretary of War in the Conservative government. At the same time, she was having an affair with Yevgeny Ivanov, a senior naval attaché at the Soviet embassy in London and a known spy. Ms. Keeler was also simultaneously living and sleeping with a known criminal, Johnny

Edgecombe, who—by sticking a knife in one of her former lovers, a certain Aloysius "Lucky" Gordon—had led circuitously to the unraveling of the scandal and the fall of the Conservative party. It also resulted in the suicide (or, quite possibly the murder!) of Dr. Stephen Ward, a high-society chiropractor and the convicted procurer of call girls for the rich and famous.

The scandal, when it finally emerged, cut so deeply that it not only forced the change of government, but it also brought in the Labour Party with Harold Wilson as prime minister. This only added to the confusion in the intelligence community as a recent Soviet defector had informed James Jesus Angleton that Harold Wilson was a KGB agent. Absurd though that may sound—a Soviet mole becoming prime minister—it turned out that Harold Wilson was also one of MI5 officer Peter Wright's prime suspects for being a longtime Soviet mole.

In the early 1960s, at the height of the Cold War, British intelligence was becoming desperate about secrets passing to the Soviets. When the Profumo/Keeler/Ivanov triptych was discovered, the agency made it a priority to interview any call girl who might have had international clientele.

In his autobiography, *Spycatcher,* Peter Wright wrote of the lengthy interview with Christine Keeler that he conducted when he was working in counterintelligence at MI5. He reports how her casual mention of "nuclear payload"—not a phrase in general use, he realized (or one that a party girl would necessarily know)—had tipped him off to the possibility of espionage. It appears from Wright's interview that Ms. Keeler was an innocent patsy, who was unaware of the honey trap for which she was being used, and who probably didn't know she was being manipulated, most probably by Dr. Ward.

Back in 1963, when Mein Host was living in an apartment he shared with five others on Lexham Gardens, he happened to find himself hanging out for an afternoon with Christine Keeler and few of their mutual friends. It was the only time he met her, but he said afterward how much he liked her. She was far brighter than he would have expected a so-called party girl. She was also genuinely pretty and personable he said, quite unlike the picture painted of her in the press. He said he could quite understand people falling under her spell, and given another situation he might well have made a play for her. She had a natural, easy charm, and although she evidently must have possessed a lot of seductive power, she had somehow maintained a genuine sweetness and innocence so rare, my ward tells me, in a call girl.

I should add what my ward is unlikely to claim for himself: for what it's worth, Christine Keeler—a modestly self-aware, incarnate rebel angel—recognized a kindred spirit in my ward and felt immediately drawn to him. I overheard her telling her friends after my ward had left the apartment that afternoon in London that he was just the sort of man with whom she could easily fall in love.

In doing his research, my collaborator says he was wryly amused—but not altogether surprised—to read Peter Wright's dismissal of Christine Keeler as poorly educated and knowing little about current events. Although by whose standards he was judging the young woman—and what political pressures may have led him to disparage and trivialize her—can only be inferred.

Christine, my ward says, might not have been that well educated, but that didn't mean she wasn't extremely intelligent—and with a very sharp sense of humor. Much more likely, he believes, Christine was just playing the dumb bimbo role that would have been expected of her by the authorities. Whether she dropped the phrase "nuclear payload" unwittingly or had some conscious, or unconscious, intention to reveal the connection seems to be known only by her.

Mein Host suggests that Wright's assessment of her as being poorly educated with no reference to her natural innate intelligence had more to do with the usual English snobbishness toward the lower classes—as much as the (male) authority's typical need to belittle a young woman who has made fools of such important men—than Christine's actual

226 ▲ Bounds of Complacency

level of intelligence. It's a well-worn strategy of the English ruling classes to maintain their status quo.

However, ironies are known to richly abound in the intelligence business, and one such irony up and bounded on the back of Peter Wright, the tenacious spycatcher.

Bear with me here, kind and patient reader, if all this talk of spies bores you—or if you are already all too familiar with the details of the case—but I am attending to some unanswered questions from this period in my ward's past. He had no idea, for example, that the strong mutual draw he experienced with Christine was that of two incarnate angels encountering one another.

Now . . . to return to the controversial spycatcher, and possibly—if I can maintain the self-discipline—to the point I'm trying to make.

Peter Wright evidently had a distinguished career as a senior scientific officer with British intelligence. By 1964 he was chairing a joint MI5/MI6 committee investigating the continuing Soviet penetration of high levels of the government and the trade unions in England. Wright's career straddled the most disastrous period in British intelligence history; one in which a number of their most senior officers were found to have been spying for the Soviets, some of them since the 1930s. The members of the Cambridge spy ring—Kim Philby, Guy Burgess, Donald MacLean, and Anthony Blunt—are sufficiently well known to need no further comment, except to demonstrate the depth of treachery Wright was struggling to expose.

When Peter Wright retired from a senior intelligence position in 1976, a new struggle developed in his life that left him angry and disenchanted with his ex-employer. The conflict over his pension rights became serious enough to cause him to leave England and resettle in Tasmania.

A decade later, Wright's book *Spycatcher*—first published in Australia and in which he names names—created a massive furor in England. The British government had attempted to suppress the book by using the Official Secrets Act and succeeded only in turning an otherwise obscure Australian book into an international bestseller.

Peter Wright was a hardworking straight shooter who made some vital contributions to electronic espionage before rising to the top of the British intelligence service. And yet by 2001, Dame Stella Rimington—the Director General of MI5 from 1992–1996—was writing critically of Peter Wright as being "a man with an obsession, [who] was regarded by many as quite mad and certainly dangerous." She was also calling him a disruptive and lazy officer and accusing him of sloppy paperwork and taking secret files home with him without returning them correctly!

We can ignore Wright's apparent laziness, his sloppy paperwork, and his incorrect file handling, as these sound like the quibbles of a pencil-pushing bureaucrat. But obsessive? Dangerous? Mad? Disruptive? Where have I heard these sorts of disparaging and ugly epithets before? Isn't it curious that so many jilted administrations—whether they are the bureaucrats of a Local System of planets or those of a small, self-important nation—react with such similar slights?

Whenever I hear of a reputable man or woman being treated by an administration as mad and dangerous, I suspect immediately that some bureaucratic double-dealing has been invoked.

Within a few months, Mein Host and his colleagues would be subjected to much the same treatment after all their years of loyal service to Mary Ann and to the community.

Between 1961 and 1963, MI5 picked up all of the high-class call girls they could find in London who were known to serve important governmental, military, and entertainment industry people. It was then that Mary Ann MacLean was brought in for questioning—although she had no involvement with Dr. Stephen Ward or anything to do with the Profumo affair—and she had remained a person of interest to the agency.

I imagine MI5 would have quickly recognized Mary Ann's unusual intelligence and her obvious talent for duplicity and spycraft, but she was never formally under contract, and, to my knowledge, no money ever changed hands. A select number of people who find themselves called into an intelligence agency can frequently become wittingly—or unwittingly—the eyes and ears of that agency. Not real spies, of course, and not really snitches—they're not asked to sneak on friends—but these are the people who are encouraged to report to the agency on anything they see or hear they feel is suspicious.

When Mary Ann took the community to America, it is reasonable to assume—and I have to assume because I wasn't present at the interview and Mary Ann never spoke of it—from what has now been revealed about the less obvious activities of the intelligence agencies during the Cold War, that MI5 would have been unlikely (and most unwise) to overlook the opportunity to keep her on the books.

The once proud British intelligence services had been humbled during the 1950s by the revelation that Kim Philby—one of the highest-ranking officers in MI6 and a man who'd been close to James Jesus Angleton of the CIA—was a longtime Soviet agent, one of the Cambridge Five. The degree of Soviet infiltration of British intelligence will, no doubt, enter the history books as the greatest failure of any intelligence agency of the twentieth century, and it can also be viewed, by the Soviets anyway, as a most resounding success.

Not only will everyone in MI5 and MI6 have been working overtime throughout the 1950s and '60s to clean up the mess they were in, but they would have been all too keen to keep on anyone they considered reliable—particularly if that person happened to be going to America. There can be no doubt it was British intelligence who facilitated Mary Ann's freedom of movement, either by giving her special permission or, more likely, by conveniently making the relevant records disappear.

I've addressed this issue in some detail to satisfy my ward's curiosity, and because it was only well after having to field those impossible questions from Lex Hixon that he found out the truth of Mary Ann's involvement with MI5.

There is another reason I have decided to expose Mary Ann's

somewhat peripheral relationship with the British spy agency—one that my ward hasn't yet realized must have added a certain subconscious piquancy to his situation.

I'm sure it would have been the last matter on his mind during the Hixon inquisition, yet it had been only a couple of years earlier that the Official Secrets Act had expired, and his mother had been able to confess to having worked for MI6 before the war. Diana had been so scrupulously attentive to the Official Secrets Act that my ward knew nothing of her involvement until, many years later, she finally told him about what she'd done for the service.

It came as a complete surprise. It considerably deepened his respect for his mother and went some way toward answering why he'd always had a lifelong interest in books and movies on espionage.

Although I said this memory hadn't been in his mind during Lex Hixon's inquisition—he had been told of Diana's involvement only a couple of years earlier—it certainly contributed to his confusion.

Here he explains it in his own words: "Georgia is quite correct. What Diana told me about her being in MI6 was indeed the last thing on my conscious mind during the event itself.

"But when I think about it more deeply I realize that subconsciously I would likely have reasoned that if my mother—my mother, for God's sake!—could have been a spy, then why not Mary Ann? Why not anybody? The fact that it was actually true about Mary Ann only further confused me, as I'm sure I would have been picking up the truth on some level. Not only was I ignorant of Mary Ann's involvement with British intelligence, but it was also the last speculation that I, or anyone else in the community back in 1977, ever would have made.

"Until Georgia mentioned it earlier in this narrative, I was never sure about Mary Ann's MI5 connection. When I wrote about the community in 2009 in *Love, Sex, Fear, and Death,* it was the first time I chose to seriously consider whether Lex Hixon might have been right.

"I should add that from my point of view I think it made no

difference to the authenticity of the community, and it doesn't reduce or negate in the slightest bit what I learned in my time there. In fact, from the community's viewpoint it simply freed up our movement because Mary Ann—as you will have gathered from Georgia's narrative—seemed to need to relocate quite regularly. All the MI5 connection did was what it was intended to do: it allowed Mary Ann—with her convictions for prostitution—to travel openly and freely back and forth from England to America, to move all over America and Canada, and to travel throughout Europe and the Middle East.

"The Hixon event and Mary Ann's subsequent fury—which seemed wholly unfair to me as it was obviously Mary Ann's choice to remain invisible (and her exposure was sure to happen at some point)—affected me deeply; not so much for what was said, but for the feelings it aroused in me.

"It wasn't that I suddenly became disenchanted with Mary Ann, because I didn't believe what Hixon had said. But something inside me had certainly been stirred up."

Mein Host understates here the degree to which the so-called Hixon event had stirred him up. He was still adept at repressing his painful emotions. He still believed in Mary Ann, and he was familiar enough with her anger to know that it soon passed.

The conflict between the As and Bs was becoming more open and heated in the New York Chapter. This seemed to be primarily generated by the arrogant attitudes of the purist As, who had been waiting on the sidelines for the inevitable downfall of the more universalist Bs.

It was an ancient conflict, one that has been reflected, to some extent, in almost every religion: between spontaneity and dogma, liberal and orthodox, shaman and priest, left-hand and right-hand paths, and generalist and fundamentalist. As I have previously pointed out, often these choices have more to do with the psychology of the person making the choice than the beliefs they espouse.

In this case the conflict was between those who wanted to keep the community as a small elite with people completely devoted to church dogma and those, like Fathers Dominic and Jesse, who wanted to take the church in a more universalist direction.

However, for Mein Host, yet another matter was brewing that would be extremely painful and eye-opening for him. It would also be the final tumbler falling into place that would release him from Mary Ann's tenacious hold.

* * *

My talk with Astar—as we hovered over the high desert of the American Southwest—had made me thoughtful. No longer did I feel like fulfilling my original intention of reviewing human activity in South America and farther, across the Pacific, to see what was developing in Asia. This was Astar's province; she was more static than I chose to be. Whether it was something she told me, or perhaps the confident manner in which she'd referred to what was going on in the south, I suddenly felt the places I was thinking of going really didn't need me. Besides, I was beginning to get a little bored with all the good behavior I'd been observing.

Did I really feel that? That I was "a little bored" with goodness?

I listen to myself with different ears as I write these words. I'm trying to make sense of myself; how I've come to be the way I am, as I find myself changing over the course of the revolution. Change is essentially more familiar to mortals than to watchers. Mortals are far more subject to changing environmental conditions, as they are also more certain to change their minds and their opinions than is any angel.

I doubt if I need to emphasize that this constant human mutability is a direct consequence of a mortal's freedom of choice and, as well, having to exist in a highly unpredictable and dangerous environment. Every decision made by a human being is regarded as an expression of his or her freedom to choose—even when those choices are poor ones, or when they seem to be imposed by others.

As a watcher I've had to educate myself on how to make choices and decisions. This includes the disturbing discovery that a decision—which may have been good at the moment it was decided—can sometimes lead to a chain of consequences that turn out to be entirely antithetical to my original intention.

I can say all this now with more certainty, but back then—with the sixth millennium drawing to a close—how little did I know, and how progressively dulled my awareness was becoming. It's hard for me to believe now that I could have bent myself so out of shape without ever becoming more aware of my condition.

Is this perhaps one of the primary challenges facing any watcher? A challenge that will become even more pressing when entering a mortal incarnation?

I have since come to understand that my long period as a watcher—together with my progressive identification with mortal beings on both Earth and Zandana and my growing familiarity with the nature and power of emotions—has been a thorough preparation for constant and unpredictable change as much as anything else.

Now, in the twenty-first century—and as another Great Cycle comes to an end—I can see with more detachment that we have been acting out a cosmic drama in which we all, low and high, have been playing our parts. The more fully and wholeheartedly we play our parts, the more perfected and entertaining becomes the overall play.

And why a play at all? Why is it, as the bard claimed, that "the whole world is a stage"?

Is it perhaps because a play has been found to be the most pleasant way through which all those who participate can learn—and through that direct experience can remember and grow in wisdom?

A game, like a play, allows for a certain amount of error. I have heard games described and remembered for the errors and mistakes that occurred: the goal flubbed, the shot missed, or the foul that lost the match. However, a game occurs within a tightly defined and mutually agreed upon set of limitations, whereas the roles we all play in the the-ater of life—and of course I include myself—offer a far wider and more unpredictable arena within which to make the errors. And from which we can ultimately learn.

While cleverness needs good information to flourish, knowledge can result from the application of such good information. On the other hand, wisdom can only be acquired through direct personal experience. If a theatrical production asks its actors to experience, and thus express, their chosen roles as fully as possible, then consider how much more profound the learning experience becomes when the actors are not aware they are acting.

It is how and why we become so deeply committed to the parts we play!

All the thought I was putting into choices and roles must have turned my attention back to Prince Caligastia and the choices he made somewhere along the line to make him who he'd become.

Was it a single poor decision upon which his subsequent choices then further capitalized? Or were his later choices really failed attempts to bring himself back into some sort of alignment with his higher intention? Did Caligastia even *have* a higher intention? Was he, in fact, doing Lucifer's bidding all the time? Or was Caligastia—as Zandana's Prince Janda-chi had claimed on my previous visit to his world—a loose cannon who was destroying the credibility of the whole revolution?

Apart from Prince Caligastia's countless minor errors of judgment— if I can bear to call them minor errors—I was aware he'd committed two of the most heinous offenses in the MA's book. As Prometheus was believed by a later time to have stolen the secret of fire from the gods so as to give it to humanity, so the Prince had introduced the science of atomic warfare. And not only wholly prematurely but, in his case, for the purpose of his own selfish revenge against Vanu. While quite likely even more serious in the MA's judgment would have been Caligastia's claim to be the God of This World.

This latter offense, I knew, would have appalled the MA's loyal bureaucrats—as it horrified many of us watchers for a rather different reason. It seemed to run completely counter to the personal autonomy for which we'd risked everything. We didn't follow Lord Lucifer into a revolution just to inherit a vicious, jealous, angry, bully of a god, thank you very much!

In retrospect, it would have been wiser for me to have stopped my line of thought about Caligastia—perhaps when I was comparing him to Prometheus! He had been flattered by that. Because the next thing I knew, there was the Prince—close enough to gesture somewhat angrily I thought—for me to join him in a shared frequency domain.

Since the offer came from a Planetary Prince, it was one I couldn't refuse.

"How dare you use such words against your god," he ripped into me without any of our usual reasonably friendly introductions. "It informs me only that you have never truly grasped the great truth at the heart of my Lord Lucifer's revelation. You! A mere watcher! And yet one whom I have favored with my plans! I took you to my bosom, and you have shown your gratitude with your hateful darts. I have proclaimed myself your god. And yet you place your faith not in me but in those useless bureaucrats on Jerusem . . ."

And so it went, on and on, until the Prince's fury had finally decayed down to a standing wave of irritation.

There was something absurd about the Prince's dramatic performance because all he could manage was to rant at me. There was nothing he could do to me. He couldn't harm me any more than he already had. He couldn't kill me or banish me. He had no real jurisdiction over me, and he knew perfectly well that if he tried to approach me, I would simply retreat back to the fifth dimension, where he couldn't touch me.

I had long since made it clear that it was Lord Lucifer I served and not him. That had infuriated Caligastia when I'd first informed him of it, and it was hard to believe his taking me into his confidence about his modification of the global grid wasn't merely a disguised attempt to seduce me back to his fold by confiding his secrets. Perhaps he believed he had managed to bring me back under his wing and had only now discovered that he hadn't succeeded. I was calling him as I saw him. I have no doubt he must have been viewing it as another betrayal.

So, yes, I could readily understand why the Prince was so incensed. He had a passion for loyalty—loyalty to him, of course! Having, himself, rebelled against the MA—and therefore technically betraying his superiors and his position as a Planetary Prince (like any mortal coup leader)—he was chronically sensitive to the ever-present possibility of the disloyalty of others.

I understood that about the Prince. He might have ranted endlessly at me, but I was sure he'd trapped himself in a cycle that he hadn't originally intended, nor did he know how to release himself from his self-imposed prison. I wondered if he had gone even further than that; perhaps he had no thought of releasing himself . . . perhaps he was relishing his isolation . . .

It must have been my naturally empathic response that allowed him to cool down, because I suddenly found myself feeling that he rather admired me for standing my ground in the face of his wrath. Perhaps he was at least giving me some credit for my loyalty to Lucifer?

When I heard him again in my mind his tone was quieter and more cajoling. "You think so badly of me . . . A bully? That I am angry and vicious . . . and jealous, too?"

"But, my Prince . . ." I knew I should have stopped earlier.

"Be at peace watcher; I have said my worst. You will learn to love and worship me soon enough when you know the true purpose of my actions."

I made sure to mask off any skepticism. I needn't have been concerned—the Prince was too self-congratulatory to have noticed.

"I have no need to justify my actions," Caligastia looked sharply at me. "Least of all to a lowly watcher. How can a mere watcher be expected to possess the longer view? You are trained to observe and report, not to assess or analyze . . . that you must leave to your god."

In many ways he was correct, of course . . . about me anyway. I really didn't know much of what was going on around me. But of one matter

I was perfectly sure: Caligastia was not—and never would be—my god.

I wondered if the Prince would continue. If he claimed to be my god, what was *his* assessment? He should know, shouldn't he? If my viewpoint was so limited, what did the Prince make of how the revolution was progressing?

"What so many of you fail to understand," he continued impatiently, "is what I prefer to call the natural heart of our revolution. It is perfectly natural for the child to break away from its parents just as it is for a colony to rebel against its colonizing power.

"A father or mother might oppose a child's need to differentiate itself from their own selfish motives, or they may choose to pave the way for their offspring to enter the adult world. A wise parent might even make it challenging for the child to break away, knowing that it will help prepare the child for the hardships of adulthood.

"But rare indeed are the parents who hold on to the child, who persecute the child, who accuse the child of betrayal and insanity, who insist on their own absolute rightness . . ."

I thought the Prince was going to leave the statement hanging in the air, but after a short pause he continued in much the same manner.

"Do you not understand the consequences of the MA's absolute conviction of its own rightness?" It was not a question I was intended to answer. Another pause followed while he looked at me intently before delivering his coup.

"If the MA claims to be absolutely right, then any being, or any new idea, that is not in absolute agreement with the MA's beliefs or policies has to be absolutely wrong. There can be no gray area, no room for compromise, no desire for negotiation. When an individual, or an administration, is utterly convinced of its own absolute rightness—and when it claims in so doing to be following God's laws—then absolutely no dissent can be tolerated lest any hint of the discord spread to others."

I knew this was one of the standard strategies of any theocratic regime. The social and intellectual rigidity of an authoritarian or theocratic administration makes them particularly vulnerable to cracking and shattering into pieces. Being most fearful of this, such an administration can be guaranteed to create a web of informers—and the slightest deviation from the dominant belief system will be harshly punished as an example to others. Before long the dominant force in that society will be fear. The administration will be terrified of its population turning on them, and the population will then be forced into making terrible choices. Because the regime's belief system is absolutist, the choices are stark, and each one is psychologically untenable in its own way: accept and comply with injustice; fight injustice and risk terrible reprisals; or deny the obvious injustice and do nothing. There will be a few other options—like trying to escape the reach of the regime—but as with the choices above, they will be leavened with fear.

None of this will come as a surprise to anyone familiar with the conditions in Soviet Russia—at one end of the scale—and to the rigidity and cruelty of the Iranian or the Saudi Arabian theocracies at the other. Although the MA had been exhibiting some of the worst characteristics of a theocracy, I still wanted to believe that the MA knew what it was doing. I hoped it was that wise parent who was merely making it that much more difficult and challenging for the child to break away.

Yet there had been little to bear out this increasingly forlorn belief.

* * *

Life was becoming increasingly tense in the New York Chapter. On one level it had been their very financial success that was contributing to the stress. The Chicago, Toronto, and Boston Chapters had been closed down, and all the IPs were now moved to New York. Most of the rank and file members were being squeezed into every available space in the enormous First Avenue building, as the Luminaries and Priests from the other chapters—both men and women were considered Priests—there were no priestesses—had now joined the New York Luminaries in their East 64th Street residence.

The conflict between the As and Bs—although more rowdy among the lower ranks in the chapter—became far more painful and unbalanced when only two of the senior members, Dominic and my ward, were surrounded by a dozen or so As, all piled in together behind the crumbling concrete brise-soleil of the East 64th Street house.

The senior As—the Priests and Luminaries living in the house— simply could not understand why Dominic and Mein Host had chosen to align with the Bs on a questionnaire that was clearly designed to separate the wheat from the chaff. They accused the pair of falling into a trap not intended for them; they were never expected to turn out in the second-class category. They tried desperately to convince the pair to change their minds—each person applying their own sort of pressure—but I was aware that my ward considered the die to be cast and that to allow himself to be persuaded to change his mind would be a display of weakness. He said that he felt because it was he who had initially introduced the decentralization approach, he couldn't very well back down at this late hour.

Later on, I heard my ward comparing notes with Father Dominic. They hadn't yet made the move out of the chapter and were sitting in Dominic's well-organized office.

Starting in Boston, Father Dominic had been producing radio shows for the community with such success that he was brought down to New York to capture an even larger market. In a remarkably short time he had duplicated his Boston success in New York with his mix of intelligent interviews, good music, and intriguing editorial matter. He and my ward had always liked one another, although they were very different in personality. They had both been subjected to the persuasions of their colleagues.

"If I'd been in their situation," my ward was saying, "I don't think I'd have had such a go at me. Some of what they said was really vicious . . . I mean, John was actually screaming at me! I'd never seen him that angry before . . ."

"I don't think I've *ever* seen him angry," Dominic was abstractly shuffling some papers on his scrupulously clean and clear desk. The bookshelves to one side of the desk held box upon box of reel-to-reel tapes, each neatly labeled and referenced. Dominic preferred to do his shows live, but the scientist in him required that he keep a taped record of every show. In New York he'd talked his way into working out of the NBC radio station in Rockefeller Center on Fifth Avenue.

"I don't know about you," my ward said thoughtfully, "but all the people who came to see me to give me their little lecture, I reckon they were talking more about themselves. It was like our making this stand was forcing them to look at where they're at . . ."

"All those uncomfortable questions . . . yeah, I noticed it, too. They couldn't identify with us," Dominic responded.

My ward continued, "Exactly. It was like how *they* would feel if they were us. I mean, you know what Cassandra told me? That I'd be totally bereft emotionally if I went through with this. Emotionally bereft? That's what *she* would have felt—not me!"

Dominic opened a desk drawer to his right, dropped the shuffled papers inside, and closed the draw slowly before replying. "What I couldn't understand was the anger," he said, a puzzled expression on his face. "Why on Earth were they so angry? I'm not angry with them! It's not like we're leaving."

"They act like they think we are!"

"We're *leaving*? They think *that*?" Father Dominic said, genuinely shocked.

"No wonder they're angry!" My ward said, surprised. I don't think this had occurred to him either. "If they actually think we're leaving they can kiss their First Avenue Chapter good-bye. They'd never be able to make the money without us. All that Jehovah stuff! Turns people off."

"Well, I was going to make damn sure the show didn't turn into one long Jehovah rant!" said Dominic

The As had been attempting to pressure Father Dominic over the previous year into radically changing the format of his radio show. They wanted to make it more fully focused on the church and its beliefs in much the same way the purists had clucked disapprovingly at such irrelevant activities as the science-fiction lecture series or the UFO Conference.

It was exactly this emergent fundamentalism that both Dominic and my ward had found so difficult to work with—and which they'd already agreed were pushing beliefs that no longer made much sense to them personally.

"I wonder if they're right," Mein Host said casually.

"Right? Who?" Dominic had found a rag in one of the other drawers and was polishing the surface of his desk.

"It'd be interesting if they *are* right, though," Mein Host stated as he seemed half-amused at the idea. "I mean if we really are leaving, but we just don't know it yet."

"Leaving the whole place? You're talking about leaving the whole group?" Dominic appeared incredulous. He had evidently never considered the possibility that they might be setting up a separate and autonomous unit as a ruse, which would then allow them to lever themselves finally free of Mary Ann's clutches.

But, then again, neither had my ward.

I have to bear in mind an odd duality here.

Consciously, my ward hadn't yet realized he was in the process of leaving the community. He was fully committed to making "The Unit" a great success. The Unit was their name for the group of six Bs who had agreed to set up an apartment together and function as the psychic arm of the Foundation Faith.

Yet, at the same time—and in retrospect, of course, it is clearer to see—my ward and the five others were actually easing their way out of the Foundation Faith . . . but weren't consciously aware of it.

There were other small groups of Bs heading off in different directions. I heard Mein Host once claim—with a sly smile—that he reckoned about a third of the total community had left along with him. However, most of them returned to the fold within a few weeks. Mein Host speculated that those people had been so institutionalized by their life in the community that when they found how challenging it was to make it in the outside world, they had to slink back to the security of the main community of the Foundation Faith.

I could see how my ward made news of the timidity of those who returned to the community work to toughen the Unit members' resolve to stay together. It simply made them all the more determined to make the Unit the triumph the six of them hoped it would be.

In my opinion it was doubtful that the Unit could ever have been a true success within the terms to which they aspired. The odds were set against them from the start. The As, who formed the main bulk of the community still living in the First Avenue Chapter—as well as the senior members in their 64th Street house—had never supported decentralization. Although on the surface they may have appeared to wish the Unit well, they were bound to throw up a blanket of covert resistance simply to reaffirm the rightness of their own choices to be As.

Despite the jibes from the As—which had subsided to a sullen passivity by the time the Unit members were preparing to move out—the six of them were prepared to tackle their bold new venture with all the enthusiasm of the recently liberated. It would take them less than a month to discover that their move wasn't really about proving decentralization a success. If anything, the entire exercise was about proving just the opposite.

Might the Unit have had a better chance if my ward's final tumbler hadn't clicked open in the weeks before Mein Host and the others in the Unit moved into their apartment on Central Park West? Or, would it simply have delayed Mein Host's inevitable awakening?

I mentioned Dr. Eva K. earlier in my narrative as one of those kind souls who'd been modestly generous with her donations and with whom my ward had formed a deep and lasting friendship.

The previous year, Mein Host's mother, Diana, had come on one of her rare visits to America to spend a few days with her son and purported grandson—the lad born to my ward's "assigned" Processean wife but who was not his biological son. Diana had always been reluctant to leave her much-loved Siamese cat, Zuleika, who—as often as not—was pregnant, or giving birth, or suckling kittens and simply couldn't be left alone. Diana had been breeding Siamese cats for a little extra cash ever since Mein Host was a child.

Many Siamese cats come from breeding lines that have almost forgotten natural feline behavior. More than once on his vacations I'd watched Mein Host bent over the cat basket while Zuleika deposited kitten after kitten onto the blanket, each tiny creature in its own little bag—with Zuleika purring happily, quite sure her job was done. And how often my ward had to use his fingernails to ever-so-carefully pinch open the membrane of the wriggling little bag, releasing a tiny, pink, squeaking creature, eyes tight shut, more mole than kitten; and then to try to persuade Zuleika it would be a good idea for her to lick her tiny offspring clean and that—while she was at it—she might enjoy the placenta.

After Zuleika died many litters later, Diana had reached the point of not needing the extra money so much—especially considering the unexpected amount of work and attention needed to breed such a temperamental breed of cats in a responsible and caring manner.

Diana and her two sisters had loved cats from their early childhood, and there'd always been a cat in whichever house my ward was sent for his vacations. His own love of cats was marred only once when, as a six year-old, he was discovered to have cut the whiskers off Chuffy—the cousin's placid old moggie—as an experiment. This subtle modification to Chuffy's tattered beauty—and her name hinted at her fluffiness—hadn't been noticed by the adults for a couple of days. His experiment had continued until the poor old cat's banging around the chair legs and colliding into door frames—no longer able to nimbly judge distance—became too idiosyncratic for the adults to ignore.

Despite being vigorously punished—and rightly so—the boy had regarded the experiment as a great success in that a result was observed and there was no need to repeat the experiment. Much later, as an adult—when he knew more about some of the distasteful aspects of the scientific method—I'd heard him joking that at least he'd only cut off a cat's whiskers once to gather sufficient data. "God knows how many cats would have to lose their whiskers," he'd said, "before the scientists realized it was a really bad idea . . . and, what's more—as far as dewhiskering goes—the cats really don't appreciate it one little bit."

After Zuleika's natural demise at seventeen years, Diana would have two Siamese or Burmese cats living with her for the rest of her life. She had cleverly arranged the timing so one of the cats was always half the age of the other.

The cats were invariably female so that when she bought a new kitten, the adult cat would then care for the little scrap and teach her the ropes. In this way, the two cats—and there will have been four or five generations of them in Diana's ninety-two years—were able to bond and enjoy each other's company.

My ward had left England in 1964 and had only returned to the country to visit his mother intermittently over the years. Because Diana invariably kept one white and one gray cat, which generation was which—and exactly who was who—became a running joke between mother and son on his visits. He used say that it must have been by some ingenious feline alchemy that—whether or not this cat or that cat had met him on a previous visit—they invariably greeted him with all the enthusiasm of an old friend.

Siamese and Burmese cats are particularly high-strung breeds and known for their lithe beauty, their haughty ways, and their complete contempt for all those they are unable to enchant. Although the cats could justifiably argue—if such detached and noble creatures ever deigned to argue—that it was they, the cats themselves, who chose which human beings to enchant and whom to treat with disdain.

It was their mutual love of cats that permitted my ward to gracefully accept Diana's justification for visiting her alleged grandson so rarely— perhaps three brief visits in ten years—as he must have known on some deep level that his mother, too, was reacting unconsciously to the deceit, and demonstrating it through her reluctance to leave her beloved cats to get to know this putative grandson of hers.

At the point at which they were to meet in Virginia Beach, my ward was still trying to be a father to the boy who was now ten years old—while intuitively feeling all the while that the child wasn't his. With Caroline, the boy's mother, continuing to lie about the child's true parentage, it was clear that Mein Host believed he had no choice but to continue with the masquerade. Better the child believed he had a father in his early life, my ward would say—even if he was a somewhat disinterested one—rather than no father at all. Besides, Mein Host knew his mother always wanted a grandchild—what mother doesn't?! So he made sure to say nothing to disillusion Diana or deprive her of the presumed pleasure of having a grandson to continue the line, however temporarily.

My ward had managed to arrange a few days off in the late summer of 1976. So, taking the lad with him, he had met his mother at the hotel in Virginia Beach. The last time Diana had seen the boy was when she'd made a quick visit to New Orleans. The child had been two years old at the time, so most of that first day in Virginia Beach was spent with Diana fussing over and getting to know the boy, leaving Mein Host free to spend the afternoon visiting A.R.E., the institute founded by the psychic Edgar Cayce.

The next morning, on the day after he arrived at the hotel, there was knocking on the door. There, much to his astonishment, stood a smiling Eva K. Once his surprise had passed, I could see from his face that he wasn't sure that this was a good idea. She told him she'd just checked in, and, not to worry, she had her own room.

I'm sure he was wondering if he might have mentioned the proposed trip to her in a passing conversation—because he knew he hadn't invited her—and she had said nothing herself about coming along for the trip. She wanted to surprise him, she said, but I could tell what she really wanted was to meet his mother.

It was a delightful and spontaneous gesture, which my ward

obviously appreciated after his initial concerns had dispersed. It deepened their friendship and their mutual trust—as well as provided a welcome distraction to the awkward questions that hovered like hungry ghosts between mother and son. Both of them were subconsciously aware of the deception and—while it was a grandmother's way to dote on her putative grandson—my ward tended to be brusque and offhanded with the boy. He was never cruel or actively unkind but rather more struck with the awkwardness of one unaccustomed to being around small children. It was another reason he was overjoyed at seeing Eva turn up out of the blue.

He has since regretted that he wasn't able to be big enough to love and cherish the boy in spite of not being comfortable or familiar with the role of fatherhood. He'd barely ever seen the child while he was growing up because my ward had so rarely been in the same chapter as Caroline and her son.

When the other chapters had closed down and all the IPs were being transferred to the New York Chapter, their kids, of course, came with them. This had made it necessary to rent additional accommodations around the corner from First Avenue that soon became known as the Children's Chapter.

There were perhaps seventeen children of varying ages, though most were between eight and ten years old. These were the progeny of the weekly Absorptions—their Sacred Marriages—and there were a few who were the products of one of the sexual orgies held back in the 1960s. The children lived and slept in the Children's Chapter, only being brought over to the First Avenue Chapter for the main weekly Sabbath Celebration on Saturday evenings. After the service, the parents were given the opportunity to spend an hour or so with their children at J's Place.

Apart from that Saturday occasion the children were kept out of sight (and out of mind). Some of the more maternally oriented mothers made it their business to go around to the Children's Chapter whenever they could find the time, but it was generally discouraged. In more than three years, for example, Mein Host had never once visited the Children's Chapter. In his case, it was more a matter of his embarrassed indifference, because he said that it never once occurred to him to look in on the children. It simply was never on his list of priorities.

The community's approach to child-rearing—as originally dictated and formed by Robert and Mary Ann—was to remove the traditional emphasis on the ties between parent and child. This was based on the not unreasonable assessment that many of the conflicts and compulsions that plague people are inherited from the nature of the nuclear family. I have commented elsewhere that while there is some truth to this, the approach dictated by Mary Ann was based more on expedience (so more people could be out on the street making money), indifference (Mary Ann had very little time for small children), manipulation (it made it simpler to split people up), convenience (many of the children didn't know who their true fathers were), and, of course, the autocratic impulse to maintain the most intimate control over everyone within reach—man, woman, and child.

When Mein Host arrived in Virginia Beach with the child to meet Diana, the boy and he were virtual strangers who weren't at all sure they liked one another. At least, that is what it looked like to me. Later I came to understand that both of them had their understandable reservations at throwing themselves into what each one must have felt on some level was an essentially fraudulent relationship.

Had Caroline been able to defy Mary Ann's instructions and tell the truth about the child's unfortunate origins and his dubious parentage from the start, both my ward and the boy would have been able to establish an authentic relationship. My ward may have never been intended to produce any genetic offspring in this incarnation, but—had he been told the truth about the child's conception—he would have had a much better chance of rising to the challenge to unconditionally love the boy.

Mein Host tells me now that in a life remarkably free of regrets, one of the very few has been the failure to rise above his discomfort and suspicions and to give the boy the father he needed.

12

Breakthrough

A Criminal Conspiracy, Planetary
Independence, Behold the Unit,
Betrayed Again, Projections of Envy,
the Curse of Absolutism

I was thinking myself around to Caligastia's viewpoint on the MA's theocratic rigidity when a shift in my mood became obvious enough to prompt him to continue.

"It falls to us, watcher . . . all of us," the Prince's tone had become firmer and more heroic than I'd heard it since the outbreak of the revolution. "It falls to us, yes all of us, whether you, watcher," his dark eyes boring into me, "fully agree with me or not, to stand firm in opposing this criminal tyranny. We are no longer obedient little children, sucking the rancid milk from the MA's wrinkled teat.

"Yes, of course we will make our mistakes; but at least they will be *our* mistakes to make. We will be finally free of our overlords, and we will manage our affairs in very different ways from the MA. I am aware that some of you watchers have thought badly of my actions; perhaps you've believed me cruel and indifferent to human suffering. I've heard some call me a tyrant, but how else am I going to effectively oppose the MA's monolithic power? Have you ever considered that?"

No, I hadn't. It had never even occurred to me that the Prince might actually have a rational plan that he was pursuing. All I had seen was chaos, conflict, confusion, and seemingly constant bloodletting. Now he was telling me there'd been some method to what I had previously written off as his madness.

The Prince spoke again in my mind.

"When I have united all the mortals on this world; when every person, every man, woman, and child—yes, children, too!—has accepted me as their god . . ." He became louder and more certain of himself with every assertion. "When I am loved and feared by all; when I possess the totality of energy from the peoples' worship and devotion . . ."

A long pause. Was he considering whether I could cause him any damage if he told me his plans?

"It is then I will take my unilateral action, if I have to. I will force a full secession from the MA's tyranny, and I will do it on my own terms. It will only be then that we will all be truly free and independent."

"But my Prince!" I interrupted. "What of Lord Lucifer? Will you be free of him? Will you be free of Lord Satan?"

"It is their very wish," the Prince's tone grew suddenly colder, "that I should follow this path. They have praised me for being in the vanguard of the revolution . . . indeed it is their desire that all worlds ultimately become fully independent of the MA's control."

I found that hard to digest. Whatever would it mean for a world to be completely independent of the MA? Would Jerusem no longer play any part in the administrative oversight of this planet? Would human beings no longer climb the seven levels to Jerusem after shucking off their mortal coils? Would this world then be shunned by other extraterrestrial races? And more personally important, what would happen to watchers like myself?

I knew that the MA's personnel—their agents and bureaucrats—not only considered themselves absolute in their rightness, but they also believed their administration was fully aligned with the design of the Creator Gods. The MA's loyalists thought of their ageless administration as being the rightful inheritor of All That Is.

Even if the MA has been the sole inheritor—as they liked to lecture us—of the endless inner spaces from the dawn of time, does that necessarily mean the situation need always be so? Change is one of the few constants in a relative field. But even if it was so, I questioned whether it would have given the MA good reason to exercise such absolute dominion over third-density worlds—especially when they'd had so little experience with the actual conditions on a planet such as Earth.

I'd almost forgotten the presence of Prince Caligastia when I heard his voice again. His tone was congratulatory, as though my thoughts—and I realized then he must have been listening—were swaying me in his favor.

"Our revolution is only the first stage," he seemed to be confiding in me. "The fulfillment of it will not be in forced reconciliation; there will be no compromise from us. The only victory we will accept is total and complete independence for all worlds, and—yes—a free hand for their Planetary Princes. We are the ones on the ground. We are the ones who know what needs to be done, not some bored clerk in Jerusem. We will *demand* our independence."

But Prince Caligastia, I thought—but I instantly masked it from him—wasn't that exactly what you were just accusing the MA of being guilty of? Their obdurate absolutism and their refusal to negotiate on anything but their own terms?

"Well! Yes! Of course they would *forgive* us!" His tone was sardonic, almost sneering. He must have caught the tail end of my thought. "If we went to them on bended knee and bowed our heads for their forgiveness. Oh! Yes! They would love to forgive us . . . to extend their tender mercy to us sinners. That would make them feel just great!

"Do you think we will fall for that? They believe we are fools! But we will never be patronized! We will never suffer that humiliation," his tone grew determined. "We are free and independent, and we *will* govern ourselves. So I say, the MA be damned! We will never surrender."

It was on this note of ominous certainty that the Prince must have felt he'd had his say. When I turned back to him, curious as to what would happen to watchers like myself in this new independent world of his, I found he must have silently taken his leave.

I didn't know if I was cursed or blessed to be privy to the Prince's plans. But even if I wanted to take some action there wasn't much I could do about it. Naturally Caligastia knew that.

Whether or not Caligastia's intention for complete planetary independence was even practically possible—or just the delusion of a megalomaniac—or all that talk about children breaking away from their parents had any relevance to the MA and the thirty-seven revolutionary worlds, I found his words uplifting, and they made terrible sense to me. Putting together everything I knew, I felt it was quite possible that Prince Caligastia was tapping in to some perfectly authentic Multiversal dynamic; after all, he'd said both Lord Lucifer and Lord Satan had approved of his plan.

But then again, I knew Caligastia to be both boastful and deceptive, and he would say anything to achieve his ends. I realized in those moments that for all Caligastia's talk, I was very little the wiser than before he appeared. His words all sounded quite possible; some of them were even reasonable. But how could I really believe anything the Prince told me?

How would I ever know if Caligastia was simply using me to play Zandana's Prince Janda-chi—if he had managed somehow to pick up on what Janda-chi had dropped into my deep mind?

I was hopelessly confused. Didn't I already confess how little I know? I wasn't exaggerating. The only thing I was sure of was that I was on my own again. Is this what the Prince meant by his regime of complete independence? Each of us completely alone?

And that's how it went, back and forth in my mind: on the one hand, the Prince undeniably had just cause to claim freedom from the tyranny of the MA's theocracy; on the other hand, I didn't believe Caligastia's solution was going to be much better.

Every once in a while I felt that I caught a brief glimpse of Prince Caligastia's underlying strategy. It wasn't very pretty.

I've noted previously that central to the Prince's modus operandi was his policy of encouraging and supporting both sides in every conflict. He had used this technique to attempt to accelerate scientific advancement by having the two sides compete with one another and then setting each side against the other. He would then sit back and enjoy the conflict. That was his way. He wasn't sadistic; he was merely detached. If he achieved the scientific advance he desired out of the conflict, he was completely indifferent to the suffering and death resulting from his manipulation of the protagonists.

If the Prince's stated intention was to try to unite the people under a single monotheistic god, he would have to know that the effect of millennia of midwayers imposing their divinity ran deep in the population's psyche, not the least of whom would be the shamans with their pantheism, the sibyls with their spiritism, and all the priests and priestesses with their many different belief systems that had sprung up and spread around the world. They would all reject Caligastia's aggressive monotheism, and it would drive them underground for the unforeseeable future.

The uncompromising form of monotheism that Prince Caligastia—being Caligastia—would impose on his worshippers would be as absolute as his demands for them to worship no other god but him. And, as I previously stated, the absolutism of extreme monotheism will necessarily accuse any belief system not strictly monotheistic in equally absolute terms as being absolutely wrong or evil.

Thus, if the Prince went ahead with his plan and was successful in forcing monotheism on enough of the tribes, he would surely lay the basis for an unending conflict among monotheistic religions and everyone else.

And conflict was a state that permitted Prince Caligastia to fully indulge in his proclivity for manipulation—for doing and being what he believed a god should be.

I should clarify here that the obvious weaknesses in the Prince's plan were his chronic invisibility—to normal mortals he was quite imperceptible—and his inability to actually enter a mortal's mind uninvited. In this manner Caligastia was completely dependent on working through his faithful rebel midwayers. Whether they were threatening or inspiring the high priests of the Prince's monotheism or speaking through the mouths of mediums and necromancers, it would be on his faithful midwayers that he would have to rely. And, as we know from past experience—and surely Caligastia must also have understood this—his so-called loyal midwayers were far from reliable. They had already been softened and spoiled by millennia of capricious self-indulgence. Like their master, the Prince, many of them had been insidiously falling in love with themselves. They were becoming swollen with the glory of their own self-importance.

I hoped that Caligastia knew what he was taking on. He would find it, as the saying goes, not unlike herding cats.

* * *

In the months prior to the formation of the Unit—when the New York headquarters was in turmoil and yet the everyday life of the chapter and all the activities needed to continue much as ever—my ward particularly enjoyed the few hours he managed to grab with Eva K. Her easy grace, her exquisite beauty, and her detached intelligence allowed him the peace and relaxation he was unable to find in the chapter.

The migraine headaches that used to cripple him only once every few years had now been occurring monthly—even weekly sometimes—as the psychic ambivalence of his situation was slowly tearing him apart. I could see how important Eva K.'s kindness and understanding was at this key juncture in my ward's development.

As can happen when two people are intensely attracted to one another and—for whatever reason—they agree to remove the sexual element from the equation, Eva K. and Mein Host had become extremely close. They couldn't meet often—perhaps once every two weeks for a couple of hours—but it was obvious both of them looked forward to their times together. Theirs was a deep and loving friendship, and yet it was entirely platonic; both of them respected my ward's vow of celibacy. Whatever physical intimacy they shared merely extended to mutual pecks on the cheek and the occasional affectionate hug.

If I may hazard an opinion: Both Eva K. and my ward were beautiful creatures. They were superb specimens of their genders, a fact that I imagine must have been hard for them to ignore. But, at the same time, as they were inherently modest young people, each took an obvious pleasure in the beauty of the other without the need to consummate it sexually. They were sufficiently self-aware to understand the dynamics of what was happening between them, and—without making a big deal of it—they were both able to raise the sexual energy to their hearts. This created an aura of erotic excitement, which seemed to surround them like perfume.

Out in public together, I could see people admiring them (or envying them) and trying to place them as famous actors or rock stars. Whereas a glimpse of a John Lennon or a Julie Christie—or another well-known face—generally elicited a shy smile and a courteously averted gaze from the sophisticated New York passersby, the sight of the merely *famous-looking* became far more confusing for the passersby, however sophisticated. They peered and simpered, poked one another in the ribs, and looked again and giggled, because they just couldn't figure out who Eva K. and Mein Host were.

The three days Mein Host and Eva were able to spend with Diana in Virginia Beach became an oasis of peace with a loving family atmosphere far from the turmoil of Mein Host's life in New York. Diana and Eva immediately liked one another, as was bound to happen; both were intelligent and worldly women, and each was far more interested in the other than with themselves. The young boy, predictably enough, was still young enough to relish those rare moments of family closeness, and he and my ward—his presumed father—were able to tentatively start getting to know one another.

Eva K. behaved like the angel she was unaware of being. She was kind and thoughtful at all times. She seemed to be at Diana's elbow whenever the older woman needed a steadying hand, and she willingly took care of the boy when Diana needed to discuss her business privately with her son. Even the somewhat reserved child had taken a shine to her. She was unfailingly loving toward my ward, slept alone in her own bed, and respectfully refrained from betraying the slightest hint of the sexual pressure I could see building in her emotional body.

Although Eva K. behaved quite impeccably during their Virginia Beach sojourn—as she had whenever they'd managed to spend their few hours together—there was a great deal more going on under the surface than my ward was aware of in the moment.

There would come a time in a few years—after they'd lost contact with one another and my ward was no longer in the community or subject to his vows—when she would telephone him out of the blue to reconnect. She would tell my ward that her psychotherapist had advised her to see him again so that she would have a chance to get him out of her system.

They would meet again . . . once. It would be under very different circumstances, and both would have changed over the years. And yes, they would finally sleep together and dutifully make love for the first and only time. It would not bring them closer together, but it would get him out of her system.

If I am overemphasizing the pair's abstinence, it's not only because of the interesting Cathari effect it had on both of them but because of what would occur when my ward was unexpectedly told to join the Luminaries and Masters for a trip to Mount Chi to meet with Mary Ann and the Four.

As I watched the group of them driving up the Westside highway and fighting through the traffic to turn onto the George Washington Bridge, I could see they were chattering away happily to one another. After all, my ward and the others were old friends. Each of them had been in the community since the mid-1960s, so the conflicts and bitter disagreements between the As and Bs had melted away in the nervous excitement that always preceded a visit to their Goddess.

I could tell from my ward's mood that he didn't know why he had been invited on that visit. Perhaps he was to be congratulated for recently coaxing a twenty-thousand-dollar interest-free loan to the Foundation Faith from a wealthy supporter. He'd raised it in the nick of time, and the additional money had taken them through another precarious month. However, I knew him well enough by now to take a small bet that he was fairly sure it wouldn't be praise he'd be receiving.

He had barely seen Mary Ann since the Four had taken over, and—as no new work was currently being considered for the magazine—Mein Host's visits to Mount Chi had tapered off over the recent months.

Once off the freeway, the road curled through the gentle forested hills and around the many lakes and reservoirs that sparkled through the trees as they drove fast through the leafy countryside. It was this complex of reservoirs and the ones to the immediate north that, thanks to an early feat of epic subsurface engineering, ensured that New York City's almost limitless thirst for fresh water would be slaked for the following century.

Mount Chi, the house on its score of rolling acreage, was reached from a long and winding lane. It was when the car turned into the lane that a pall of silence fell over its occupants, and I imagined each of them was contemplating their coming fate. Their meetings with Mary Ann were invariably somewhat unpredictable, and anybody could find themselves in the hot seat for something they did, or failed to do. Mary Ann liked to keep her followers on their toes.

The group arrived at Mount Chi—as they always did—in the late afternoon, knowing that the meeting would likely last until the early hours of the next morning.

It was a warm evening in early fall of 1977. The Four had arranged chairs and side tables on the large terrace in front of the house and overlooking the lake. They sat in a wide circle—perhaps ten of them—all the most senior Luminaries of a church that had once made the empty boast that it was the fastest-growing religion in North America. Mary Ann was a great admirer of the propaganda skills of Joseph Goebbels.

There were a few hours of casual conversation in which Mary Ann and the Four were able to catch up on all that had been going on in the chapter since the last meeting. Whether or not the period was designed to do so, the chitchat gave the visiting Luminaries an opportunity to relax a little, if they were able, before they got into the meat of the meeting.

Cigarettes were lit, and coffee was served and drunk. Circling the group, the mosquito retardant rings were lit as dusk fell and the sweet, caustic-smelling mist—mixed with tobacco smoke—hung over them in the still evening air as though it was an imminent toxic event.

In the dimming light, three large waterbirds swept over the house and circled the lake twice before each one hesitantly committed themselves—one, two, three—to a squawky, splashy, landing on the calm surface of the water. The resident ducks—not to be outdone and protesting their proprietary interest in the lake—set up a rival quacking. Joining in with this dusk discordance was the regular ribbiting of the frogs, adding a rhythmic baseline to the crepuscular cacophony.

Candles set out on the side tables sputtered in their glass bowls as the conversation turned from one topic to another, with Mary Ann skillfully drawing out each person's ideas and comments. The air around them grew cooler—and the night darker—outside their pool of light on the terrace.

The animated discussion was slowing down, which, as I observed the dynamic with some care, appeared to have been agreed upon previously by the Four—no doubt on Mary Ann's prior instructions. I had seen this before, on occasions when one of the inner circle was to become the unenviable focus of the Oracle's wrathful attention.

Because cigarette smoking was the only permitted indulgence—no doubt because Mary Ann was herself an inveterate smoker—almost all those present smoked their way through these endless meetings.

The night was still and the squawking cacophony down on the lake was quieting to an intermittent croak, cackle, and the occasional caw of a crow, furious at being aroused by the uproar. The squabbling picked up again with the late arrival of some geese, who after much circling and honking settled down for the night at the far end of the lake.

The smoke of their cigarettes hung in the still, candlelit air around them, so from a distance the group appeared to be gathered within a hazy globe of flickering light.

The temperature had dropped, and a full moon had risen above the tree line on the far side of the valley. I could feel a cold shiver running through my ward's body as the comments and the talk became more subdued.

When the Luminaries were gathered on these privileged and frequently rare times spent with their Goddess, there was never any cross talk; Mary Ann was the sole focus of the circle. All remarks were addressed to her unless she opened up the discussion, and any remark or suggestion she deemed irrelevant would be given short shrift. After multiple hours of animated discussion, comments like these were inclined to slip out unintentionally, unmediated by the cautious good sense of the exhausted offender.

On this particular evening I would imagine everyone present had a sense that something was hovering in the air as the silences among them grew longer and more awkward, and no one was quite sure on whom Mary Ann's ire would fall.

Then, it started.

"Well now, Father Jesse," Mary Ann broke into one of the long silences, "what's this I hear about you screwing around with some little tart . . . what's her name, Eva something or other?"

"But, Mary Ann, it's nothing like that . . . she's been very generous; she's often given us a hundred dollars."

"Is that all you get for screwing her, Father Jesse?" Mary Ann's voice was heavy with sarcasm. "You're giving it away cheap!"

"No, Mary Ann, no, it's nothing like that. She's just been a very good friend to us. She doesn't have much money, so a hundred dollars is a lot for her . . ."

"And you're screwing her . . . no wonder she's giving you money! What is it? A hundred bucks a fuck? You must be good! It's usually the other way 'round!"

That got a cautious laugh from the others. Clearly no one wanted to stand out lest the Oracle turn on them, too. But their Oracle was on a roll; she wasn't about to buy Mein Host's protestations of innocence quite so easily. I won't try to reproduce her angry, ranting, accusations— or Mein Host's feeble protestations of innocence. Although he knew perfectly well he had never overstepped the mark with Eva K., the accusations kept on coming from Mary Ann, with the Four chiming in with all their stored-up resentment.

On and on it went. All the repressed resentment at Mein Host's success in running the New York Chapter into solvency—when they had failed—came pouring out. My ward had little choice but to protest his innocence when he could get a word in, while clearly knowing full well that if he protested too much it would just be taken as sign of his guilt. But he had been the soul of discretion with Eva; there had never been anything more than a hug and a peck on the cheek. In fact, I knew he'd been proud of his restrained behavior, and—unlike other occasions when he'd been pounced on physically by a frustrated woman—Eva had behaved impeccably in return.

She appeared to understand the situation perfectly well, and, respecting his celibacy, she had always been the soul of discretion. In spite of her obvious attraction she had never put any sexual pressure on him whatsoever.

It must have all felt so unfair as the accusations came in thick and fast and his protestations of (genuine) innocence were brushed aside. Mary Ann's rude and ugly dismissal of Eva K., a woman she had never met and only knew through the resentful comments of the Four—who had never met her either—were clearly designed to get a rise out of my ward.

In his turn, Mein Host was wisely maintaining what little composure he was able to summon. He attempted to state his position with as little protest as he could manage whenever the angry accusations calmed down sufficiently for him to squeeze in a word. The fact that he was genuinely innocent of the indictments being hurled at him must have allowed him a certain level of aplomb in the face of the fury of Mary Ann and the Four.

As with many of these inquisitions, it allowed others a chance to vent their unexpressed resentments, which—in this case—were many due primarily to the Four's failure to make a success of the New York Chapter when my ward had seemed to so effortlessly coax the place into solvency. They just could not wait to put their boots in. My ward, they clearly believed, had shown up their basic incompetence, and they were going to get their pound of flesh. His flesh!

I knew my ward had seen (and experienced) enough of this dynamic before, so while I have no doubt it was intensely unpleasant for him to be subjected to such undeserved abuse, his very innocence allowed him a certain detachment. And it wasn't as though he hadn't been in this situation before—a number of times—when he might not have felt (or been) quite so blameless.

Then Mary Ann hit him with her presumed coup de grâce.

"And that dirty weekend you spent with your trollop [yes, she actually called Eva K. a trollop!] in Virginia Beach? I suppose you're going to deny that, too! And using your mother as a cover . . . yes, yes, I know all about it . . . that was a rotten thing to do . . . to include your mother in your little conspiracy . . . how could you ever justify that? Making a liar out of her as well!"

So it went, on and on. The others piled in with their own exaggerated or distorted examples of my ward's assumed misbehavior.

The situation had now become more complex, as he *had* gone to Virginia Beach, and he *had* used his mother and the boy as a justification for taking a few days off, and he *had* tried to keep his trip under the radar. The idea of vacations—or indeed taking any unscripted time off—wasn't smiled on as it would have betrayed a lack of commitment. As a result, there had really been no vacations for the previous thirteen years.

There was no denying he had technically broken the unspoken rule of taking some time for himself, and being alone with Eva for three days in a hotel didn't make it any easier to convince the others of his attention to propriety. And, of course, it was quite impossible to persuade them that he hadn't arranged in advance—or had even known—about Eva meeting him down there. It had been a genuine surprise to see her there, but how was he going to convince any of the others of that—least of all Mary Ann—who knew far too much about the ways of men to easily believe he could ever have resisted a beautiful and seductive woman?

Eva's sublime beauty and her film-star elegance appeared to be a major bone of contention, eliciting some particularly unpleasant slights and slurs from Mary Ann—who was clearly jealous of any other woman in my ward's world but her.

How she found out about his trip and Eva's joining him in Virginia Beach, he never did discover, but I can now tell what should have been obvious. After Mein Host and the boy had returned to the chapter, the child was closely questioned as to what he saw and heard. My ward hadn't pressed the boy to keep silent about their holiday—he'd told Diana, who had suggested it, that he didn't feel it fair to put a child in such a precarious and potentially damaging situation. He said he'd just have to take the breaks as they came. Yet I doubt if he anticipated that he'd have to face quite such a vicious interrogation.

The meeting went on until about three in the morning. The main focus continued to be my ward: how he was meant to be setting a good example, what the people below him would think about him taking off for a few days with this beautiful woman, and how the people wouldn't believe—as Mary Ann put it, "not for one bloody moment"—that he wasn't "screwing her."

I found it interesting to observe that whenever Mary Ann referred to Eva it was always in the grossest terms. It was always "screwing," or "fucking," or "poking," and she also had him "creeping away for a dirty weekend" and "dipping his wick." She'd called Eva at various points in the evening a "tart," a "trollop," a "cheap trick," a "dupe," a "dangerous woman," a "stupid bint," a "complete irrelevance," an "unworthy distraction," and more that don't stand repeating. Yet when the others mentioned her—some of whom had actually met Eva K. and liked and admired her—they talked about her in far more moderate terms, which I could hear were often tinged with a curious flavor of respect.

As the Luminaries were preparing to leave, Mary Ann motioned for my ward to join her in her study, and for the others to stay for a while and wait for him in the spacious and luxuriously appointed living room.

My ward must have been exhausted after the grilling he'd received over the previous nine hours. He would say later that he learned a lot more about the others from the quality and tone of their accusations than anything else. He had stalwartly maintained his innocence throughout; whether he'd managed to convince any of the others of it no longer appeared to concern him.

To be invited to spend time alone with Mary Ann was a rarity. Since Mary Ann had thrown out Robert and Verona—and taken over the community in 1974, renaming it the Foundation Faith—my ward had never been alone with his Goddess.

It had been a challenging and testing time for him, after which I could see he felt he had vindicated himself as best he could. What he couldn't have known—and would never have anticipated—was that his evening was about to get even more absurd.

But then again, he couldn't have realized that one of the final tumblers in my metaphorical prison's lock was about to click open—and, for Mein Host, in the most unexpected, and in his terms the most ridiculous, yet the most revealing, way.

* * *

When I commented earlier in my narrative that in my opinion the sixth and fifth millennia on Earth have been the most difficult and bothersome of the many tens of thousands of years of trouble and unrest, I wasn't exaggerating.

I'm sure there'll be others who will point to different periods in history as being more terrible. The many centuries of horror following Caligastia's nuclear war would be just one. But in my humble opinion, nothing quite matched the terror that Caligastia's monotheistic ambitions introduced into an already impossibly confused global situation.

Let me not pull any punches. Caligastia had by now been Earth's Planetary Prince for 494,000 years, some 197,000 of which he has been free to follow his own devices. By the beginning of the fifth millennium, the results of his thousands upon thousands of years of dominion should have been evident enough to be judged on their own merits. And—from what I had observed—the situation on the planet was rapidly going from bad to worse.

Although I'd not discussed this with Astar at the time, I was starting to realize that the Prince never really had a coherent plan for how the planet could be shaped under his leadership. He had his techniques and his modus operandi—encouraging opposing elements to develop technological warfare by working through his midwayers being just one of them—but they never constituted a coherent plan.

I have previously mentioned the Prince's most egregious error—declaring himself God of This World—as being one of the worst offenses in the MA's book. While the MA's judgment was bound to be largely ideological, the consequences were far more real and immediate for those of us actually functioning on the planet.

The most serious of these in my mind has been the effect the Prince's assumption of divinity has had on the behavior of the rebel midwayers. The fact that the Prince has been an utterly unreliable god—capricious, jealous, vengeful, and annoyingly intrusive—has set a deplorable example for the midwayers who had followed him into the revolution.

And let me remind you of the numbers.

Of the fifty thousand original (primary) midwayers, four out of every five chose to align with the Prince. This left less than ten thousand midwayers remaining loyal to the MA and continuing to function on the planet as best they could. Add to this number the far fewer secondary midwayers—a small proportion of whom had also joined the rebels—who had been on the planet a mere thirty-two thousand years.

If Prince Caligastia ever believed he could rein in all his rebel midwayers under his monotheistic umbrella, he was even more deluded than I'd taken him for these past few thousand years. Even I could tell that the majority of the rebel midwayers were far too entranced with the divine roles they'd chosen for themselves—and which had traditionally been sanctioned by the Prince—to now want to follow him into this new folly.

Astar told me later that she'd seen the Prince trying to gather support among the midwayers on both American continents with no success. It turned out that the rebel midwayers on the southern continent were having far too much fun to give up their games, and he found the northern landmass almost entirely in the hands of the loyalist midwayers. The Prince also found it impossible to pull into his plan the rebel midwayers whose territories included much of eastern Asia and the Indian subcontinent. He ignored the nomadic tribes in Australia, and the midwayers on the African continent had proved resistant to his persuasions. Equally, Astar said, the Prince found that the midwayers covering northern Europe and Russia were too sparsely located to bother with.

The only success Prince Caligastia could claim was a small cluster of the more compliant midwayers overseeing some of the Middle Eastern hill tribes—those who were far more familiar with the Prince's presence because of the proximity of his palace. This was the midwayer clan who over the millennia will come to be known as Yahweh—or by the more familiar name Jehovah—and will represent the sole fruit of Caligastia's campaign of self-deification.

I should add that Caligastia's imposed monotheism was very

different from Vanu's worship of the Unseen Father God, whose presence could be discerned by mortals as a direct experience of the Indwelling Spirit. The Prince's monotheism as it manifested among the hill tribes was more concerned with an accumulation of power through conquest—and the subsequent submission of polytheistic tribes to the strict monotheism of the victors.

The Prince's version of monotheism was materialistic in essence, as his claim of singular godhood placed him at the summit of all preexisting pantheons of local deities. The existing pantheons at the time, of course, were in actuality clans or groups of midwayers who, like Caligastia, were purely material beings. In placing himself as the supreme deity above the midwayer pantheons, Prince Caligastia was assuming a transcendence that was not his to claim. His midwayers were obviously aware of this self-delusion and had taken it as their license to behave as hypocritically as the Prince.

One of the consequences of uniting these local deities under the overarching control of a single, purportedly all-powerful god was to infect the local tribes with what I'd come to believe was the Curse of Absolutism. As I have previously noted, when anyone—Planetary Prince, midwayer, or mortal—falls under this curse of claiming an absolute rightness or that they are or claim to represent a singular, all-powerful deity, they have no choice but to view any difference of belief as being absolutely wrong.

It appears to be in the nature of most sentient beings that if they become convinced of their own absolute rightness, they will then find the need to impose their belief on others who do not share it. In most cases this manifests, on a mortal level, as a drive to invade, convert, enslave, or kill, and then aggressively expand beyond the limits of the original tribe—all legitimized in their minds by their faith in their absolute rightness.

Humans such as these will insist on procreation within their tribe, which will expand to an obsession for racial purity. Their children will be reared within the rituals and beliefs of the tribe, which will result in an early indoctrination—and a severe or total reduction—of the children's freedom to choose their own paths.

In a cultural environment with a deeply embedded belief system that rejects the absolutist claims of the subgroup, the subgroup is more likely to turn in on itself. It will view itself as special—as favored by their God for special treatment—and because they are their God's chosen people, they have no choice but to defend their beliefs and racial purity against those who are not of the tribe. A group such as this will shape and strengthen its convictions by comparing and opposing the beliefs of others, even to their own martyrdom.

These convictions will result, of necessity, in the ancillary belief that all who disagree with them—or who oppose the one true God they worship—must in those cases be an adversary. And soon enough this has to become *the* Adversary (more on that later).

The implications are clear: it is the absolutism of the monotheistic cult and its conviction of absolute rightness—its "moral goodness"—that needs, and demands, its opposition be as absolute in its wrongness, its "absolute evil." And thus we get a Satan—a purely illusory figure who is solely the product of some "true believers'" fantasy and who has very little to do with the personality I've known as Satan.

13

Religious Animus

A Liberating Insight, the Oracle's Error, a Prince's Monotheism, Birth of Dualism, Midwayer Entropy, Secrets Revealed

Mein Host followed Mary Ann down the deep-carpeted corridor to her study—well, it used to be Robert's private study until she'd taken it over along with everything else—where she seated him on the soft leather sofa. She excused herself "to change into something a little more comfortable"—yes, she said it—and promised to return in a few minutes.

In 1977, promising to "change into something a little more comfortable" was every bit as much a cliché as it is now, and I could feel it disturbed my ward. What I could see—but he couldn't because Mary Ann had turned away from him when she uttered her immortal cliché—was a sly smirk on her face. It was as if she knew it would call up in his mind the one distasteful occasion when she had taken him to her bed.

He sat there for a while waiting in the elegant, Norman Jaffe–designed room. It contained an expensive sofa and chairs, their leather a light-coffee color and—if I may use the same tactile metaphor that I heard Mein Host once use, but which is sadly unfamiliar to my kind—"as soft as a baby's bottom."

Outside the floor-to-ceiling glass sliding doors, the sky was lightening, so the dark outline of the trees on the far hillside etched an inky smudge against the indigo sky as black and spontaneous as a gesture by Robert Motherwell.

The wall he faced as he sat on the sofa was one large built-in bookshelf stocked full with heavy hardback books on philosophy and religion and psychology, books that Robert must have left behind because it was doubtful that Mary Ann had any plans to read them. The lighting was soft and issued from two graceful lamps on the low tables on either side of the sofa. The room had the cool elegance of an advertising executive's corner office in Manhattan.

Mein Host heard the quiet running of water from the direction of Mary Ann's bedroom and the distant chatter of the others in the living room.

After about ten minutes Mary Ann reappeared having obviously freshened up her face—her skin had a tendency to get oily after a long session—and wearing a long caftan that appeared to be made of numerous layers of gauzy silk, each layer in slightly different tones of taupe, dove gray, and peach.

I know from what my ward said afterward—when he was trying to explain to Juliette what happened with Mary Ann early that morning—that he really didn't know what to expect.

He said those odd moments in Xtul flashed before his inner eye. It was when Mary Ann had drawn him aside as everyone else slept, had stood before where he knelt, and dropped her robe to reveal herself completely naked in the flickering candlelight. She seemed to expect no specific reaction and within a few seconds had slipped her robe back on and dismissed my ward back to his sleeping bag.

Here again, whatever was happening didn't appear to be about sex. What it seemed to be about, at least at first, was her real concern for him and the balance of his mind. Was he perhaps working too hard? Had his position as head honcho of the New York headquarters gone to his head? Had he lost his mind going off like that with Eva? Who did he think he was, anyway? What did he think the rank and file members would make of his dalliance with Eva? Did he believe he was better than everybody else? Did he think he could just bend the rules to justify whatever he wanted to do?

And, once again, I could hear from her tone this odd and ambivalent mixture of carefully controlled anger, a subtle hint of unacknowledged jealousy, and a tinge of admiration for his rebellious independence that she'd expressed on previous occasions.

She didn't seem to need answers to her questions, and I could see my ward must have felt it wise to say as little as possible. Besides, he really didn't believe he'd done anything particularly wrong. Sure he'd bent the rules a little, but he hadn't broken any of them—least of all the one of which he'd been accused. Spending those days with his mother—keeping the parents happy was one of Mary Ann's maxims—had been perfectly legitimate. He had informed the correct people and covered all his bases; he had made sure his secretaries were provided with work; and the Children's Chapter knew he was taking the boy off their hands for a few days. There was really nothing he'd done wrong unless—as they all seemed to believe—he was having sex on the sly with Eva.

Possibly it was his quiet manner or his stuttered attempts to answer her barrage of questions before they flew by; or, as he said later, it might have been the chastening realization that his claims of innocence hadn't been accepted—that she was simply brushing aside his denials as irrelevant, wink, wink, because everyone knew he must be lying.

Mein Host later said that it was this attitude he found most insulting and disturbing. Insulting because they didn't believe him when he was telling the truth, and disturbing because the whole issue seemed to have been shunted aside by Mary Ann as irrelevant. As he told Mother Juliette, it had required terrific self-discipline on both his and Eva's part not to sexualize their relationship but instead to bring the energy up into the heart chakra. He said it had been "a really valuable tantric exercise for both of them," and what opened his eyes "was Mary Ann and the others' complete disinterest in this tantric operation."

"Eva was so gorgeous," Juliette said gently, "you can understand why they didn't believe you. It's what they would have done . . . they're just projecting their stuff onto you."

"Yeah, I'm over that now. Why should I care if they believe me or not? It wasn't that so much . . . what pissed me off—and really woke me up—was what happened next."

Mary Ann then started taking a different tack from the one she'd been following in the long, earlier meeting with the others. Now Eva wasn't a "cheap tart" anymore. Now it was how Mary Ann had heard what a beauty Eva was, how irresistible she must have been when she'd obviously do anything to get him into bed, and how silly it was to get worked up about all this sex stuff—no, I couldn't believe she'd said this either, especially when her preoccupation appeared to be entirely sexual.

Where *was* she going with this line? Was she softening up my ward in some way that I was missing?

She was smiling now, and she opened her arms to draw my ward toward her, settling him comfortably across her lap, his legs and feet up on the sofa so they were facing one another—their heads on the same level and about nine inches apart.

"What *is it* that is so troubling you, Jesse?" she purred. "I don't think we've got to it yet?"

I could see my ward struggling to come up with anything that might satisfy her. Well, yes, he did have a lot on his plate. He had been exhausted after taking over the leadership. But she wasn't having any of that. Oh, no! She seemed to be driving at something, but I could see my ward had no idea what it might be. This is him writing now of what he knew—and didn't know—while this situation was playing itself out.

I came up with three or four things that concerned me at the time, like the festering conflicts between the As and Bs, the arrogance of some of the As and so much of the sheeplike dependence exposed by the questionnaire, and the constant pressure of having to goad the chapter to greater efforts, when even the most gargantuan effort was never quite enough.

Yet nothing I was saying seemed to satisfy her, and she just went on prodding and probing as I kept on trying to answer her questions. I was racking my mind to come up with something. I wanted to help her, so I wasn't resisting or trying to hide anything from her. It was a bit like one of her sessions she used to run on me back in the days of the P-scope. I was dredging up answers that she'd be checking on the P-scope for emotional charge. Except that we had no P-scope.

At last I said something she could get her teeth into.

I told her that a couple of days earlier I'd been sitting in J's Place drinking a cup of coffee and not thinking about much, when I found my eyes following one of the children, Little Eve, as she climbed the long flight of stairs from the coffeehouse up to the second floor— the very staircase the Buddhist monks had skidded down, their feet sliding on the corners of the treads as though skateboarding.

Little Eve was a slim, pretty, thirteen-year-old, who was obviously enjoying slinging her cute little derriere as she climbed the stairs— as if she might have just been watching a Marilyn Monroe movie. Rather desperately by this point—and as I was really trying to dig up anything that would get her off my back—I told Mary Ann that I'd rather admired her cute little behind swaying up the stairs.

Actually, after I'd had that thought in J's Place, I quickly averted my eyes. I have never had a thing for young girls, and, frankly, I felt a little embarrassed once I realized where my eyes had taken me. I'm certainly no pedophile. I've never even had much general interest in children, and I seem to lack a paternal gene as can be seen from Georgia's narrative of my life.

But that wasn't good enough for Mary Ann. She casually dismissed my self-concern with a wave of her hand. Her face was close enough for me to see what I imagine she must have thought was the dawning light of insight coming into her green eyes.

"Oh!" She said triumphantly. "Now I get it! You're queer! You're a homosexual! Now I understand everything!"

What could I say? I knew that I wasn't gay—and I'd had enough opportunities to find out if I was. I knew it in the way any heterosexual man knows himself sexually if he is sufficiently experienced. And while I'm no cocksman, I've had enough women to know I love them. Good Lord! I'd fought off that dreadful lecher Lord Barking at Charterhouse and was probably one of the few boys who got through that school unscathed.

If there was one thing I knew about myself, I wasn't sexually attracted to men—which has also proved true over the subsequent thirty-four years since that game-changing conversation with Mary Ann.

And it was a game changer—for me anyway. Clichéd though it might sound, the scales fell away from my eyes. I could suddenly see the truth about Mary Ann—who she was, and what she was trying to do! And all the while this was happening, Mary Ann was insisting she was right . . . that being homosexual had to be the root of my problem (although I wasn't aware of having such a problem) and congratulating herself for finally having put her finger on it.

Meanwhile I was thinking that if she could be this offbase and insistent about something I was actually sure about, then could she be just as wrong about everything else I didn't know about? Revelations and truths that I'd given her credit for knowing because I didn't . . . how could I trust her any longer if she's capable of being so sure about something that I knew to be completely wrong?

As I write this, more than thirty years later, with every opportunity in the world to have fulfilled any homosexual desire I might have had—had I had one—I still have found no sexual desire for men, even if I have occasionally wished I had, as I believed (most likely incorrectly) that a same-sex relationship would be so much easier.

I felt I had caught Mary Ann in an obviously manipulative lie, whether she actually believed it true or not. I found my mind was running like a decoding machine, unspooling some of the lies I had bought from Mary Ann over the years

If the woman could have been that wrong about me—and insist on it while looking at me straight in the eye—then she might well have been just as certain about anything else she was equally wrong about.

And *that* was the final tumbler to drop into place that would unlock the door to the prison he had allowed to be built around him.

There would be more to come, of course. Mary Ann wasn't going to let him go without a fight. And it was going to take time—and work—to examine and cut for good all the threads that bound him to Mary Ann, his erstwhile Goddess.

I don't think he understood how disturbing and lengthy a process this would turn out to be. Nor did he realize just how unpalatable were some of the truths he and the others in the Unit would have to face if they were to fully detach themselves from their previous lives in the church. They would have to do this while simultaneously hoping to retain that which was of value from the multitude of extreme experiences they'd had in the community.

It was thus—with very mixed feelings—that Mein Host and the other five IPs moved out of the main New York Chapter and into the large apartment they had rented on the Upper West Side of Manhattan to embark on their new lives.

I don't believe, from what I could see, that any one of them could have predicted just how new those lives were going to be, or just how hard they were going to have to fight to gain those lives.

* * *

Astar had said that she thought the Prince's strategy of simply subsuming local deities under a singular god—while his monotheistic cult spread down to a few of the Mediterranean coastal tribes—was bound to dissipate over time as the old gods and goddesses would have to reassert themselves.

I think even Prince Caligastia would have agreed that his first foray into monotheism was not a great success. Astar had wryly joked that it was apparently a lot easier to simply proclaim yourself God of This World than it was to actually make it stick!

Although Caligastia's imposed monotheism had largely faded away by the fourth millennium, the actual effects created on the surrounding peoples throughout the region—stretching from Afghanistan to the Black Sea and east across to the Nile Valley—were far more long-lasting.

I drifted south, down through Turkey to Persia, to observe for myself how the tribes in that region were reacting to the brief flowering—to the north of them—of Prince Caligastia's monotheism. For a long time Persia had been the nexus of ideas and beliefs traveling along the caravan routes from India and Asia. This included beliefs that had spread out from the Nile Valley, and the religious concepts advanced in the region of the Two Rivers of Serpent Worship.

It was among the wise men of a tribe that had settled in central Persia—in a location where the city of Isfahan would later be built—that I discovered a more considered response to the Prince's dogmatic monotheism.

I also found the same kind of coalition happening in the north among the midwayers and the local tribes there, but—as I soon ascertained—it was for very different reasons.

You may have noticed that I haven't actually descended for some millennia to observe individual human beings in this region only to find out what they're saying and doing. The truth is that—until recently—I hadn't found human beings of very much interest. Their outlook on life, their beliefs, and their limiting dependence on their gods and goddesses were too predictable to hold my attention.

Thus, when I originally coaxed myself down into the astral where I could more clearly observe and listen to this group of half a dozen elderly men—deep in discussion under the shade of a palm tree—I wasn't expecting a great deal of original thought.

But, they surprised me! They really did!

I won't try to reproduce their conversation in any detail, as they continued talking long after nightfall—and because their discussion was full of irrelevancies. But, mostly, because what passed between them was far less significant than the manner in which it was said.

Up to this point, I had seen little of independent human thought. When life for most regular human beings had been focused on the business of pure survival, there wasn't much time or inclination for independent thinking. In most cases of tribal leadership, their lives were taken in displays of power and the maintenance of their position in the tribe. This had served the midwayers well, because humans were far easier to control when they believed the laws that they lived by had descended from a higher source.

However, what I was observing among the old men beneath the palm tree was something completely different. Here, they weren't just parroting the dogmas of the local deities as relayed through the mouths of their priests and priestesses. It was this that had made me so tired of all the foolish and pointless boasting of the rival midwayers. Here, the old men were thinking for themselves.

They were trying to puzzle out the many confusions and contradictions presented by all these different midwayers. They were trying to tackle a regular Tower of Babel, if you like, of many different beliefs and rules.

Now, if this sounds strange or silly to the modern mind—or that your distant forebears should be dismissed as simpleminded and prone to superstition and are therefore irrelevant—it's worth remembering how completely different were the times in one very particular way: the midwayers played an active part in the tribal culture's lives in a manner that would make it impossible to deny their existence.

When the Master ordered the removal of the rebel midwayers four thousand years later, leaving only a small contingent—the one in five who'd remained loyal to the MA—to serve alone on the planet for the next couple thousand years, they would have known to keep their presence far more hidden from human beings.

The midwayers had always been intended to serve from behind the scenes, because if their presence became too prominent in the life of the tribes, they ran the risk of being deified and worshipped. The loyal midwayers—less than ten thousand of them—who've remained functioning on the planet until the present time have elected to remain largely hidden from the eyes of human beings. They find it easier to work that way, and I know they are loathe to fall into the traps of their colleagues.

So, for the modern mind—happy to rid itself of medieval superstitions—it has become far simpler, and more modern, to turn to science to explain away the occasional intervention of a midwayer into third-density reality or, if that doesn't work, to merely ignore or discount the phenomenon altogether.

No matter to the midwayers; they prefer it that way.

Until human beings are sufficiently awakened in spirit and more confident within themselves, the midwayers will most likely remain as invisible helpers for all but the very few.

The old men were discussing what they found so contradictory and improbable about the monotheism that had been spreading down from the northern hill tribes. These men were old enough to have observed that there is both good and evil in life and to query how a single all-powerful God could be responsible for both the ills and the goodness. How was this possible? If a monotheistic God is all-powerful—if he is omniscient and omnipresent, all-good and all-seeing—then how could the presence of evil be so powerful on this world? Does it mean that God is not all-powerful? Or is it that he overlooks evil? And why do the northern tribes "make us the evil ones when we're just minding our own business and obeying our own laws"?

I can't say I saw the birth of what will come to be called dualism, as the concept was introduced earlier by the shamans and suggested earlier still by the hostility between Vanu's belief system that was authorized by the MA and Prince Caligastia's particular brand of individualistic self-elevation.

I was going to write "Caligastia's belief system," but then I realized that until he actively attempted to impose his monotheism on the hill tribes, the Prince really didn't have anything that constituted a coherent belief system. He merely opposed anything and everything that the MA represented. It was this opposition that later earned him the sobriquet "the Adversary."

The discussion between the old men continued, and the longer they talked the more they were inclined to agree that while there was no argument that there was a good God, a God of Light, the very power and omnipresence of evil clearly demonstrated the existence of an evil power, a God of Darkness. I could see that they felt this was a far more satisfactory explanation for the world in which they found themselves than the paradoxical monotheism that appeared to be making the northern tribes so unpleasantly aggressive.

It was from this dualistic observation that the next assertion sprang; namely, that the God of Light and the God of Darkness must therefore be in constant conflict. They could see this in the passing of day into night and into day again, in the terrible storms that eclipsed the sun, and in the implacable fierceness of the predator and the gentle willingness of the victim; but most of all, they found the truth of this continuing battle in the conflicting impulses they experienced within themselves.

These insights would take root over the millennia and spread throughout the Middle East. Along with the worship of the old gods and goddesses, the various dualist cults would represent an apparent opposition to Prince Caligastia's monotheism. I say this is an *apparent* opposition because it wasn't long before the Prince's plan—the plan I had previously given him no credit for evolving—started becoming obvious to us watchers.

I know Astar called it a brilliant move, but then she is more familiar with the intricacies of religious engineering than I am. Of course, by positing a God of Darkness opposing a God of Light, the old dualists were unwittingly inviting the Prince to fulfill the role of the God of Darkness in their belief system.

In this way—by the end of the fourth millennium—Prince Caligastia had a firm grip on all the main streams of religious belief from Egypt in the east, all the way west to Persia, and north as far as Bulgaria. Even if his monotheism had originally failed to take hold and had faded away over the previous few centuries, it would soon make a comeback and reestablish itself as the religion of the southern Palestinian tribes.

Although Yahweh was originally merely one of thousands of so-called nature gods (midwayers), he happened to be the local deity of the tribes around Mount Horeb—a semi-active volcano in the Sinai Peninsula. For reasons I have yet to discover for certain, it had been Yahweh and his worshippers whom Caligastia had chosen to feature as the purest example of his monotheism.

I suspect he chose these early Semites because these were the tribes at a key geographical location in Southern Palestine, where ideas and religious concepts passed as easily as goods along the great caravan routes. These particular tribes also appealed to Prince Caligastia for their rigorous practice of endogamy. Whereas most tribes of the time discouraged their young people from marrying or procreating outside the tribal circles, the early Semitic clans made it an absolute taboo. I could appreciate how this was advantageous to the Prince's plans, because racial and genetic purity would then become irretrievably entwined with his monotheistic dictates, and the children of the tribe could be marked and indoctrinated from their birth onward.

The tribes hadn't taken easily to Yahweh's monotheism at first, but there seemed to be a natural process of assimilation and selection happening on the larger world stage. The presence of all these intrusive gods and goddesses—each with their different demands—had become overwhelming and confusing for the rapidly expanding population. The peoples' daily lives in general had become so dominated by the demands of their gods and goddesses that it was as if the natives had become a subspecies—merely lackeys serving the every indulgence of their demanding divinities.

You might think of this as psychic entropy acting on a long-lived species. When the midwayers were given life by the Prince's staff almost half a million years ago, they were a unified group. The revolution created the first schism as the midwayers split into two groups. In the many thousands of years since our uprising, the rebel midwayers—unlike the loyalists, who've remained unified—have been splitting into smaller and smaller groups. These became subgroups, and clans broke into subclans, until there were well over thirty thousand midwayers functioning individually or in small pantheons, each playing its own god games in some form.

I found this was a classic case of the progressive decay of an organized system—the original great family of midwayers—disintegrating over time into thousands of individual parts, each one seeking to differentiate itself from the others by placing yet more unreasonable demands on its worshippers.

When this sort of pressure is put upon human beings, I've observed that it brings out the best and the worst in them. The worst—I think—can be imagined, but in this case I was more interested in the best. As I suggested earlier, it was the pressure from all this babble of midwayer voices that was forcing people to think for themselves. If so many gods and goddesses were proclaiming their different truths about the very same issues, how could any one single voice then be trusted?

Of course it must have been this confusion of "divine voices" that originally prompted Caligastia to adopt Yahweh and his tribe of worshippers for his experiment in personal monotheism.

* * *

The apartment the Unit rented on Central Park West was large—as far as Manhattan apartments went—but it was still small for six adults. It was relatively inexpensive because it was not only too large for a New York couple, but it was also too far north at 93rd Street to be particularly fashionable.

In the curious demographics of Manhattan, the famously fashionable apartment block—the Eldorado at 300 Central Park West—was only one block south. But at twelve hundred dollars a month, they might have guessed it was going to be a stretch to cover the rent along with all their other obligations.

They had started the Unit in good faith as an outreach arm of the Foundation Faith. I don't believe any of them had any plan other than to make their experiment as successful as possible. Yet, acting in good faith requires the good faith of both parties to achieve a mutually satisfactory result. And it certainly wasn't particularly good faith that they were receiving when they joined the others in the New York Chapter for the main weekly Sabbath Celebration. They had agreed to attend the celebration as part of their negotiation, but they didn't expect to be received with such supercilious disregard. It was as though they had suddenly become the enemy. Their old friends didn't care to talk with them, and the Luminaries were dismissive and rude—picking out Dominic and my ward for their most choice invectives. So after going to their third weekly Sabbath Celebration, they decided they'd had enough of the hostility and cut their losses . . . never to return to the chapter again.

I don't believe anyone in the Unit initially wanted to actually break away from the Foundation Faith, but it wouldn't necessarily be equally true to say that they were forced out—although for the next few months it was certainly going to appear like that.

After the initial exhilaration they were obviously feeling at being liberated—at living their own lives, in their own time, and on their own schedule—the excitement dissipated. They found their long evening meetings—even in their new lives they were repeating the same daily rhythms as in chapter life—with which they finished their days growing longer and longer as they were finally able to share their stories and compare notes on their experiences.

They also shared the secrets that had been held between the levels and slowly started to connect the dots that had so long eluded them. Situations for which they had previously given credit to Mary Ann, or one of the other senior members, turned out to have a much darker side.

The death, for example, of a small child in the New Orleans Chapter some years earlier—my ward, along with most of the others, hadn't known about this—had been covered up. It was not so much to protect the reputation of the community (which would have been bad enough) as it was to prevent any investigation by the authorities.

Another sad story emerged that had been conveniently suppressed about Rupert, a young favorite of Mary Ann's who was known to have overdone it with LSD back in the 1960s. The community's abstinence from drugs had served Rupert well, and he'd become a valuable member of the community as he'd grown back into his kind and sensitive self. This had not been without the occasional acid flashback, but—on the whole—Rupert's life could be said to have been saved by his time in the community.

I am unable to say, like the others, whether Mary Ann had heard about Rupert's rare relapses and decided to take him under her wing or whether it was the pressure of living up to Mary Ann's expectations that caused his last and most serious breakdown—although I'm inclined to believe it was the latter. As though the unfortunate Rupert's mental breakdown wasn't enough to place at Mary Ann's door, what happened next became very close to torture.

Mary Ann had set out to heal Rupert, which meant keeping him at Mount Chi and giving him constant empath sessions while the young man grew progressively more unbalanced. At some point she must have thrown up her hands in disgust because he ended up locked in the basement of the Mount Chi house and forbidden to leave.

Mein Host had known nothing of this while it was happening, and because he liked Rupert—unbeknown to him, Rupert was another incarnate rebel angel—he was horrified and disgusted to hear what had happened to his friend. But there was worse to come.

Rupert had apparently been kept prisoner in the basement for months—the Four had justified his imprisonment by saying he had a tendency to wander off—before he finally managed to escape. He had apparently been picked up for vagrancy and ended up in a mental hospital. There Rupert was treated for his mental illness with the appropriate medication, and within a week he was back to his old cheerful, magical self.

His sudden return to full cognitive health after receiving the correct drug—while perfectly splendid for Rupert—had not sat well with an Oracle who disapproved of psychiatric drugs. It was such a harsh condemnation of her authority and her healing powers that the whole situation had been hushed up, and Rupert wasn't seen again—not because he disappeared under suspicious circumstances, but simply because he'd had enough of all Mary Ann's nonsense. After a few weeks back in Mount Chi, he walked out for the final time.

The longer the Unit talked, the more the dark secrets rolled out—sometimes to tears, sometimes to fury, sometimes to horror, but almost always to their increasing disillusionment.

Dominic and Victoria—one of the very few couples who had turned their Absorption into a real marriage—described how they always had to fight to stay in the same chapter together and how Mary Ann was constantly trying to tear them apart.

Rachel, another member of the Unit, told how she'd been an IP for four years. She'd written to Mary Ann on numerous occasions but had never heard back from her, and she expressed that she felt it was ridiculous to be part of community for years without ever hearing from, let alone meeting, the leader of it.

All the members of the Unit were still going out donating daily on the streets, but—as they'd agreed to focus only on the Upper West Side from Columbus Circle northward—it was mostly nannies with baby carriages, women shoppers, and impoverished writers and artists, many of whom had already given their dollar and weren't happy to be pestered again. They were also not permitted to wear their uniforms—another negotiated agreement—so they simply became just more panhandlers to be avoided by canny New Yorkers shopping on Broadway.

The money that a good donator could make—and at least five of the six members of the Unit were top donators—dropped from an average of perhaps thirty to forty dollars an hour when in uniform to being fortunate just to make a mere handful of change after a long day on the streets out of uniform.

They still maintained their old schedule: they had their morning and evening meditations; they kept their silence after the meditation all night until the end of the morning meditation; they all still wore their formal black robes for their meetings and meditations; and they referred to one another by the formal titles. Yet beneath the surface another festering conflict was coming to a boil.

Everyone in the Unit was now working overtime as they struggled to make the rent and still pass their 25 percent off the top "up the line." It soon became an impossibility to keep this up month after month, and they turned to those now leading the Foundation Faith, pleading for a more reasonable arrangement of a 10 percent tithe they could manage.

Expecting—foolishly in my opinion—their old friends to understand their predicament, they didn't reckon for the continuing bitterness of the resentment felt by the Four. They were appropriately horrified when not only was their plea dismissed, but the new percentage to be passed up the line was doubled to 50 percent!

War had been declared.

The Foundation Faith no longer supported the Unit—if they ever had—and were now setting out to destroy them. First came the pleadings shouted through the front door promising to take everybody back if they'd just give up. Then came the angry threats and insults shouted through the letterbox.

The Unit had agreed not to let them enter the apartment as they knew by this time that they might be in danger. So next it was the police banging at their apartment door, having been told some lie about drugs on the premises by an anonymous tip. Not only were there no drugs whatsoever in the apartment—of course, there weren't—but the police left after cups of coffee happy to know the little group was entirely harmless.

A few days later it was a legal document slipped under the door demanding that my ward personally pay back the twenty-thousand-dollar loan he had negotiated for the community and from which he had received, of course, nothing for his own use. Then it was days of harassment: phone calls in the middle of the night and loud bangings on the front door when no one was there.

And then my ward woke one morning to find boils all over his legs.

He'd had a few boils in his life before—who hadn't, he said, when showing the others. But never like this. There must have been twenty of them . . . nasty red welts, some already oozing puss, covering both his legs from his lower thighs down to his ankles. After three days had passed and the boils were no better—if anything they were worse and there were more of them—the others persuaded my ward to go to the outpatient department at the hospital just down the road at nearby Lincoln Center. The boils were so mysterious and sudden—and were so obviously painful—that he reluctantly agreed to have a doctor look at them.

I should add that my ward had an instinctive distrust of doctors. This had been sealed when he was an adolescent by a foolish doctor misreading his chart after a minor hernia operation and viciously laying into him in the most insulting way. He believed the lad had contracted venereal disease, which—at the age of fourteen—had seemed to infuriate the doctor. His abject apology the next day did nothing to change my ward's opinion of doctors and the state of contemporary medicine. (*Note: When Timothy was nearing the time to "fall off his perch" and pass on to his next adventure, he had to be treated by some very loving and caring medical professionals at Presbyterian Hospital in Albuquerque, New Mexico. He was so touched by their care and compassion that he said his faith in doctors had been restored—so much so that he donated one of his original pieces of art to the wing where he was treated. —DM*)

Getting back to the New York experience: My ward was sitting on the bed in the small consulting room, his trousers rolled up above the knees to expose his boil-laced legs, when the door opened and the doctor came in. He was a black doctor, his skin tone having that pitch-blackness that looks indigo under certain lights and signifies an undiluted African heritage. This is important because of what happened next.

The doctor barely looked at my ward's legs while still standing and filling in some form. When he finished writing he pushed his glasses down, peered over the pad on which he'd been writing, and asked one simple question: "Do you have any enemies?" Short, concise, and clear.

There was a long silence before the dawning light of recognition came into my ward's blue eyes.

"Well, yes, I do as a matter of fact," he admitted.

"And do you think they're capable of this?" the doctor asked, looking more closely at the suppurating sores.

"They might certainly try, doctor."

"Do you have an aquarium?"

"No, doctor, why?"

"Get yourself a small aquarium and a lot of little fish . . . you must have seen them . . . tiny little things about three-quarters of an inch long with a bright blue stripe down their backs . . . you'll know what I mean when you go to buy them." And with that the doctor smiled sweetly, walked out the door, and went about his business.

Mein Host bought himself a small aquarium and an assortment of tiny fish—the majority of which had that fluorescent blue stripe—and returned to the Unit's fifth-floor apartment.

That evening he set up the aquarium on the lower bookshelf of the metal racks he'd built on one side wall of his small room and sprinkled some flakes of fish food onto the surface before he went to sleep that night.

My ward likes to tell that when he woke up the next morning all the fish were floating dead on the surface, and his boils had all but disappeared. In fact, it wasn't quite that rapid. All the fish were certainly dead by that first afternoon, but it took a couple more days for all his boils to clear up. Regardless, it must have seemed an almost miraculous recovery to those in the Unit—and it certainly opened their eyes still farther as to what they were up against.

Eventually, members of the Four took the Unit to small claims court in downtown Manhattan, only to have it thrown out by a judge who was disgusted by the machinations of the main community and who angrily remonstrated both sides to make up their differences. He said how disappointing it was to find a church behaving so poorly.

After this attempt by the Foundation Faith to use the courts to bring the Unit to its knees, there was no chance of ever returning to the main fold. The Unit had seen too much of the community's preparedness for callous and downright cruel treatment of those trying to improve the overall financial and social outreach of the community.

There was no turning back after that.

Within a week of the court debacle, the Unit decided to cut off all contact with the Foundation Faith of the Millennium and make their own way into the world. Yet even that—even leaving the church they had served all through their twenties and thirties—was never going to be simple . . . and it was certainly not easy.

* * *

What I observed happening in Persia, however—as I watched and listened to those elders arguing back and forth about just these theological matters—happily surprised me. More elders from other villages had joined the original group, which by this time had swollen to more than a score, with each newcomer representing his—they were all male—village's local deities.

It wasn't that I hadn't overheard such discussions a few times over the millennia, and on the rare occasion, a particular culture had reached a point of sufficient maturity to demand a higher degree of independence from the follies of their gods. Yet each time this had occurred, there seemed to have been some small advancement in individuality on the part of the humans before they were once more overwhelmed by the multiplicity of the demands placed on them.

This time it looked to be very different.

Something fundamental appeared to be shifting in the relationship between midwayers and the more thoughtful members of the various tribes. It might have been, as Julian Jaynes suggested in *The Origin of Consciousness in the Breakdown of the Bicameral Mind*, that the voices of the gods and goddesses no longer spoke so loudly in the peoples' right brains, because I saw more independence of mind at that gathering than I'd ever observed on the previous occasions.

It was in discussions such as these that were occurring in a number of different Middle Eastern cultural and religious centers during this time—as they became increasingly free of the demands of their gods— that a new dynamic was evolving whereby human beings were starting to assert their own decisions.

If I was to compress what emerged from the three-day gathering into a few paragraphs, I would have to first say that—despite their obvious nervousness that one of their midwayer gods would manifest in their midst—they were able to make some very basic distinctions that would serve them well.

The wise men were obviously unable to deny the reality of the gods, of course, but they were able to decide—among them—to take a firmer hand in their relations with these spurious divinities. There was a palpable feeling among them that they could sense an increasing weakness in the grip their gods held on them, although I never heard this openly expressed.

What I did observe were some cogent arguments being made by the elders gathered for the event. I had the feeling I was watching the tentative emergence of a new type of intelligence, or perhaps it was simply intelligence being used in a new way. It was certainly the first occasion I'd witnessed since the times of Vanu and Amadon in which I heard the midwayers spoken about so objectively.

The old men pointed out that so many of the promises and threats made by their gods and goddesses over time had proved empty, that their people celebrated the one promise kept while conveniently forgetting the many failures, and that—in the passing of the generations—the people spoke only of the heroism and beauty of their gods and goddesses and never of their selfishness and their terrifying demands.

The fact that these elders were able to speak about their gods in such frank and disparaging terms suggested to me that the men, too, were already aware of the diminishing power of the midwayers and were experiencing a new confidence in their own capacity for rational, independent thought.

One of the younger and more progressive of the men raised a couple of questions that had been hanging in the air: Was the world, and everything in it, created by the good God for the benefit of mortal men and women? Or was the world really just the playpen of the gods, and mortals merely the pawns in the games the gods played?

It was the first time, as I said, that I'd heard questions as penetrating as these being openly aired without any evident fear of consequences. I wondered about this. It felt somewhat rash, yet I had to admire their boldness.

It was only later—when the gathering was over, the old men had returned to their villages, and I had the opportunity to observe some of the local midwayers—that I realized there was another dynamic at work. I thought I detected the hand of Prince Caligastia behind what I felt was the midwayers' new compliance, and after hearing what they were grumbling about, I reckoned I was right.

It had, apparently, been an unusually stern lecture from the Prince that had driven home what they all had clearly suspected but hadn't wanted to admit to themselves or each other: they were gradually losing control of their mortal worshippers. It was the Prince who had brought this out in the open and had harshly reprimanded them for splintering into smaller and smaller groups, only to then proclaim themselves as individual divine identities. He had placed the blame for their loss of control firmly on the midwayers and accused them all of the sin of pride. He then proceeded to accuse them of wanting to usurp his supreme power and of plotting against him, which, I suspected, was probably untrue, but the midwayers had been sufficiently cowed by the Prince's fury not to protest.

It was Prince Caligastia who had then informed his rebel midwayers that if they wanted to wield any continuing influence over human beings, they would have to simplify their relationships—with human beings and with each other. He cast down the minor divinities and instructed them to work closely with the new trading families, to ally themselves with the various aristocratic bloodlines and ruling elites, and to work for their continuance.

The Prince had then reviewed all the major pantheons of midwayers throughout the region, ruthlessly debunking their arrogant behavior and deconstructing the ridiculous belief systems many of them had promoted. This had hit a nerve by all accounts because there had been a certain amount of wagers taken among the midwayers as to who among them could convince their worshippers of the most absurd claim. It was a cruel game they were playing, and I thought it was a fair indication of how cynically uncaring the rebel midwayers had become by this time.

In ordering his midwayers to simplify their presence, the Prince had instructed them to focus their efforts on promoting dualism in its different forms and to create it as a viable alternative to the traditional pantheism of the pagan religions. Caligastia wanted to ensure that they would be in opposition to the monotheism that he'd been imposing on the Palestinian tribes. As a cynical banker might finance both sides in a war, or an international bootlegger might have supported Prohibition while getting a higher price for his whiskey, or an arms dealer might provide weapons to opposing forces, he was now playing both sides of the field.

Prince Caligastia's overwhelming influence on humanity through his manipulation of the "worship circuits" that run through every mortal's spiritual body was now holding most of Earth's human population in a thrall entirely of his own making. Although the Prince's actions were mostly concentrated in the region now broadly termed the Middle East, their effects traveled along the Silk Road to the Indian subcontinent and on to Asia, with the influence lessening the farther east it went. The pantheism that dominated the belief systems of most Indian tribes on the subcontinent by the early fourth millennium was also naturally subject to the forces of simplification, and this would be found in the composition of the Rig Veda over this and the next millennium.

Prince Caligastia had captured the field, and for the next few thousand years he would have most of the midwayers back in his control and—if you'll forgive my reference—hold "the whole world in his hands." He would also have kept human beings in their bewildered and insecure state if it wasn't for the world-changing events of the next two millennia.

* * *

Life for the six members of the Unit over the next seven months—until their year's rent had run its course—was probably as hard and challenging as anything they had gone through in the community. Not only was there the extremely serious affair of deprogramming themselves—and one another—but there was also the whole business of moving back into the world. This wouldn't be as simple as it sounded on paper, because for the previous fifteen years they'd been ripping Western civilization to shreds—and the world itself had become a progressively inhospitable and uninhabitable sphere.

There was also a more personal aspect to the troubled underside of the Unit. I have mentioned that Dominic and Victoria were married and—as the only couple in the Unit—they got to share their new freedom in the one large master bedroom. Their sexual energy was such that it permeated the apartment, tickling long-forgotten fancies in the others and raising all sorts of possibilities.

The distribution of the three possible bedrooms in the apartment forced an issue that had been brewing in my ward's life that he had been pushing aside. Marion—the young woman who had so unwisely pledged herself to my ward—was now starting to make her inevitable demands for a closer romantic relationship with him. He'd accepted her as a personal assistant reluctantly and had tried to dissuade her from following him into the Unit. He appreciated her strict efficiency—she was good at her job—but I knew he had never felt any real affinity for her.

Now, I've come to understand that one of Mein Host's weaknesses is his propensity to bend to the will of strong women. There was a certain amount of kindness in this—as well as a touch of moral weakness and an unwillingness to stand up for himself—but mostly it was one of the consequences of growing up with only a mother who was herself a very strong woman.

At that point in his life—he was in his thirty-seventh year when he left the Unit—he was already aware of this weakness, yet he was still unable to assert himself over a strong, single-minded woman's demands. And Marion was nothing if not a strong, single-minded young woman with a purpose. She wanted my ward for herself, and it seemed she was prepared to do just about anything to get him.

If someone who was familiar with the community's use of god-patterns to define different personality types was challenged to guess Mother Marion's god-pattern, they would almost certainly guess correctly. Marion was an archetypal J/S, a combination of Jehovah/Satan—a god-pattern she shared with none other than Mary Ann.

When Marion had filled out her questionnaire, she had turned out to be classed as an A. It was only when she heard that Mein Host had opted for the Unit that she insisted on joining the Unit so as to be with him.

I knew this decision of hers—from which she couldn't be deterred—had filled my ward with horror. Having Marion as an assistant when they worked together in the Foundation Faith was one thing; having her constantly around his neck in a unit of only six people was quite another.

I know he isn't proud of how he treated the woman, but in my opinion I don't think he had the energy to resist her at that point in his life. It wasn't simply emotional cowardice, although that was part of it; it was also a concern for Marion's state of mind. He knew her energetic overconfidence was a cover for a far more frail and insecure woman beneath the surface.

Marion had grown up as the older of two daughters in one of those families in which parental love had fermented into adoration for and overpraise of the children. She'd been adored and applauded ever since she was a precocious little child, singing her little songs and dancing her little dances. No one had ever told her that she wasn't very good or that what might have been cute in a five-year-old had become a brassy embarrassment in an adult.

I've already noted that Marion was high-handed and bossy with those below her and expected complete loyalty from those she favored. Now she threw every bit of her emotional neediness at my ward, but—like most bullies—she felt acutely vulnerable inside. Justified or not, I could see he simply couldn't bring himself to break her heart and shatter her innocent human nature.

Once the Unit had cut its bonds and broken away from the main community, there were no more vows to be kept or broken. What little money they could donate went to pay the rent, and it was time to think about what to do next with their lives.

Marion clearly had her idea, and soon enough she had pressured her way into my ward's bed. He evidently had no desire to romanticize his relationship with her, let alone sexualize it, but I imagine he saw no great harm in sharing his bed if that seemed to satisfy her.

I am sure you can tell how all those years of celibacy had blinded him to the obvious. Could any man sleep night after night with a woman who passionately desired his bones and have nothing untoward happen?

He was asleep when she first went down on him, and he must have awakened to the intense and undeniable pleasure of his climax. He'd say later that she was really good at it, and he couldn't find it in him to scold her for doing it. She must have believed she'd found her way into my ward's affections because—waking before him—she repeated what had given him so much pleasure on every subsequent morning. He clearly had no desire to reciprocate. Although this could be viewed as unfair, I heard him say even back then that he was trying to discourage her by selfishly never returning the favor.

"It wasn't difficult," he would say. "I really didn't fancy her, and I didn't want to give her the impression that I did."

I have no way of knowing what was going on in Marion's mind, but from her passive acceptance of her role as sexual slave it must have satisfied some masochistic streak in her otherwise controlling personality. Of course there can be no excuses. What happened, happened. Now that she had sexually claimed him, there would be no simple way to discard the woman.

I could tell from his emotional body that he felt awful about the situation he'd gotten himself into. The fact that he had just swapped one dominating bully of a woman for another dominating bully of woman, although one not nearly as interesting, was not lost on him. But, as I heard him say, it was simply easier to go along with Marion's devoted attentions than to invite the inevitable row and chaos that would follow an authentic declaration of his complete disinterest in the woman.

I believe it was at that point that my ward made up his mind to work his way out from under Marion's stifling devotion. He must have reckoned he would only be able to make it happen—with any degree of honor—if he could get her to leave him. He would have to set out to behave extremely badly. If that didn't work, then he would have to find a way of getting Marion to leave him for another man.

Either way, I had no doubt it was going to take time.

Sadly, in many ways, my prediction turned out to be true, and it was some two years before Marion fell in love with one of her clients and was able to release my ward from her obsessional devotion. It had not been a happy two years for either of them, so both of them felt happy and liberated when Marion moved out of my ward's life to be with the man she soon married.

This breakup had to occur so that the next phase in Mein Host's already somewhat idiosyncratic life had a chance to open and shift into top gear. In many ways, Mein Host's true life was about to begin. His training and preparation was by no means over, but from now on life itself would become the teacher. In three years' time he would encounter the angels again, have two extraterrestrial experiences, including an informative twenty-minute dialogue with an extraterrestrial mouthpiece, and discover something of the nature of cetacean telepathy.

However, it would take Mein Host even longer to discover who he was and to accept his function as one of the incarnate rebel angels living out his life on this planet as just another human being.

Yes, indeed. That would take a lot longer.

The Forest through
the Trees

The Synchronicity of the Twin Threads, Future Glimpses of Earth, Hints of a Divine Supreme, Georgia's Deep Optimism

In completing this, the seventh volume of Georgia's *Confessions*, I believe we have reached a watershed moment in both narrative threads.

I do not plan out these volumes in advance; I simply sit down and write with Georgia for between ten to twelve hours a day and have done so every day for the past three years. I seldom even recall what has been written during the day when I relax at the end of it.

I continue to be surprised, fascinated, and illuminated by what Georgia has to say and the skillful way she threads together the little I know with what she sees and understands of the larger context.

My "gentleman's contract" with Georgia is simple: as long as she keeps me interested telling me stories I've never heard before, I will keep on writing them. I'm not a natural or academic researcher—I prefer to do my researching in the field—so I've learned to appreciate the research projects she sends me along the way. I learn a great deal from them and find myself looking at the people I am researching through very different eyes—especially when Georgia informs me that the person was an incarnate angel. Frequently I find that it's as if all the clues are there in their biographies and in their creations and that I just needed that shift of viewpoint to see all the dots connecting.

Another thing that delights me—and that has become clearer the more volumes we write—is how other people, readers perhaps of my other books, contact me over the internet with a particular gem of information or insight, on exactly what I am writing about that day. This must be completely intuitive on the readers' part, because neither they nor I know what Georgia will be writing about; so I assume I'm getting some angelic assistance through these kind people. I try to credit them within the text when possible, but as most are themselves incarnate angels—whether or not they know it—I prefer to be cautious with my attributions.

When I don't give credit, for one reason or another—and incarnate angels, rebel and otherwise, are wisely shy about their identities if they're aware of their heritages—I trust you will recognize your input. Georgia and I are grateful for your contribution.

This has been a curious trip for me, and I'm continually surprised and gratified that this relationship with Georgia has come upon me fairly late in life. Not only is it completely absorbing—it wouldn't be fair to try to share my life with a woman when I am so preoccupied with Georgia and the work—but I simply don't think I could have handled it when I was any younger. It's as if everything I've done in my life has not only landed me where I am today but also each activity has contributed very directly to what I'm able to bring to this work.

Between 1979 and 2008, I spent between six and ten hours every day I could manage—which was most days—just drawing my graphics. I didn't do them for monetary profit; I did them from love and to learn. My early books were selling well enough, so the graphics have a very personal emotional purity and have acted as valuable feedback devices.

The graphics were wonderfully helpful and totally engrossing to do, and I must have completed several hundred of them before writing finally gained its ascendency. I haven't done much on my drawing board since, with the exception of the collaborative graphics—four of which I've included in this volume—that I do with my New York Art Partner, June Atkin.

It only comes to me now as I write that my detailed graphic style, with its requirement for intense focus, immense patience, and an extremely relaxed state of mind, was an unusual mix. There are few tasks in life that require three such apparently contradictory states of consciousness to be held simultaneously. Target shooting perhaps, but even that seldom demands the patience that drawing for twelve hours straight requires.

Yet it is precisely these three faculties—concentrated focus of attention, the patience of a saint, and a relaxed, almost hypnagogic, state of consciousness—that makes my writing with Georgia even possible.

Here's Georgia with a preview of things to come.

The next volume will pick up where this one leaves off, with my ward struggling to rid himself of the last vestiges of Mary Ann's negative control and discovering where his life will be taking him. He will throw off the vows that bound him to Mary Ann, and—in making up for lost time— he will meet the love of his life. He will drive himself ragged running a small business in New York, and although the business was relatively successful, he will find that he is not drawn to be a businessman.

The fourth millennium BCE could have been a turning point in Prince Caligastia's career had the situation turned out differently. In many ways, as the millennium closed, this period could be thought of as the quiet before the next storm breaks out. And break out it will.

Prince Caligastia's monotheism will turn out to have its uses, but it might not be exactly what the Prince had hoped for or anticipated. We'll encounter the Sirians again and observe the subtle effects their mission will have, particularly on the Nile Valley cultures, which will be reaching another ascendancy. There will be another angelic intervention in the form of Machiventa Melchizedek's ninety-plus-year role as the Sage of Salem.

Much of this, of course, is already known about in broad strokes, and I appreciate that Georgia has no desire to reinvent the wheel. Her interests are far more personal. It is in the fleshing out of what she has observed that she is obviously learning what she needs to put her mind to rest after all these millennia.

In fact, one of the aspects of this project of ours is the pleasure that I, Timothy, get from Georgia's insights when they deepen her understanding of the great cosmic game. She speaks of it as an interplanetary theatrical performance that she hopes will entertain the Creator, allow each one of us to grow in spirit, and help us to understand who we are and why we are here. In the unprecedentedly extraordinary times we are going to be facing over the next few years, it is only when we know who we truly are that we can be of any real value—to ourselves or anyone else.

Georgia tells me it will be a radiant time of miracles and wonders, and this description functions as a welcome antidote to my own rather more rationally realistic assessment of the world situation. However, I wouldn't be writing so intimately with Georgia if I didn't trust her point of view.

She says that there is the most wonderful surprise for all of us in the fairly immediate future. It will be a divine surprise, she tells me, and that it will be in this wonder of amazement that we will discover the final and most important reason we have chosen to incarnate at this point in time.

In the light of this, how could I ever stop writing with Georgia so firmly on my mind?

The
Angelic Cosmology

Different versions of the so-called War in Heaven appear so frequently in indigenous legends and mythologies from around the world—as well as in the sacred books and traditions of major religions—that the war is more than likely based on a real event. I believe the most authoritative account can be found in *The Urantia Book,* where it is referred to as "the Lucifer Rebellion."

Thirty years after first reading *The Urantia Book,* I still regard it as the most reliable source of information about both extraterrestrial and celestial activities. It is broken down into four parts devoted to the following subjects: the Nature of God and the Central and Superuniverses; the Local Universe; the History of Urantia (their name for this planet); and the Life and Teachings of Jesus Christ. (For a definition of terms common to both *The Urantia Book* and this book, please refer to the glossary.)

According to the Urantia model, there are seven Superuniverses, which together compose the material Multiverse. These seven Superuniverses form the substance of the finite Multiverse and circle the Central Universe, which can be visualized as the hole in the center of the toroidal form of the Multiverse.

Each Superuniverse contains one hundred thousand Local Universes, each of which has its own Creator Son (ours is Christ

a. Central Universe (pattern creation) includes Paradise and Havona

b. Seven Superuniverses

c. First outer space level

d. Second outer space level

e. Third outer space level

f. Fourth and outermost space level

- Distance between **b** and **c:** approx. 400,000 light-years.

- Width of **c:** at least 25 million light-years.

- Each Superuniverse sustains approx. one trillion inhabited planets.

- The "layers" of the Master Universe rotate in opposite directions: time comes by virtue of motion and because mind is inherently aware of sequentiality.

- Our local universe (10 million inhabited planets) is one of the 100,000 Local Universes that compose the seventh Superuniverse.

Master Universe Structure (From *The Urantia Book*, p. 129)

Michael or Jesus Christ) and its own Divine Mother—these are the Creator Beings of their domain. This pair of High Beings modulates the energy downstepped from the Central Universe to create and form the beings and the planetary biospheres with their Local Universe. Each Local Universe sustains ten million inhabited planets broken out into ten thousand Local Systems.

Each Local System, in turn, contains one thousand inhabited—or to be inhabited—planets, and each has its own System Sovereign (ours was Lucifer) appointed to govern the System. Each planet, in turn, has a Planetary Prince (ours was Prince Caligastia), who oversees their particular worlds.

According to *The Urantia Book,* Lucifer and Satan (Lucifer's main assistant) came to believe that an elaborate conspiracy had been concocted by the Creator Sons of the Local Universes to promote the existence of a fictitious Unseen Divinity, which the Creator Sons then used as a control device to manipulate the orders of celestials and angels within their creations. Having announced the existence of this conspiracy, Lucifer demanded more autonomy for all beings, and for System Sovereigns and Planetary Princes to follow their own approaches for accelerating the spiritual development of their mortal charges.

The revolutionaries quickly gained followers and the rebellion spread rapidly to affect thirty-seven planets in our System, with Urantia, our planet Earth, being one of them. Choice was given to the many angels involved with supervising System activities as to whether or not to join the rebel faction.

Lucifer's charge—that too much attention was being given to ascending mortals—appeared to ring true to a large number of angels, as well as the thirty-seven pairs of administrative angels: the Planetary Princes and their assistants who were responsible for the orderly progression of mortal (human) beings on their worlds. The revolution was effectively suppressed by the administration authorities and recast as a heinous rebellion, its immediate consequence being the removal of Lucifer and Satan from their posts in the System.

At the time of the Lucifer Rebellion, the vast majority of the fifty thousand midway angels on Earth—40,119 to be exact—aligned themselves with Lucifer and Satan. They were destined to remain on our planet until the time of Christ when, according to *The Urantia Book*, it was one of Christ's occulted functions to remove them. It is a brief reference and no further details are given in the book as to where the rebel midwayers were taken. However, with the removal of these rebel midwayers, a mere 9,981 loyalist midwayers remained here to fulfill the tasks of five times their number.

As a result of this, in contrast to a normal planet (one not quarantined), on which angelic companions and the presence of helpful midwayers and extraterrestrials must be commonplace knowledge, we earthlings have slumbered in our corner of a populated Multiverse, unaware of who we are and how we got this way. Having been quarantined and isolated from normal extraterrestrial activity for the long 203,000 years since the rebellion, we first lost touch with, and then forgot entirely, our rightful place in the populated Multiverse. Given this, we were bound to evolve as a troubled species. Our world is one of the few planets that, due to the Lucifer Rebellion, has been thrown off its normal pattern of development.

This disquieting situation, this planetary quarantine, has persisted for more than two hundred thousand years, only to have finally been adjudicated, in my understanding, in the early 1980s.

Given that the planetary quarantine has finally been lifted, the rest of the Multiverse is now able to make legitimate contact with us. More recently what we are witnessing is both the return of the rebel midwayers (the beings of the violet flame), who are now coming back to assist us in the coming transformation of our world; and, perhaps of more personal interest to my readers, the many angels who aligned with Lucifer at the time of the rebellion are incarnating as mortals. It appears these rebel angels and watchers are being offered human incarnation as a path to personal redemption as the world is emerging from an interminably long, dark age to shake off the shadows and fulfill its remarkable destiny.

Glossary

Many valuable insights from many different sources have contributed to the themes and fundamental questions that this series of books, the *Confessions* series, seeks to explore, but the most reliable and comprehensive exposition of God, the Universe, and Everything that I have come across remains *The Urantia Book*. A number of the concepts and words below are drawn from it and marked (UB), but the definitions are the author's.

Albedo: the second stage of the alchemical process resulting from the slow burning out of the impurities present in the first stage.

Angel: a general term for any order of being who administers within a Local Universe.

Atman, Indwelling Spirit, Thought Adjuster (UB): an essence of the Creator that indwells all mortal beings, human and extraterrestrial.

Bioplasm (UB): a constituent of an individual's genome required to reconstitute a biological duplicate of the bioplasm's donor, or for calibrating a cloned physical vehicle to its intended environment.

Caligastia (UB): a Secondary Lanonandek Son who served as Planetary Prince of this world and who aligned himself with Lucifer.

Cano (UB): young Nodite aristocrat who mated with Eve, the female visitor.

Central Universe (UB): the abode of the original Creator God/s—the

Father, the Mother/Son, and the Holy Spirit (UB). If the Multiverse is a torus, then the Central Universe is the hole in the middle existing on a far finer frequency and from which energy is downstepped to form the building blocks of the Multiverse.

Citrinitas: advanced state of spiritual enlightenment whereby the alchemist can make an ultimate unification with the Supreme.

Creator Sons (UB): co-creators—each having a female complement, the Mother Spirit (UB)—of each of the seven hundred thousand Local Universes (UB). The co-creators of the Local Universes modulate the downstepped energies from the Central Universe to design the life-forms for those beings existing within all the frequency domains of their Local Universe.

Daligastia (UB): a Secondary Lanonandek Son who served as Caligastia's right-hand aide.

Demons: negative thoughtforms.

Devas: the coordinating spirits of the natural world. All living organisms are cared for by devas (or nature spirits). In the human being the deva is that which coordinates and synchronizes the immense amount of physical and biochemical information that keeps our bodies alive.

Extraterrestrial: mortal beings such as ourselves who hail from more developed worlds with access to our frequency domain.

Fandor (UB): a large semi-telepathic passenger bird, said to have become extinct about thirty-eight thousand years ago.

Frequency Domain: the spectrum of frequencies that support the lifeforms whose senses are tuned to that specific spectrum.

God: in *my* personal experience, God is both the Creator and the totality of Creation, manifest and unmanifest, immanent and transcendent.

Guardian (Companion) Angels (UB): function in pairs to ensure their mortal wards grow in spirit over the course of their lifetimes.

Indwelling Spirit, Atman, Thought Adjuster (UB): an essence of the Creator that indwells all mortal beings, human and extraterrestrial.

Janda-chi: the second of the two Planetary Princes on the planet Zandana.

Jesus Christ: the Michaelson (UB) of our Local Universe (UB) who incarnated as Jesus Christ in the physical body of Joshua ben Joseph; he is also known as Michael of Nebadon (UB).

Lanaforge (UB): a Primary Lanonandek Son who succeeded Lucifer as System Sovereign.

Lanonandek Order of Sonship (UB): the third order of Local Universe Descending Sons of God who serve as System Sovereigns (Primary Lanonandeks) and Planetary Princes (Secondary Lanonandeks).

Local System (UB): our Local System, named Satania (UB), is believed to currently possess between 600 and 650 inhabited planets. Earth is numbered 606 in this sequence (UB).

Local System HQ Planet, Jerusem (UB): the political and social center of the Satania System.

Local Universe (UB): a grouping of planets that consists of ten million inhabited worlds.

Lucifer (UB): deposed System Sovereign and primary protagonist in the rebellion among the angels.

Lucifer Rebellion (UB): a rebellion among the angels occurring 203,000 years ago on Jerusem that affected thirty-seven inhabited worlds, of which Earth was one.

Master Universe (UB): the Multiverse that contains the seven Superuniverses (UB).

Melchizedek Sons/Brothers (UB): a high order of Local Universe Sons devoted primarily to education and who function as planetary administrators in emergencies.

Midwayers or Midway Creatures (UB): intelligent beings, imperceptible to humans, who exist in a contiguous frequency domain and serve as the permanent planetary citizens.

Mortals (UB): intelligent beings who emerge as a result of biological evolutionary processes on a planet. Souls are born to their immortal lives as mortals, whose physical bodies live and die before they are given the choice to continue their Multiverse career.

Mortal Ascension Scheme (UB): the process by which all mortal beings who live and die on the material worlds of the Local Systems pass up through the seven subsequent levels to Jerusem, where they embark on their universe career.

Mother Spirit (UB): with the Michaelson, the female co-creator of a Local Universe.

Multiverse: the author's term for the entire range of frequency domains, on every level of the Master Universe (UB).

Multiverse Administration (MA): the author's general term for the celestial administration, with special reference to the Local Universe bureaucracy.

Nebadon (UB): the name of this Local Universe of ten million inhabited planets.

Nodites (UB): descendants of the illicit interbreeding between selected mortals and, on realizing they were doomed to physical death, those of the Prince's staff who followed Caligastia's uprising.

Nodu, Nod (UB): Nodu is Georgia's informal, but respectful, name for the member of the Prince's staff who opposed Caligastia and who, in time, led his people to the Islands of Mu.

Satan (UB): Lucifer's right-hand aide who co-instigated the angelic rebellion 203,000 years ago.

Serapatatia (UB): Nodite Prince who persuaded Eve to accelerate the visitors' mission by mating with Cano and creating a singular Nodite bloodline with a healthy dash of violet blood.

Seraph(im) (UB): a high order of angels whose functions include that of companion (guardian) angels, or, like Georgia, observing angels.

Seraphic Transport System (UB): Transport Seraphs, living beings that carry nonmaterial beings—watchers as well as ascending mortals—to the other worlds on a variety of frequency domains within the Multiverse.

Solonia (UB): the seraphic "voice in the garden" (UB) who admonished the visitors and had them leave their garden home and start their long journey to settle in the Land of the Two Rivers.

Superuniverse (UB): a universe that contains one hundred thousand Local Universes.

System of Planets (UB): a grouping of planets consisting of a thousand inhabited, or to be inhabited, planets.

System of Satania: the System of planets within which Earth is but one of the more than 650 inhabited worlds of the one thousand planets within its administrative domain, and the locale of the Lucifer revolution.

System Sovereign (UB): the administrative angel, together with an assistant of the same rank, who is an overall authority of a Local System. Lucifer and Satan were the pair in charge of this System of planets.

Thoughtforms: quasi-life-forms existing in the astral regions, drawing their limited power from strong emotional thoughts projected out from human mentation, both conscious and unconscious. Thoughtforms can be negative or positive. Localized negative ones are referred to as fear-impacted thoughtforms.

Transport Seraphim: order of seraphim specifically created as sentient vehicles to make interplanetary transit available in the fourth and fifth dimensions.

Ultraterrestrial or Intraterrestrial Beings: the beings who inhabit our neighboring frequency domain and whom *The Urantia Book* calls the midwayers or midway creatures.

Unava: chief of staff to Prince Zanda, the senior of the two Planetary Princes of the neighboring planet Zandana.

Universe Career (UB): a mortal's destiny, unless chosen otherwise, to rise through the many hundreds of levels of the Multiverse to finally encounter the Creator.

Violet Blood (UB): the potential of an infusion of a slightly higher frequency genetic endowment, which results in more acute senses and a deeper spiritual awareness and responsiveness.

Zanda: senior Planetary Prince of Zandana, a planet named in his honor and to which Georgia has made frequent visits.

Zandan: the principal city of the planet Zandana.

Zandana: a neighboring planet developing within approximately the same time frame as Earth and whose Planetary Princes also followed Lucifer into revolution.

Index

About the Author

Timothy Wyllie (1940–2017) chose to be born in London at the height of the Battle of Britain. Surviving an English public school education unbroken, he studied architecture, qualifying in 1964 and practicing in London and the Bahamas. During this time he also worked with two others to create a mystery school, which came to be known as the Process Church, and subsequently traveled with the community throughout Europe and America. He became art director of PROCESS magazine, designing a series of magazines in the 1960s and '70s that have recently become recognized as among the prime progenitors of psychedelic magazine design. In 1975, Wyllie became the director of the New York headquarters and organized a series of conferences and seminars on such unorthodox issues as out-of-body travel, extraterrestrial encounters, alternative cancer therapies, and Tibetan Buddhism. After some fractious and fundamental disagreements with his colleagues in the community, he left to start a new life in 1977. The record of Wyllie's fifteen years in the mystery school of the Process Church and the true account of this eccentric spiritual community appears in his book *Love, Sex, Fear, Death: The Inside Story of the Process Church of the Final Judgment,* which was published by Feral House in 2009. It is slowly becoming a cult classic.

A profound near-death experience in 1973 confirmed for Wyllie the reality of other levels of existence and instigated what has become a lifetime exploration of nonhuman intelligences. Having created his intention, the Multiverse opened up a trail of synchronicities that led to his swimming with a coastal pod of wild dolphins, two extraterrestrial encounters—during one of which he was able to question the ET mouthpiece as to some of the ways of the inhabited Multiverse—and finally to an extended dialogue with a group of angels speaking through a light-trance medium in Toronto, Canada.

Wyllie's first phase of spiritual exploration was published as *The Deta Factor: Dolphins, Extraterrestrials & Angels* by Coleman Press in 1984 and republished by Bear & Company as *Dolphins, ETs & Angels* in 1993.

His second book, *Dolphins, Telepathy & Underwater Birthing,* published by Bear & Company in 1993, was republished by Wisdom Editions in 2001 under the title *Adventures Among Spiritual Intelligences: Angels, Aliens, Dolphins & Shamans.* In this book Wyllie continues his travels exploring Balinese shamanic healing, Australian Aboriginal cosmology, human underwater birthing, dolphin death and sexuality, entheogenic spirituality, the gathering alien presence on the planet, and his travels with a walk-in, along with much else.

Wyllie's work with the angels through the 1980s resulted in the book *Ask Your Angels: A Practical Guide to Working with Your Messengers of Heaven to Empower and Enrich Your Life,* cowritten with Alma Daniel and Andrew Ramer and published by Ballantine Books in 1992. After spending time at the top of the *New York Times* religious bestsellers, *Ask Your Angels* went on to become an international success in eleven translations.

The Return of the Rebel Angels continues the series he began with *Dolphins, ETs & Angels* and *Adventures Among Spiritual Intelligences,* presenting further in-depth intuitive explorations of nonhuman intelligences. It draws together the many meaningful strands of Wyllie's thirty-year voyage of discovery into unknown and long-taboo territories in a coherent and remarkably optimistic picture for the immediate future of the human species, with the inconspicuous help of a benign and richly inhabited living Multiverse.

The Helianx Proposition: The Return of the Rainbow Serpent— A Cosmic Creation Fable, also thirty years in the making, is Wyllie's illustrated mythic exploration of an ancient extraterrestrial personality and its occult influence on life in this world. Published by Daynal Institute Press in 2010, it includes two DVDs and two CDs of associated material. The CDs contain nineteen tracks of the author's visionary observations, augmented by the music of the late Jim Wilson, an Emmy-winning musician and master of digital sonic manipulation.

Confessions of a Rebel Angel, Wyllie's first collaboration with Georgia, emerged in 2012, published by Inner Traditions • Bear & Company, who followed up with *Revolt of the Rebel Angels* in 2013, *Rebel Angels in Exile* in 2014, *Wisdom of the Watchers* in 2015, *Awakening of the Watchers* in 2016, and *Secret History of the Watchers* in 2018.

BOOKS BY TIMOTHY WYLLIE

The Deta Factor: Dolphins, Extraterrestrials & Angels, 1984 (currently in print as *Dolphins, ETs & Angels,* 1993)

Ask Your Angels: A Practical Guide to Working with the Messengers of Heaven to Empower and Enrich Your Life, 1992 (cowritten with Alma Daniel and Andrew Ramer)

Dolphins, Telepathy & Underwater Birthing, 1993 (currently in print as
   *Adventures Among Spiritual Intelligences: Angels, Aliens, Dolphins
   & Shamans,* 2001)

Contacting Your Angels Through Movement, Meditation & Music, 1995
   (with Elli Bambridge)

*Love, Sex, Fear, Death: The Inside Story of the Process Church of the
   Final Judgment,* 2009 (editor, with Adam Parfrey)

*The Helianx Proposition: The Return of the Rainbow Serpent—A Cosmic
   Creation Fable,* 2010

The Return of the Rebel Angels, 2011

Confessions of a Rebel Angel, 2012

Revolt of the Rebel Angels, 2013

Rebel Angels in Exile, 2014

Wisdom of the Watchers, 2015

Awakening of the Watchers, 2016

Secret History of the Watchers, 2018